DATE DUE

GRASS-ROOTS RECONSTRUCTION IN TEXAS, 1865–1880

# GRASS-ROOTS
# RECONSTRUCTION IN
# TEXAS, 1865–1880

RANDOLPH B. CAMPBELL

LOUISIANA STATE UNIVERSITY PRESS

BATON ROUGE AND LONDON

Designer: Melanie O'Quinn Samaha
Typeface: Sabon
Typesetter: Impressions Book and Journal Services, Inc.
Printer and binder: Thomson-Shore, Inc.

Portions of some chapters were first published as follows, and are reprinted with permission: Chapter 2 as "Reconstruction in Colorado County, Texas, 1865–1876," *Nesbitt Memorial Library Journal*, V (January, 1995), 3–30; Chapter 3 as "A Moderate Response: The District Judges of Dallas County During Reconstruction, 1865–1876," *Legacies: A History Journal for Dallas and North Central Texas*, V (Fall, 1993), 4–12; Chapter 4 in Randolph Campbell, *A Southern Community in Crisis: Harrison County, Texas, 1850–1880* (Austin, 1983); Chapter 5 as "Reconstruction in Jefferson County, Texas, 1865–1876," *Texas Gulf Historical and Biographical Record*, XXXI (Fall, 1995), 10–28; Chapter 7 as "Reconstruction in Nueces County, 1865–1876," *Houston Review*, XVI (Fall, 1994), 3–26.

LIBRARY OF CONGRESS CATALOGING-IN-PUBLICATION DATA

Campbell, Randolph B., 1940–
Grass-roots reconstruction in Texas, 1865–1880 / Randolph B.
Campbell.
p.  cm.
Includes bibliographical references and index.
ISBN 0-8071-2194-0 (alk. paper)
1. Reconstruction—Texas.  2. Texas—Politics and
government—1865–1950.  I. Title.
F391.C27  1997
976.4—dc21        97-17335
CIP

# CONTENTS

# MAPS

# ACKNOWLEDGMENTS

It has taken so many years to research and write this study that, not having kept a log of all the individuals who helped in one way or another, I may fail to recall everyone who should be thanked for assistance. To anyone so neglected I apologize and plead poor memory rather than deliberate intent.

Richard G. Lowe, my friend and colleague who teaches the Civil War and Reconstruction courses at the University of North Texas, deserves special thanks for listening patiently to innumerable rehearsals of my thoughts on how this study should be done and for providing a critical reading of the whole. Cecil Harper, Jr., my first doctoral student at UNT, believed in this project from the beginning and encouraged me on the occasions when it seemed to be going nowhere. I also wish to thank my friends Donald E. Chipman of UNT, Walter L. Buenger of Texas A&M University, and Carl H. Moneyhon of the University of Arkansas at Little Rock for their unfailing support and encouragement.

The following people provided special assistance in locating particularly hard to find research materials in local depositories: Robert Wooster of Texas A&M University, Corpus Christi, Brian Hart of Del Mar College, JoAnn Stiles of Lamar University, Bill Stein of the Nesbitt Memorial Library at Columbus, and Robert Schaadt of the Sam Houston Regional Library and Research Center at Liberty. William T. Block, Jr., graciously shared with me his deep knowledge of Jefferson County's history. Patrick Williams, a doctoral student at Columbia University, provided invaluable assistance in clarifying the byzantine political life of Nueces County and South Texas during the Reconstruction era. Melinda Smith, a master's student at UNT, shared her research and findings on postwar Dallas County. As always, three members of the library staff at the University of North Texas—Richard L. Himmel, David Lindsey, and Martin Sarvis—did everything possible to locate materials and make them available to me. Erin Wise of the Center for Instructional Services at UNT prepared the maps. The Faculty Research Committee at the University of North Texas gave financial support to this project at its inception, and the Texas State Historical Association awarded it the Coral H. Tullis Research Prize.

Finally, there is the obligatory, but very accurate and just, disclaimer: The persons whose assistance I have acknowledged brought valuable sources to my attention, questioned my interpretations, and caught many of the errors that invariably appear in such historical studies. Any omissions, weaknesses, and errors that remain are my own responsibility.

GRASS-ROOTS RECONSTRUCTION IN TEXAS, 1865–1880

# INTRODUCTION

Reconstruction after the Civil War dealt primarily with two issues—restoring across the South governments loyal to the United States and determining how African Americans would be treated as freedmen. Efforts to attain those ends provoked furious controversy beginning in 1865 and continuing into the 1870s. When it ended, Reconstruction had returned all the states to their proper constitutional relationship within the Union and allowed at least one generation of black men to enjoy full citizenship and equal rights. At the same time, however, the era deepened the negative attitude most white southerners held toward government and strengthened their determination to deny equality to blacks.

Historians have given Reconstruction the attention that it deserves, provoking considerable controversy themselves along the way. As Henry Steele Commager and Richard B. Morris noted in their introduction to Eric Foner's 1988 synthesis for the New American Nation Series, "Probably no other chapter in American history has been the subject, one might say the victim, of such varied and conflicting interpretations." Virtually all these studies, however, have focused on Reconstruction at the national level or in one of the southern states. Few academic historians have sought to determine how the issues of the era came home to people at the local level. When Foner looked for work other than national or state in focus, he could find only a few scattered case studies, some examinations of urban areas, and chapters in general histories of counties.[1] Heretofore, no one has attempted a systematic examination of Reconstruction at the county level across an entire state.

For several reasons counties are the appropriate units for a study of Reconstruction at the grass roots in Texas from 1865 to 1880. First, the state was overwhelmingly rural during the nineteenth century, making county rather than city governments the level of political organization closest to the great majority of Texans. Control of the key offices in county government became a vital issue in most localities in 1865 and remained a subject of contention into the 1870s. Second, much of the process of Reconstruction, such as voter registration and the elections of delegates to constitutional conventions and of state legislators and executive officers, had to be carried out on a county-by-county basis. Thus this study is based on an in-depth examination of six counties—Colorado, Dallas, Harrison, Jefferson, McLennan, and Nueces—all of which were created as units of local government in Texas well before the Civil War (see Map 1).

The region of Texas settled primarily by migrants from the Old South before 1861 and therefore most affected by the Civil War and Reconstruction comprised only the eastern two-fifths of the modern state. Even then, however, it was about the size of Alabama and Mississippi combined and at the time of secession had 105 organized counties stretching from the Red River to the Gulf of Mexico and from the Sabine River to near the ninety-eighth meridian. The region enjoyed enough cultural and political unity that a strong majority of its white population supported secession and the Confederacy; nevertheless, there was great geographic, demographic, and economic diversity among the counties.[2] A brief look at the six counties examined in this study clearly reveals these differences.

Colorado County, located in south-central Texas, was a slaveholding, cotton-producing area with a population that was 45 percent black in 1870. Like some other counties in that area and in the hill country, however, Colorado also had a sizable minority of German immigrants. Dallas County, in north-central Texas, had no efficient transportation outlet before the early

1. Eric Foner, *Reconstruction: America's Unfinished Revolution, 1863–1877* (New York, 1988), xvii. The list of books and articles in Foner's bibliography shows how little has been done in the history of Reconstruction at the local level.

2. Randolph B. Campbell and Richard G. Lowe, *Wealth and Power in Antebellum Texas* (College Station, Tex., 1977), 13–17; Walter L. Buenger, *Secession and the Union in Texas* (Austin, 1984), 117–77.

Map 1

Texas in 1870

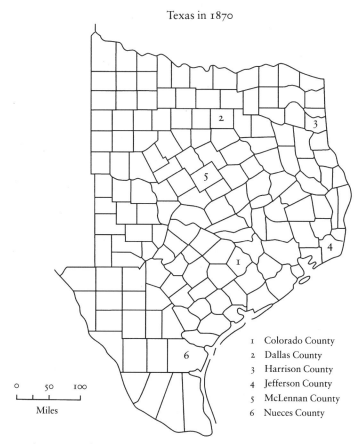

1  Colorado County
2  Dallas County
3  Harrison County
4  Jefferson County
5  McLennan County
6  Nueces County

0        50       100
Miles

Map by Terry G. Jordan

1870s and consequently grew no cotton and had relatively few freedmen (16 percent of the population in 1870). Its population came largely from the Upper South and old Northwest. By contrast, Harrison County, located on the border with Louisiana in northeast Texas, had a highly developed plantation economy, a white society heavily influenced by lower southerners, and a population that was 67 percent black in 1870. Jefferson County, situated in the southeastern corner of the state, did not grow cotton, but it offered enough opportunities in other work that freedmen constituted 26 percent of its population in 1870. It also had a notable number of residents of French ancestry and of foreign birth. McLennan County, in central Texas, entered the Cotton Kingdom during the 1860s and 1870s. Its 1870 population was 34 percent black. Finally, Nueces County, located on the Gulf Coastal southwestern frontier, relied on commerce and ranching; its population was only 8 percent black in 1870. A significant proportion of the people in Nueces County were of Mexican heritage.[3]

These six counties, although well distributed geographically across antebellum Texas, cannot be presented as "typical" of the state or any of its regions. They obviously differed from one another extensively, and in some cases even varied notably—in ethnic makeup or the availability of transportation outlets, for example—from the counties adjoining them. To raise the number of counties examined to twelve or twenty-four (although it would create a book of unmanageable size) still would not ensure that those studied necessarily were "typical" or "representative." Therefore, the Reconstruction-era stories of Colorado, Dallas, Harrison, Jefferson, McLennan, and Nueces Counties are presented as case studies that permit reasonably precise comparisons of how the various regions of Texas experienced the years from 1865 to 1880. This approach is at least suggestive concerning Reconstruction at the local level across the state as a whole, and it provides an opportunity to analyze the impact of differing geographic, demographic, and economic circumstances on the major events and developments of that period in the Lone Star State.

A study such as this may be organized in one of two ways. It can take a fully chronological approach and present information on developments in all the counties as Reconstruction unfolded, or it can use a topical approach and tell the story of each county separately before offering a general sum-

3. Statistics on the demographic and economic characteristics of each of the six counties are documented in the following chapters.

mary and conclusion. Diversity so outweighed uniformity in the Reconstruction experience of these six counties that only the topical approach could avoid a mass of confusing detail on each phase. Thus the study begins with a factual overview of the era from 1865 to 1880 to provide a context for events and developments at the local level, proceeds with a chapter on each of the six counties, and concludes with a summary of what the events in those localities suggest about the basic nature and impact of Reconstruction at the grass roots in Texas.

In the largest sense, this study represents an attempt to answer three groups of questions. First, how did Reconstruction as it developed at the national and state levels come home to the people of these six counties? What actually happened? Who, for example, held the key offices in county government during each phase of Reconstruction? What were their partisan affiliations, and how was their tenure received by local residents? Such basic information may seem elementary, but anyone seeking to uncover it will quickly see why there are so few studies of Reconstruction at the local level. Second, how much change during each phase of the era did Reconstruction bring to the lives of the major groups involved—conservative whites (defined as former secessionists and those Unionists who opposed equal rights for blacks and congressional intervention), freedmen, and Republicans? Did conservative whites find themselves stripped of political power and their counties ruined economically? Were members of the economic elite of 1865 displaced by a new upper class? Did African Americans gain anything other than to keep the freedom brought to them in 1865? What did Unionists who became Republicans gain as a result of the opportunities provided them as supporters of the victorious United States? Third, how much did Reconstruction vary from one county to another? Did politics develop along classic "Radical Republican" versus "Conservative Redeemer" lines in all counties? Did the experience of blacks differ notably in particular counties? If there were significant variations from one locality to another, what factors accounted for the differences?

This third group of questions concerning diversity in the grass-roots experiences of Texans between 1865 and 1876 brings up a final, and essential, introductory point. Reconstruction differed so much between counties that the effect of this study may appear at first glance to be the destruction of any useful generalization about the period for the state as a whole. It is impossible to conclude that Reconstruction at the grass-roots level across

Texas lasted for a certain period of time, ended in a particular way for largely the same set of reasons, and had an unvarying impact on the people involved. Indeed, readers are likely to decide that all generalizations have disappeared in a welter of confusing and conflicting detail. This need not be the case, however, if attention is focused on the role of certain conditions in shaping Reconstruction in each county. These key local conditions include the presence of federal authority in the form of troops and Freedmen's Bureau agents; the involvement of scalawags as leaders of the developing Republican party; the rate of population growth and economic expansion; the proportion of foreign-born residents; and the proportion of freedmen in the total population. In the end, an examination of Reconstruction at the grass roots in Texas reveals great complexity and diversity and explodes facile generalizations, but it also provides evidence for useful conclusions about the local conditions that determined how most citizens experienced the events and developments that did so much to shape their state's politics and society for the next century and beyond.

# I

# A CHRONOLOGICAL OVERVIEW
# OF RECONSTRUCTION IN TEXAS

The decision to secede from the United States came easily for the great majority of Texans in 1860 and 1861 because their state, regardless of its southwestern location, was essentially southern in economy, society, culture, and politics. Natives of the South headed more than three-fourths of all Texas households in 1850 and 1860, and the state rapidly joined the Cotton Kingdom during the last antebellum decade. Cotton production rose from 58,072 bales in 1850 to 431,463 in 1860, an increase of 643 percent. Slavery, of course, held the key to this development. During the 1850s the slave population of Texas rose from 58,161 to 182,566, an increase of 214 percent. By 1860 slaves constituted 30 percent of the total population, and more than one-quarter of all households owned bondsmen. These percentages of slaves and masters did not equal comparable statistics for states such as South Carolina and Mississippi, but very nearly matched those for Virginia. In this sense, Texas as the newest slave state in the Union was very similar to the oldest.[1] Thus when the "Black Republican" Abraham Lincoln, whom most white southerners regarded as a dangerous enemy of slavery, won the election of 1860, Texas readily joined the secession movement. Even the opposition of the state's greatest hero, Gov-

---

1. Campbell and Lowe, *Wealth and Power in Antebellum Texas,* 29; Richard G. Lowe and Randolph B. Campbell, *Planters and Plain Folk: Agriculture in Antebellum Texas* (Dallas, 1987), 19; Randolph B. Campbell, *An Empire for Slavery: The Peculiar Institution in Texas, 1821–1865* (Baton Rouge, 1989), 1–2, 55, 190.

ernor Sam Houston, could not sway voters from approving disunion by a vote of 46,153 to 14,747 on February 23, 1861, and joining the Confederate States of America in March.[2]

Texas escaped the terrible destruction of the Civil War for a simple reason—United States troops never invaded and occupied the state's interior. Coastal areas from Sabine Pass to Brownsville fell to invading forces at various times beginning in 1862, but when the war ended in the spring of 1865, all inland towns, plantations, and farms remained untouched. Texans paid a huge price for the war, of course, primarily in terms of lives lost and ruined in the Confederate army and, to a lesser extent, in the privations of families left at home. The conflict also disrupted the cotton trade and drained essential livestock from plantations and farms. Nevertheless, Texas in 1865 had nothing to compare with the scenes of devastation in Old South states such as Virginia and South Carolina.[3]

Reconstruction in Texas began at the close of the Civil War during the late spring of 1865. The last battle of the war, ironically a Confederate victory, took place at Palmito Ranch in the Rio Grande valley on May 13. Gen. Edmund Kirby Smith surrendered the Trans-Mississippi Department of the Confederacy at Galveston on June 2, and the first occupation troops arrived at that city on June 19. Gen. Gordon Granger immediately announced the Emancipation Proclamation (making "Juneteenth" forever a day of celebration for Texas blacks), and the army began the work of paroling former Confederate soldiers. Federal civilian authority arrived at Galveston on July 21 in the person of Andrew Jackson Hamilton, President Andrew Johnson's appointee as provisional governor of Texas.[4]

A. J. Hamilton was a native of Alabama who had come to Texas in 1846, served two terms in the state legislature during the early 1850s, and been elected to the United States House of Representatives in 1859. A committed

2. Buenger, *Secession and the Union in Texas*, 117–77; Joe T. Timmons, "The Referendum in Texas on the Ordinance of Secession, February 23, 1861," *East Texas Historical Journal*, XI (Fall, 1973), 15–16.

3. Succinct accounts of the Civil War era in Texas include Allen C. Ashcraft, *Texas in the Civil War: A Résumé History* (Austin, 1962); Stephen B. Oates, "Texas Under the Secessionists," *Southwestern Historical Quarterly*, LXVII (1963), 167–212; and Bill Winsor, *Texas in the Confederacy: Military Installations, Economy and People* (Hillsboro, Tex., 1978). Rupert N. Richardson, Ernest Wallace, and Adrian Anderson, *Texas: The Lone Star State* (5th ed.; Englewood Cliffs, N.J., 1988), 213–25, provides a good textbook account.

4. Charles William Ramsdell, *Reconstruction in Texas* (New York, 1910), 26, 39–40, 55–57; Campbell, *Empire for Slavery*, 249–51.

Unionist of the Sam Houston school, Hamilton refused to support the Confederacy and left Texas from 1862 until 1865. When he returned as an agent of Presidential Reconstruction, his primary responsibility was to restore state government and bring Texas back to its proper constitutional position in the Union.[5] This meant registering eligible voters, defined as those who could take the oath of amnesty promising future loyalty to the United States, and electing a convention to revise the state constitution in recognition of changes such as the end of slavery. Once the constitutional convention completed its work, voters would again go to the polls to approve the new fundamental law and elect state and local officials under its terms. At the same election, voters would choose United States representatives; and the new state legislature, once it assembled, would select United States senators. When the president approved these steps and Congress indicated its approval by seating the new representatives and senators, Presidential Reconstruction in Texas would be complete.[6]

During the summer of 1865, Governor Hamilton appointed interim state officials such as a secretary of state and attorney general and named judges to reopen the state's district courts. Also, to restore local government on an interim basis in the more than one hundred Texas counties, the governor appointed key officials such as county judges (usually called chief justices), sheriffs, and commissioners. In all cases, of course, he sought to appoint men of known loyalty to the Union. On August 19, 1865, while in the midst of appointing interim officials, the governor issued a proclamation ordering the registration of voters in preparation for electing the constitutional convention.[7]

Federal authority arrived at Galveston in yet another form on September 5, 1865, when Brevet Brig. Gen. Edgar M. Gregory reached his headquarters as the state's first assistant commissioner of the Bureau of Refugees, Freedmen, and Abandoned Lands. Established by Congress under the Department of War, the Freedmen's Bureau, as it was generally called, had the

5. Walter P. Webb, H. Bailey Carroll, and Eldon Branda, eds., *The Handbook of Texas* (3 vols.; Austin, 1952, 1976), I, 759; Ramsdell, *Reconstruction in Texas*, 55–56. John L. Waller, *Colossal Hamilton of Texas: A Biography of Andrew Jackson Hamilton, Militant Unionist and Reconstruction Governor* (El Paso, Tex., 1968), is a thin account of Hamilton's career.

6. Ramsdell, *Reconstruction in Texas*, 55–58; Richardson, Wallace, and Anderson, *Texas*, 229–34.

7. Ramsdell, *Reconstruction in Texas*, 59–62; Carl H. Moneyhon, *Republicanism in Reconstruction Texas* (Austin, 1980), 23–25.

primary responsibility of helping blacks adjust to freedom. Providing relief for the destitute was a relatively minor problem, but the bureau's efforts in supervising labor contracts, establishing schools, and protecting freedmen against violence made it extremely controversial. By January, 1866, Gregory had twenty-one sub-assistant commissioners, generally called agents, serving in towns such as Marshall, Waco, and Columbus, and the bureau was on its way to becoming a major force in Reconstruction Texas. By July, 1867, the bureau would have seventy agents working in the field across the state.[8]

In mid-November, 1865, Governor Hamilton called for an election on January 8, 1866, to choose delegates to the constitutional convention. The convention met in Austin from February 7 until April 2, when it completed the Constitution of 1866. The delegates declared the secession ordinance null and void (without any reference to whether or not it had ever been a valid act), repudiated public debt incurred during the war, and recognized (but did not ratify) the Thirteenth Amendment by removing slavery from the constitution. The convention also promised basic rights of person and property to freedmen, but denied them the right to vote, hold office, serve on juries, or attend public schools.[9]

During the convention and the period between its adjournment and the election on June 25 to approve the new constitution and elect officials, a significant division developed among those who had assumed leadership in reconstructing the state. One faction, generally termed Radical Unionists and including Governor Hamilton, favored a total condemnation of secession and took a moderate stance toward the freedmen. Their candidate for governor, Elisha M. Pease, a native of Connecticut who had held that office from 1853 to 1857, favored granting the franchise to literate blacks. The other faction, known as Conservative Unionists, was led by James W. Throckmorton, a noted opponent of secession in 1860–1861 who served as an officer in the Confederate army once the war began. This group wanted to restore the Union with as little change as possible and refused to consider

8. William L. Richter, *Overreached on All Sides: The Freedmen's Bureau Administrators in Texas, 1865–1868* (College Station, Tex., 1991), 3–4, 21, 38, 156.

9. Ramsdell, *Reconstruction in Texas*, 85, 89–106; Barry A. Crouch, "'All the Vile Passions': The Texas Black Code of 1866," *Southwestern Historical Quarterly*, XCVII (1993), 21. Constitutional guarantees of such rights as owning property and entering into contracts depended, of course, on action by the state legislature.

enfranchising the freedmen. Conservative Unionists tended to accuse their opponents of "radicalism" and a willingness to cooperate with northern Republicans in punishing the South and elevating the former slaves. Radical Unionists retaliated with charges that the conservatives were disloyal and planned to punish true loyalists in Texas.[10]

Conservative Unionists easily won the gubernatorial election on June 25, 1866, because they appealed to former secessionists as well as to those who had opposed disunion but were against extending equal rights to blacks or making radical changes. Throckmorton received 48,631 votes to 12,051 for Pease, and conservatives, defined at this point as Unionists like the new governor and former secessionists, gained total control of the new state legislature. The Eleventh Legislature assembled on August 6, Throckmorton took office three days later, and on August 20, President Johnson issued a proclamation declaring that the rebellion had ended in Texas and returning control of the state to civil authorities.[11]

One of the new legislature's first acts was to elect Oran M. Roberts and David G. Burnet as Texas' United States senators. Roberts had presided at the secession convention in 1861 and held the rank of colonel in the Confederate army. Burnet, a much older man, had not endorsed disunion, but he had supported the Confederacy and was bitterly critical of the Radical Unionists. During the late summer and early fall, the state district judges elected on June 25, fourteen of whom in a total of twenty had been officers in the Confederate army, opened their courts. At the same time, county officials chosen on June 25, many of whom had supported secession and the war, took over local governments. Presidential Reconstruction thus appeared to have ended with the restoration of governments controlled by a combination of conservative Unionists and former secessionists, with the latter holding the upper hand.[12]

10. Ramsdell, *Reconstruction in Texas,* 108–12; Moneyhon, *Republicanism in Reconstruction Texas,* 42–47. The platforms of the Radical Unionists and the Conservative Unionists in 1866 are found in Ernest William Winkler, ed., *Platforms of Political Parties in Texas* (Austin, 1916), 95–99.

11. Ramsdell, *Reconstruction in Texas,* 112–17; Moneyhon, *Republicanism in Reconstruction Texas,* 47–50; Richardson, Wallace, and Anderson, *Texas,* 232. The vote totals reported for the governor's race vary slightly from source to source. The totals given here are from Mike Kingston, Sam Attlesey, and Mary G. Crawford, *The Texas Almanac's Political History of Texas* (Austin, 1992), 61.

12. Randolph B. Campbell, "The District Judges of Texas in 1866–1867: An Episode in the

In the meantime, however, Congress under the leadership of Radical Republicans was moving successfully to block Presidential Reconstruction and take control of the process. Disgusted at the lack of penance among white southerners, the mistreatment of loyalists in the South, and the refusal to accord freedmen any semblance of equal rights, Republicans in Congress during late 1865 refused to seat the representatives and senators sent to Washington by states reconstructed under President Johnson's direction. Texas, although it was the last state to complete Presidential Reconstruction, acted in essentially the same way as the other southern states and provided additional ammunition for the Radicals. For example, both U.S. senators elected in 1866 strongly opposed the Republicans, and the Eleventh Legislature passed the sort of special laws discriminating against freedmen that had become notorious across the South as "black codes." The first reports from Freedmen's Bureau agents in Texas indicated that many blacks were still held in near slavery or suffered violence that made a mockery of freedom. Republicans, using as their primary weapons the attitudes of southerners and conditions for blacks and Unionists in the old Confederacy, swept the mid-term congressional elections in the fall of 1866 and took control of both houses with a two-thirds majority. In March, 1867, Congress passed the first of four Reconstruction acts that in effect began the process anew, this time under the direction of the United States army. Texas would have to register eligible voters (black as well as white), elect a convention to write a new state constitution, establish state and local governments under that constitution, ratify the Fourteenth Amendment, and elect new United States representatives and senators. Then, if Congress approved, it could return to the Union.[13]

Congressional Reconstruction called for dividing the South into five military districts and placing each under the command of a general in the army. Texas and Louisiana composed the Fifth Military District under the overall command of Gen. Philip Sheridan, who was then stationed at New

---

Failure of Presidential Reconstruction," *Southwestern Historical Quarterly,* XCIII (1990), 360–64; Campbell, "Grass Roots Reconstruction: The Personnel of County Government in Texas, 1865–1876," *Journal of Southern History,* LVIII (1992), 106, 112–13; Webb, Carroll, and Branda, eds., *Handbook of Texas,* I, 252–53, II, 484–85.

13. The best overview of the congressional takeover of Reconstruction is found in Foner, *Reconstruction,* 221–80. The Texas black code is detailed in Crouch, "'All the Vile Passions,'" 13–34. The laws in question did not mention race, but everyone understood that they applied only to freedmen. The early reports of Freedmen's Bureau agents are described in Richter, *Overreached on All Sides,* 20–22.

Orleans. Sheridan officially took charge on March 19, 1867, and ordered both states to keep their present military commanders. This meant that Texas remained under the immediate direction of Gen. Charles C. Griffin, a West Point graduate who, like Sheridan, stood ready to deal firmly with ex-Confederates. Within two months, the two generals made it very clear that the Throckmorton-led government of Conservative Unionists and se-cessionists established in 1866 had become strictly provisional in the eyes of Congress and the military. In mid-April, Sheridan ruled that the governor could not appoint anyone to fill vacancies in elective offices or call for elections for any purpose. No elections will be held, the general said, until directed by the military commander.[14]

Later that month, General Griffin, in response to numerous complaints from Unionists about their treatment in Texas courts, issued an order requiring all jurors to swear the test oath of 1862 that they had never voluntarily supported the Confederacy. Obviously this requirement made the great majority of white men in Texas ineligible to serve. Governor Throckmorton considered the jury order "outrageously wrong" and sent protests to General Griffin and President Johnson. District judges, knowing of the governor's attitude, reacted largely as they chose. Some complied as fully as possible with the directive, and others simply closed their courts without making a genuine effort to find jurors.[15]

Thus the worst fears of conservatives (defined from 1867 onward as those who opposed the Republican party both nationally and in Texas) concerning Congressional Reconstruction came true from the outset. The first critical step in repeating the process of reconstruction was the registration of voters according to guidelines established by Congress and interpreted by Generals Sheridan and Griffin. The Reconstruction acts called for registering all adult males, white and black, except those who had ever sworn an oath to uphold the Constitution of the United States and then engaged in rebellion (and the very small number of men who had held high civil or military offices in the Confederacy and could not register until they received a special pardon from the president of the United States). Sheridan interpreted these restrictions stringently, barring from registration not only all pre-1861 officials of state and local governments who had supported the

14. William L. Richter, *The Army in Texas During Reconstruction, 1865–1870* (College Station, Tex., 1987), 52, 73–74; Ramsdell, *Reconstruction in Texas*, 94–96.
15. Campbell, "District Judges of Texas in 1866–1867," 368–74.

Confederacy, but also all city officeholders and even minor functionaries such as sextons of cemeteries.[16] In May, Griffin divided the state into fifteen registration districts, each of which had two supervisors and included six to eleven counties designated as subdistricts. The general also appointed a three-man board of registrars for each county, making his choices on the advice of known Unionists and local Freedmen's Bureau agents. In every county where practicable, a freedman served as one of the three registrars.[17] Registration began in most counties during June or July, continued for several months, and resumed for a week in late September.[18]

On December 16, 1867, Gen. Winfield Scott Hancock, who had taken over command of the Fifth Military District in November, ordered an election to be held February 10–14, 1868, to choose delegates to the constitutional convention. Hancock also directed the boards of registration in all counties to reopen their books from January 27 to January 31, 1868, for a revision of the existing rolls and the addition of newly eligible voters. Final registration amounted to approximately 59,633 whites and 49,479 blacks. It is impossible to say how many whites were rejected or refused to register (estimates vary from seventy-five hundred to twelve thousand), but blacks, who constituted only about 30 percent of the state's population, were significantly overrepresented at 45 percent of all voters.[19]

While they supervised registration in preparation for the election of a constitutional convention, commanders of the Fifth Military District and the District of Texas further demonstrated the provisional nature of state and local government by the wholesale removal of officials elected in June, 1866. Congress gave the military virtually unlimited powers of dismissal and appointment on July 19, 1867, and Sheridan waited less than two weeks before removing Governor Throckmorton as an "impediment to the

---

16. Ramsdell, *Reconstruction in Texas,* 146, 161–65.

17. A copy of General Griffin's order of May 16, 1867, is found in Governors' Papers: James W. Throckmorton, Archives Division, Texas State Library, Austin (hereafter cited as Governors' Papers: JWT). All six counties involved in this study had a freedman serve on the Board of Registrars. For the story of a black registrar in San Augustine County, see Randolph B. Campbell, "The Burden of Local Black Leadership During Reconstruction: A Research Note," *Civil War History,* XXXIX (1993), 148–52.

18. The dates of voter registration in each county beginning in 1867 are found in the county-by-county List of Registered Voters in Texas, 1869, Archives Division, Texas State Library, Austin.

19. Ramsdell, *Reconstruction in Texas,* 195–96; William A. Russ, Jr., "Radical Disfranchisement in Texas, 1867–1870," *Southwestern Historical Quarterly,* XXXVIII (1934), 40–52.

reconstruction" of Texas. The general's order of July 30 named former governor and unsuccessful 1866 Radical Unionist candidate, Elisha M. Pease, to replace Throckmorton. Sheridan soon began to unseat state district judges, and on August 27, he authorized General Griffin to displace all county officials deemed disloyal. Taking charge of both the Fifth Military District and the District of Texas when Sheridan left the former command on September 5, 1867, Griffin discharged all five justices of the Texas Supreme Court and three more district judges before he died of yellow fever on September 15. His successor in Texas, Gen. Joseph J. Reynolds, took at least as dim a view of former secessionists and Confederates holding office, and within two months replaced more than five hundred county officials. Governor Pease gathered information and made recommendations to the general, who in turn ordered the removals and appointments. By late November, 1867, when General Hancock, a Democrat who had little use for the Radicals, took over the Fifth Military District and exerted a restraining influence on his subordinate in Texas, military authority had substantially altered the personnel of state and local government elected in June 1866.[20]

The election of a constitutional convention between February 10 and February 14, 1868, resulted in nearly a total victory for Texas' fledgling Republican party, which had organized during the previous year and held its first state convention on July 4, 1867. Encouraged by chapters of the Union League, more than four-fifths (82 percent) of the newly enfranchised blacks went to the polls, voting overwhelmingly for the convention (36,932 to 818) and Republican delegates. By contrast, only 31 percent (18,379) of registered whites voted, probably because conservative leaders had given contradictory and confusing advice before the election. At first, because the Reconstruction acts required participation by at least half of all voters registered at the time of the election, conservative spokesmen urged whites to register and then refuse to vote. Just before the election, however, they became uncertain of the Republicans' strength and changed tactics, advising whites to vote no on the convention but to support conservative candidates in case the meeting won approval. Of the whites who voted, 10,622 opposed the convention, and 7,757 voted for it. The latter group probably rep-

---

20. Ramsdell, *Reconstruction in Texas*, 168–75; Moneyhon, *Republicanism in Reconstruction Texas*, 68–69; Richter, *Army in Texas During Reconstruction*, 124–26. The names of all individuals removed and appointed are recorded in the Election Registers, 1867, Records of the Secretary of State, Archives Division, Texas State Library, Austin.

resented the extent of white support for the Republican party in 1868, an indication that conservatives, if they organized and turned out their vote, still could control Texas.[21]

When the constitutional convention assembled in Austin on June 1, 1868, seventy-eight of its ninety members were Republicans. Southern-born whites, or scalawags, made up the bulk of these delegates. Only twelve, including six whose states of birth could not be determined, may be classed as carpetbaggers, and nine were black. Obviously the Republicans could dominate the twelve conservatives in the convention and write any kind of constitution they wished, so long as they remained unified. From the outset, however, factionalism disrupted their efforts and indeed threatened to prevent the writing of any constitution.[22]

The most important division among Republicans in the convention involved a split between moderates led by former provisional governor A. J. Hamilton and radicals led by Edmund J. Davis. A native of Florida, Davis came to Texas well before the war, lived at various times in Corpus Christi, Laredo, and Brownsville, and was a state district judge in 1860. He opposed secession to the extent of forming the First Texas Cavalry that served with Union forces in Texas and Louisiana. Davis ended the war as a brigadier general and returned to Corpus Christi, where he was elected a delegate to the constitutional conventions of both 1866 and 1868–1869. When the latter convention organized, he became its presiding officer.[23]

Moderate and radical Republicans fought most bitterly over three issues: a provision called *ab initio* that would have declared the ordinance of secession null and void and as a result revoked all acts by the state government from 1861 until 1867; the disfranchisement of former Confederates; and the division of Texas to create a new western state. *Ab initio* had great importance because its passage would invalidate measures such as an 1864 act allowing six Texas railroads to pay part of their debts to the state school fund in depreciated wartime paper rather than in specie as originally required. Disfranchisement raised the emotional issue of punishment for secession and, of course, promised to strengthen the Republican party. The

21. Moneyhon, *Republicanism in Reconstruction Texas,* 78–81; Ramsdell, *Reconstruction in Texas,* 195–99.

22. Randolph B. Campbell, "Carpetbagger Rule in Texas: An Enduring Myth," *Southwestern Historical Quarterly,* XCVII (1994), 590, 592; Ramsdell, *Reconstruction in Texas,* 200–201; Moneyhon, *Republicanism in Reconstruction Texas,* 82–86.

23. Webb, Carroll, and Branda, eds., *Handbook of Texas,* I, 469–70.

creation of a new state in West Texas would probably benefit Republicans even more because unionism was much stronger there than in East Texas. Radical Republicans favored all three measures, while moderates opposed them. Only one issue—the violence that had plagued Texas since June, 1865—unified all members of the new party. The convention's Committee on Lawlessness and Violence compiled a report showing that 509 whites and 468 blacks had been murdered since the war and suggesting that most of these killings involved conservatives' hatred of loyalists of both races. Two Republican leaders, Colbert Caldwell and Morgan Hamilton, took the report to Washington to support their appeal for greater federal intervention on behalf of Unionists and freedmen.[24]

The convention settled only the *ab initio* question, by rejecting the radical position, before it ran out of funds after three months. It then ordered the collection of a tax to finance another session and recessed from August 31 until December 1, 1868. During the second session, which ended in February, 1869, moderate Republicans aided by the conservatives defeated the radicals on the other two major issues and completed the new constitution. Texas was not divided, and the Constitution of 1869 (often referred to as the "radical constitution") had no significant provisions for disfranchisement. Adult male blacks and virtually all adult white men could vote, once a voter registration system was created. The most striking change brought by the constitution involved the centralization of power in Austin, especially in the hands of the governor. Elected to a four-year rather than two-year term as under previous constitutions, the governor would appoint the secretary of state, attorney general, and all the judges of the supreme court and state district courts. County government changed notably, too, in that the commissioners' court composed of the chief justice (county judge) and four county commissioners was replaced by a five-man county court composed of five justices of the peace elected by precinct. The justice residing in the precinct containing the county seat would act as the presiding officer.[25]

24. Moneyhon, *Republicanism in Reconstruction Texas,* 86–93; Ramsdell, *Reconstruction in Texas,* 206–29.

25. The convention ended with so much bitterness between moderate and radical Republicans that the constitution had to be put into its final form by a committee of delegates appointed by Gen. Edward R. S. Canby, commander of the Fifth Military District. All the key provisions, however, were settled by the convention. Moneyhon, *Republicanism in Reconstruction Texas,* 93, 100–103; Ramsdell, *Reconstruction in Texas,* 229, 242–60. The entire text of the Constitution of 1869 is found in H. P. N. Gammel, comp., *The Laws of Texas, 1822–1897* (10 vols.; Austin, 1898–1902), VII, 395–427.

The conflict between moderate and radical Republicans carried beyond the convention and into the election to ratify the new constitution and choose officials under its terms. Both sides sought aid from U. S. Grant, winner of the 1868 presidential election in which Texas had not participated, and Congress. A. J. Hamilton and the moderates, hoping to continue the advantage they held at the end of the convention and appeal to white conservatives as well, sought an early election and quick readmission to the Union. Davis and the radicals, needing time to solidify their hold on the black vote through the Union League and also to prevent an alliance of moderates and conservatives, urged delay in the vote. Congress put the decision in Grant's hands, and the president wound up supporting the radicals. He delayed until July 15 in calling the election and then set the voting for November 30–December 3, 1869. This, plus the decision by General J. J. Reynolds, a personal friend of Grant's and commander of the Fifth Military District, to support Davis rather than Hamilton greatly improved the chances of a radical victory.[26]

In the meantime a second period of removing local officials and replacing them with military appointees affected many county governments across the state. The first round of removals, which took place in late 1867, generally saw officials replaced because they were disloyal or "impediments" to Reconstruction. This second course of dismissals was in response to an act of Congress on February 18, 1869, requiring all governmental officials in states still not restored to the Union—Texas, Georgia, and Virginia—to swear the test oath of 1862 that they had never voluntarily supported the Confederacy. Many local officeholders who had served to the general satisfaction of Unionists, blacks, and the military could not swear such an oath and had to be replaced in April and May, 1869, further upsetting conservatives at the whole process of Congressional Reconstruction. Indeed, most whites found little to be pleased with in public life during this period except the closing of all local offices of the Freedmen's Bureau in the state at the end of December, 1868.[27]

The gubernatorial campaign between A. J. Hamilton, who had an-

26. Moneyhon, *Republicanism in Reconstruction Texas,* 103–16; Ramsdell, *Reconstruction in Texas,* 261–67, 274–78.

27. County-by-county removals and appointments in 1869 are found in Election Registers, 1869. The act requiring the test oath of local officials is in *Congressional Globe,* 40th Cong., 3rd Sess., Pt. 3, Appendix, 327. Richter, *Overreached on All Sides,* 287.

nounced his candidacy on March 18, and Davis, the nominee of a Radical Republican convention in Houston held June 7–8, got underway in September, 1869. Hamilton received an important boost on September 30 when provisional governor E. M. Pease, seeing that General Reynolds was likely to replace moderates who held local offices with radicals friendly to Davis, resigned and publicly attacked the military's continuing interference in local government. Pease's action stung Reynolds to the point that he made few removals in late 1869 and at the same time let informed voters know that his friend Davis stood for military involvement and delay in ending Reconstruction. The general did not appoint a replacement for Pease, choosing instead to handle the functions of the office himself until after the election.[28]

A final revision of voter registration lists, made November 16–26, added more whites than blacks to the rolls, bringing the totals to 78,648 and 56,905 respectively. Whites constituted 58 percent of the eligible voters, but in the election of November 30–December 3, only slightly more than one-half went to the polls. This was a far higher participation rate for whites than in the election of the constitutional convention in 1868, but a larger proportion of eligible blacks (approximately two-thirds) went to the polls. Whites may have stayed away rather than vote for a moderate Republican, or they may have, as some claimed, thought that Texas would not be allowed to return to its proper constitutional relationship with the Union unless Davis won. In any case, their absence from the polls allowed blacks in eastern and central counties and white voters in the western part of the state to make the difference. The new constitution easily won approval by a vote of 72,466 to 4,928, but the contest for governor was very close. According to the returns certified by General Reynolds, Davis defeated Hamilton by 39,901 to 39,092, a margin so thin that the loser would always believe that he had been cheated. Fortunately for Davis, radicals also would have working majorities in both houses of the new state legislature, the twelfth. Republicans also won three of Texas' four congressional seats; the fourth going to a Democrat who, ironically, was a carpetbagger.[29]

On January 8, 1870, General Reynolds appointed E. J. Davis and all the

28. Winkler, ed., *Platforms of Political Parties in Texas,* 117, 119–21; Moneyhon, *Republicanism in Reconstruction Texas,* 116–17; Ramsdell, *Reconstruction in Texas,* 278.

29. Ramsdell, *Reconstruction in Texas,* 283–87; Moneyhon, *Republicanism in Reconstruction Texas,* 122–26. County-by-county returns for the 1869 election were printed in *Senate Miscellaneous Documents,* 41st Cong., 2nd Sess., No. 77, pp. 38–79.

other state officials elected the previous month to act as a provisional government while the state took the final steps for restoration to the Union. The general also called a provisional session of the Twelfth Legislature to ratify the Thirteenth, Fourteenth, and Fifteenth Amendments and elect United States senators. At a brief session February 8–24, 1870, the legislature ratified the amendments and elected two Radical Republicans, James W. Flanagan and Morgan Hamilton (A. J. Hamilton's brother) to the senate. Congress then passed a bill that President Grant signed on March 30, ending military Reconstruction in Texas. On April 16, 1870, General Reynolds turned over all authority to civil officers. The Twelfth Legislature met in a called session for the inauguration of Governor Davis on April 28, and the slightly more than three years of Congressional Reconstruction in Texas came to an end.[30]

Immediately after his inauguration, Davis outlined an ambitious program aimed especially at securing law and order, and the legislature remained in special session until August 15, 1870, to deal with his recommendations. A militia bill passed in late June created a state militia composed of all able-bodied men aged eighteen to forty-five. The governor as commander-in-chief could call the militia into state service to police any county in which regular law enforcement could not be handled by constituted civil authorities. A second law-and-order measure that passed in June established a state police force of 258 men headed by a chief of police but also under the ultimate control of the governor. All local law enforcement officers had to aid the state police in their activities. Individuals accused of felonies by the state police or regular law enforcement officials were tried in state district courts, and there, too, the legislature increased the power of the governor. The Constitution of 1869 provided that the chief executive would appoint district judges, but made no provision concerning the number of judicial districts. So, on July 2, the legislature increased the number of districts from seventeen to thirty-five, giving Governor Davis an opportunity to appoint thirty-five loyal Republicans to key positions in the state's justice system.[31]

30. Ramsdell, *Reconstruction in Texas*, 285–92; Moneyhon, *Republicanism in Reconstruction Texas*, 127–28, 134.

31. Moneyhon, *Republicanism in Reconstruction Texas*, 135–42; Randolph B. Campbell, "Scalawag District Judges: The E. J. Davis Appointees, 1870–1873," *Houston Review*, XIV (1992), 77.

Governor Davis also called the special session's attention to the constitutional mandate that the state create "public free schools" for all children aged six to eighteen in Texas. To this end, an act of August 13, 1870, designated each county as a school district with the local justice court acting as a school board. The perpetual school fund created by the constitution (all lands and monies previously set aside for education plus all revenues from future sales of public lands, one-quarter of the income from general taxation, and a one-dollar poll tax on all males aged twenty-one to sixty) was to be used to pay teachers, and school buildings would be financed by a 1 percent property tax levied by the local justice court/school board.[32]

Little came of this measure immediately, and on April 24, 1871, during its regular session, the Twelfth Legislature passed a new public school law creating a highly centralized system more to the liking of Governor Davis. Under the new law all supervisory power rested in a state board of education composed of the governor, superintendent of public instruction, and attorney general. The superintendent of public instruction appointed supervisors for each state judicial district who in turn designated the counties in their districts as school districts and appointed five supervisors for each. County supervisors could levy a 1 percent property tax for building and maintaining schools in in their districts. Overall, this centralized school system, which proved to be expensive, gave great power to the governor, especially since he appointed the attorney general and the first superintendent of public instruction who served on the state school board.[33]

The special session of the Twelfth Legislature in 1870 also passed three other pieces of legislation aimed at enhancing the position of the governor and maintaining Republican control of the state. First, an enabling act of June 28 permitted Davis to appoint replacements to most state, district, and local offices that were vacant at that time or became vacant before the next regular election. Second, the legislature gave the governor control of the voter registration system by empowering him to appoint a registrar and a three-man board of appeal for each county in the state. Third, the legislature passed a law postponing mid-term congressional elections that should have been held in the fall of 1870, and state elections due in the fall of 1871, until November, 1872. This allowed Republican congressmen elected in

32. Gammel, comp., *Laws of Texas*, VI, 287–92, VII, 417–18.
33. Carl H. Moneyhon, "Public Education and Texas Reconstruction Politics, 1871–1874," *Southwestern Historical Quarterly*, XCII (1989), 395.

1869 to go unchallenged in 1870 and local officials such as sheriffs who had won two-year terms in 1869 to hold their offices for at least an extra year.[34]

The Twelfth Legislature met in regular session from January 10 to May 31, 1871, but with the exception of the new public education bill, passed little legislation having the significance of the laws enacted in 1870. In any case, by mid-1871, Governor Davis and the legislature faced a rising tide of criticism from both conservatives and moderate Republicans such as A. J. Hamilton. This attack utilized the themes of tyranny and taxes and contained a strong element of racism. The conservatives said that the militia law and state police force gave the governor dictatorial power; moreover, some 40 percent of state policemen were black. State and local taxes had risen to unprecedented levels due to the expenses of an enlarged central government, efforts to improve roads and bridges, and the establishment of the public school system. Moderate Republicans, conservative Unionists, and former secessionists called a taxpayers' convention in Austin for September 22–25, 1871, at which representatives of ninety-four counties approved a report condemning virtually every action of the Davis administration to that date. Faced with an increasingly organized opposition, and having failed to build a large constituency among the state's whites, virtually all of whom could and would now vote, Republican government in Texas had a very limited life expectancy by the fall of 1871.[35]

The first important Republican defeats came in special congressional elections called for October 3–6, 1871. Originally planned for 1872, these elections had to be held in 1871 because the Forty-first Congress—to which representatives had been elected in 1869—expired on March 4, 1871, and the Forty-second Congress would meet in December of that year, well before the date Republicans in Texas had hoped to choose new congressmen. The Democratic party organized on a statewide and district level and took all four seats in Congress. During the election, Governor Davis responded to a riot in Limestone County by declaring martial law and sending in state militia who had to be paid by means of a special tax on local property holders. This action may have been necessary, but it only added to the conservative charges of tyranny and taxes.[36]

34. Gammel, comp., *Laws of Texas*, VI, 191–92, 198–205, 302–13.

35. Moneyhon, *Republicanism in Reconstruction Texas*, 152–62; Ramsdell, *Reconstruction in Texas*, 301–309; Richardson, Wallace, and Anderson, *Texas*, 242; Winkler, ed., *Platforms of Political Parties in Texas*, 128–40.

36. Moneyhon, *Republicanism in Reconstruction Texas*, 162–67.

The Twelfth Legislature held a relatively short and uneventful session from September 12 to December 2, 1871, and the two parties spent most of the next year preparing for a general election to be held November 5–8, 1872. In the presidential race, the first for Texas voters since 1860, the Democrats endorsed the Liberal Republican candidate Horace Greeley in opposition to the incumbent Republican U. S. Grant. The state also had to elect United States representatives for the Forty-third Congress, one-third of the state senate (state senators under the Constitution of 1869 served six-year terms staggered so that one-third faced reelection every two years), and a new state house of representatives. Finally, the election had to fill the positions of local officials, such as sheriffs, who were limited to two-year terms under the constitution but had held office since winning in 1869. Candidates and campaigners for both parties worked hard across the state and, as in 1871, the Democrats won overwhelmingly. Greeley carried the state in the presidential election, and Democrats won all six congressional races, including two at-large seats that had been awarded to Texas by redistricting after the census of 1870. State legislative races were even more damaging to the Davis administration, as Democrats won control of both houses of the Thirteenth Legislature. Thus by 1873 Republicans still had strongholds in the governor's office and the judiciary, but conservatives confidently expected the next gubernatorial election to bring total "redemption" to Texas.[37]

The Democrat-controlled Thirteenth Legislature met from January 4 to June 4, 1873, and rejected all efforts at reconciliation by Governor Davis. Over his veto, it repealed the state police act, limited his use of the militia, and reduced the appointive powers of the governor's office. A new public education law, also passed over Davis' veto, decentralized the system and placed strict limits on the power of local boards to raise taxes for schools. Finally, the legislature called a one-day general election for state and local officials to be held on December 2, 1873, in the various precincts in each county rather than at the county seat, the site of all elections since 1867.[38]

The Republicans renominated Davis and pointed out that the Thirteenth

37. *Ibid.*, 168–82; *Report of the Secretary of State of the State of Texas, for the Year 1872* (Austin, 1873), 62–75; Kingston, Attlesey, and Crawford, *Political History of Texas*, 75; Election Registers, 1872.

38. Moneyhon, *Republicanism in Reconstruction Texas*, 183–85, 192; Richardson, Wallace, and Anderson, *Texas*, 244.

Legislature controlled by Democrats had increased taxes, added to the state debt, given eighty thousand acres of public lands to railroads, and destroyed the school system. Democrats, however, needed only to remind most white voters that Republicans were the party of Congressional Reconstruction, blacks, centralized "tyranny," and taxes. Their nominee, Richard Coke of McLennan County, overwhelmed Davis at the polls by an official total of 85,549 to 42,633. Black voters, due in part to intimidation, did not turn out as in earlier elections, but even if they had, Coke would have won easily.[39]

Davis accepted defeat and prepared to leave office at the end of his term on April 28, 1874 (four years after his inauguration), but some Republican partisans raised a constitutional question that the governor felt obligated to pursue. The issue arose over the provision in the constitution providing that "all elections . . . shall be held at the county seats of the several counties until otherwise provided by law; and the polls shall be open for four days." Those who wanted to challenge the election argued that the semicolon made the two clauses independent; hence the legislature had no constitutional power to change the length of the election from four days to one. The Texas Supreme Court, which was composed of Davis appointees, ruled the election unconstitutional in a decision known as the semicolon case. In the meantime, Democratic leaders demanded that Davis resign on January 8, 1874, four years to the day after General Reynolds had made him provisional governor following the election of 1869. When he refused, the Democrats decided to have the legislature meet, inaugurate Coke, and take power until the federal government intervened. On January 11 Davis asked President Grant for aid in holding his office and preserving peace until the problem could be solved, but received a curt refusal. The president pointed out that Davis had signed the election law in question and disregarded the governor's argument that he could not ignore a decision by the state supreme court. Coke was inaugurated on January 15, and Davis, with no federal support forthcoming, had no choice except to resign from office four days later.[40]

With Davis' resignation, the judiciary was the only branch of government remaining in the hands of Republicans. A constitutional amendment

39. Moneyhon, *Republicanism in Reconstruction Texas*, 185–91; Kingston, Attlesey, and Crawford, *Political History of Texas*, 61.
40. Moneyhon, *Republicanism in Reconstruction Texas*, 191–94.

adopted at the election on December 2, 1873, however, increased the membership of the supreme court from three to five justices and allowed Coke to appoint an entirely new court in January, 1874. The governor also filled the positions of fourteen district judges, most of whom resigned or were removed by the state legislature during 1874 and 1875. In all cases, of course, Coke appointed Democratic replacements, bringing virtually the entire government of Texas under the control of "Redeemers."[41]

Not satisfied with having removed Republicans from government, conservatives also believed it necessary to replace the "radical" Constitution of 1869 with a more appropriate fundamental law. In early August, 1875, voters approved a convention and elected ninety delegates, three from each senatorial district. More than 80 percent of the delegates (seventy-five) were Democrats, and they wrote a constitution reflecting their dislike for centralized, activist, expensive state government. Governors would serve two-year terms and have no control over other elective state officers and local officials. Even the salary of the chief executive was reduced—from five thousand dollars a year to four thousand. The legislature would meet biennially, rather than annually as under the 1869 constitution, and legislators would be paid five dollars a day for the first sixty days of a session and two dollars a day thereafter. The legislature could not incur indebtedness greater than $200,000. Courts and judges would have much less power than under the Republicans. The supreme court would hear appeals on civil cases only, and a new court of appeals had jurisdiction in all criminal cases. The number of district courts was reduced from thirty-five to twenty-six. All judges were to be elective: district judges for four-year terms and higher court judges for six-year terms. Constitutional provisions concerning public schools also reflected the conservatives' attitudes in that they decentralized the system and left support largely up to local government. The constitution abolished the position of state superintendent of education, authorized legislative support amounting only to a one-dollar poll tax and not more than one-quarter of property taxes, and had no provision concerning local school taxes. The convention approved its handiwork by a vote of fifty-three to eleven on November 24, 1875.[42]

41. The constitutional amendment is found in 40 *Texas Reports* 19. Coke's appointments to the supreme court and the district courts are found in the Election Registers, 1874–1875.

42. J. E. Ericson, "The Delegates to the Convention of 1875: A Reappraisal," *Southwestern Historical Quarterly*, LXVII (1963), 22–27; Winkler, ed., *Platforms of Political Parties in*

Voters went to the polls on February 15, 1876, to ratify the new constitution and elect state and local officials under its terms. The Democratic
state convention took no official position on the document while renominating Coke for the governorship, whereas the Republican convention
unanimously opposed it and nominated William M. Chambers to oppose
the incumbent governor. Coke won easily by an official total of 150,581 to
50,030, a much greater margin of victory than he had over Davis in 1873.
The constitution was somewhat less popular than the governor, probably
because conservatives in counties with large black populations wanted it to
include a poll tax limitation on the suffrage, but it won approval by a vote
of 136,606 to 56,652. On April 18, 1876, the new constitution went into effect, sweeping away the last remaining vestiges of congressional directives,
military rule, and Republican government. In the words of the Dallas *Herald,* "Today [April 18] without a single murmur every single officer known
to the State Government of Texas quietly surrenders up his position. Today
the organic law which for four years has controlled the destinies of Texas is
buried with the eternity of years that are no more, and the new Constitution, fresh from an overwhelming revolution by the people, takes its place."
Reconstruction thus ended, but the era left a deep, seemingly permanent
imprint on the Lone Star State.[43]

---

*Texas,* 163–73; Richardson, Wallace, and Anderson, *Texas,* 250–54. It should be noted that at
least forty delegates to the convention, most of whom were Democrats, also belonged to the
Patrons of Husbandry, better known as the Grange. This organization of farmers strongly opposed taxes, government expenditures, public schools, and corporations. Therefore, Democrats who belonged to the Grange had an additional reason to rewrite the Republicans' constitution of 1869.

43. Winkler, ed., *Platforms of Political Parties in Texas,* 173–79; Richardson, Wallace, and
Anderson, *Texas,* 254–55; Kingston, Attlesey, and Crawford, *Political History of Texas,* 61;
Dallas *Herald,* April 22, 1876.

# 2

## COLORADO COUNTY

In many ways antebellum Colorado County typified the slaveholding, cotton-producing Old South. Families in Stephen F. Austin's "Old Three Hundred" settled along the Colorado River, the county's namesake, in 1822 and established the future seat of county government, Columbus, in 1835. Mostly Anglo in ethnic origin and coming primarily from the older southern states, these settlers introduced slave labor to cultivate the rich blackland soil and quickly brought Colorado County into the Cotton Kingdom. By 1860, the county had 306 slaveholders, representing 39 percent of all families, and 3,559 slaves, constituting 45 percent of the total population. Fifty-two slaveholders qualified for the title "planter" by owning at least twenty bondsmen. Four of these men held more than one hundred slaves, ranking them among the state's great planter elite. The county's 14,438-bale cotton crop in 1859 surpassed the output of all but four others in Texas. In 1860, Texas' first railroad, the Buffalo Bayou, Brazos, and Colorado Railway, reached Alleyton just to the east of Columbus, providing a commercial link with Houston and even more encouragement to the expansion of slavery and cotton production.[1]

1. Brief descriptions of Colorado County, Columbus, and the Buffalo Bayou, Brazos, and Colorado Railway are found in Webb, Carroll, and Branda, eds., *Handbook of Texas*, I, 240, 378–79, 382. Stephen F. Austin apparently surveyed Columbus in 1823, but the town was not established under that name until the mid-1830s. William B. DeWees, *Letters from an Early Settler of Texas* (1852; repr., Waco, Tex., 1968), 42; Houston *Telegraph and Texas Register,*

## Map 2

## Colorado County

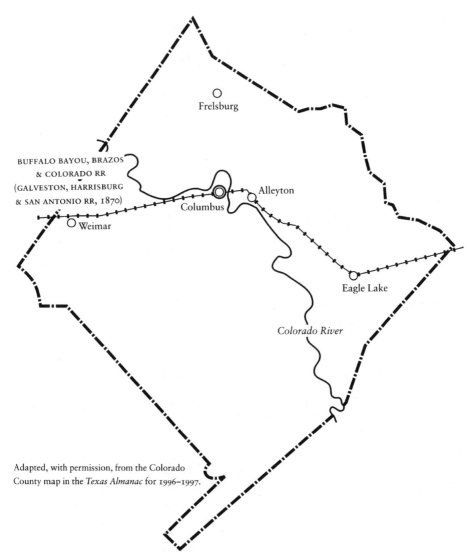

Frelsburg

BUFFALO BAYOU, BRAZOS
& COLORADO RR
(GALVESTON, HARRISBURG
& SAN ANTONIO RR, 1870)

Columbus

Alleyton

Weimar

Eagle Lake

Colorado River

Adapted, with permission, from the Colorado
County map in the *Texas Almanac* for 1996–1997.

Colorado County differed, however, in one very important way from most other areas of Texas that had joined the Cotton Kingdom. Its population included not only southern-born whites and African Americans, but also a significant minority of German immigrants. Germans began to settle in northern and northeastern Colorado County during the 1830s and 1840s. They established Frelsburg, which gained a post office in 1847, and several smaller towns, including Bernardo and Mentz, and gave antebellum Colorado County a strikingly multi-ethnic population. In 1860, it was 45 percent black, 30 to 35 percent Anglo (primarily southern-born), and 20 to 25 percent German. The Germans, of course, did not share the cultural heritage of their southern-born neighbors, and most did not have the capital to acquire slaves and participate in the cotton economy even if they wished. Consequently, they generally opposed secession in 1860 and 1861, and their role in Reconstruction, especially after the freedmen became voters, promised to be vital.[2]

Given Colorado County's commitment to slaves and cotton, its voters, except for the German immigrants, should have tended toward the pro-southern extremism typical of most plantation areas of the state during the late 1850s. This was not the case, however, and was probably due in part to the influence of the *Colorado Citizen*. Established in Columbus in 1857 by James D. Baker and his two brothers, the newspaper consistently took a moderate position until after the election of Abraham Lincoln in November, 1860. It endorsed the Unionist, Sam Houston, for governor against the Calhoun Democrat, Hardin R. Runnels, in 1859, and Houston carried the county by a vote of 345 to 275. In the presidential election of 1860, the

May 2, June 2, 1837. Information on the population and slaveholding is from the Eighth Census of the United States, 1860, Schedule 1 (Free Inhabitants) and Schedule 2 (Slave Inhabitants), National Archives, Washington, D.C. A listing of the county's largest slaveholders is in Campbell, *Empire for Slavery*, 274. Statistics on cotton production are from U.S. Bureau of the Census, *Agriculture of the United States in 1860; Compiled from the Original Returns of the Eighth Census* (Washington, D.C., 1864), 140–49.

2. Webb, Carroll, and Branda, eds., *Handbook of Texas*, I, 647; Colorado County Historical Commission, *Colorado County Chronicles: From the Beginning to 1923* (2 vols., Austin, 1986), I, 374; Terry G. Jordan, *German Seed in Texas Soil: Immigrant Farmers in Nineteenth-Century Texas* (Austin, 1966), 40–43, 94–95, 110; Charles Deaton, comp., *Texas Postal History Handbook* (Austin, 1980), 98. Foreign-born residents, mostly German, amounted to 15 percent of Colorado County's population in 1860. The estimate that Germans made up 20 to 25 percent of the total is based on the fact that children born to German immigrants after they arrived in Texas would have been reported in the census as native born. U.S. Bureau of the Census, *Population of the United States in 1860; Compiled from the Original Returns of the Eighth Census* (Washington, D.C., 1864), 484, 487–89.

*Colorado Citizen* supported the Constitutional Union party ticket headed by John Bell rather than the Southern Democratic candidate, John C. Breckinridge. Bell lost Colorado County, but he received 41 percent of the vote (394 to 569 for Breckinridge), a far better showing than the Constitutional Unionists made statewide. Once Lincoln won the election, however, the *Citizen* endorsed disunion rather than submission to a "Black Republican." County voters sent T. Scott Anderson, an avowed secessionist, to the convention in Austin and on February 23, 1861, approved leaving the Union by a vote of 584 to 330.[3]

The secession referendum demonstrated a clear division within Colorado County. Areas populated largely by southern-born slaveholders voted overwhelmingly for secession. Eagle Lake in the southern part of the county, for example, voted yes, 106 to 1. By contrast, a majority of the no votes, 195 of the 330, came from the two heavily German precincts in northern and northeastern Colorado County. Frelsburg voted 154 to 22 against disunion, and the polling place for Bernardo and Mentz reported the rejection of secession by a 41 to 10 margin. The only other precinct with significant opposition to leaving the Union was Columbus, which cast 201 yes and 93 no votes, the disapproval coming primarily from town-dwelling Germans and Unionists native to the Upper South.[4]

Fortunately, the division between Unionists and secessionists did not lead to serious repression or violence in Colorado County once the Civil War began in 1861. In fact, the price of conflict remained relatively small throughout the next four years. Several companies of Colorado County soldiers saw heavy action and suffered severe losses—Capt. John C. Upton's company in the 5th Texas Infantry (Hood's Texas brigade) being the best example—but hundreds of men volunteered for service in home-guard units and fought no major battles. Also, the county, like all interior regions of Texas, escaped federal invasion and, although the site of considerable Confederate supply activity, was not occupied by either a defending or attacking army. In at least one way, the war even proved an economic boon as Alleyton became the eastern terminus for a cotton-exportation route that ran from south-central Texas to the Mexican port of Bagdad on the Gulf of

3. *Colorado County Chronicles*, I, 79; *Colorado Citizen* (Columbus), July 23, 1859, September 1, 1860, January 5, 12, February 16, 1861; Kingston, Attlesey, and Crawford, *Political History of Texas*, 54, 72; Timmons, "Referendum in Texas on the Ordinance of Secession," 15.

4. Election Record, 1854–1866, County Clerk's Office, Colorado County Courthouse, Columbus, Tex.

Mexico below Matamoros. During 1863, observers reported that Alleyton looked like a boom town; its streets filled with cotton sellers and buyers, speculators, and teamsters.[5]

The Confederacy's surrender in the spring of 1865 brought uncertainty and fear to many in Colorado County. Everybody is "mighty down in the mouth," wrote a young woman on June 11. We have little basis for hope, she continued, "for it is the Yankeys who are dealing with us, and who have proven themselves to be the most cruel race that ever existed." The actual arrival of Federal troops two weeks later, however, proved less frightening than expected. The *Colorado Citizen* described the officers of the 23rd Iowa Infantry that occupied Columbus on June 24 as "mild, generous, and forebearing" and their troops as "disciplined" and "orderly." Local residents crowded into the courthouse to take an oath of loyalty to the United States, and Reconstruction got off to a quiet start.[6]

The tranquility of June, 1865, doubtless reassured most whites in Colorado County, but at least one important Unionist did not like the prospect of a lenient Reconstruction. Kidder Walker, a native of Kentucky, wrote from the Frelsburg area to express his displeasure to provisional governor Andrew Jackson Hamilton. "The poor," Walker wrote, "must be made a political element. The light must penetrate the darkened cabin. This class must learn to think and act independently, or the aristocracy will lead them as before. . . . I am decidedly of the opinion," he concluded, "that every seceded state should go through a military probation before its ultimate civil reorganization." Walker was not known as an extremist—he had served as a county commissioner before the war—but the views that he expressed were too radical in June, 1865, for more than a handful of northern Republicans in the United States Congress and certainly too radical for President Johnson and his appointees such as A. J. Hamilton. Reconstruction under presidential direction from 1865 through 1867 would be far more moderate.[7]

On August 9, 1865, Governor Hamilton, as the first step in restoring civil

5. *Colorado County Chronicles*, I, 100–22; Winsor, *Texas in the Confederacy*, 17, 37, 42, 81–82.

6. Caledonia "Callie" Wright to Miss Jodie H. Wright, June 11, 1865, in Josepha Wright Papers, Eugene C. Barker Texas History Center, University of Texas, Austin; *Colorado Citizen*, July 6, 1865, quoted in Galveston *Daily News*, July 14, 1865.

7. Kidder Walker to Andrew Jackson Hamilton, June 5, 1865, Governors' Papers: A. J. Hamilton, Archives Division, Texas State Library, Austin (hereafter cited as Governors' Papers: AJH). Walker was a county commissioner in 1860. See Election Registers, 1860.

government to Colorado County, appointed a county judge, sheriff, four county commissioners, and other local officials. These men were to govern until the planned constitutional convention could prepare Texas for re-admission to the Union. Hamilton chose Unionists rather than members of what Walker called the "aristocracy" to run local government, but his appointees were generally southern-born, longtime residents of the county. John D. Gillmore, the interim county judge, was a native of Kentucky who worked as a gunsmith before the war and owned no slaves. James B. Good, Hamilton's appointee as sheriff, was also a nonslaveholding native of the Upper South (Tennessee). In the 1860 census, Good reported his occupation as an agent for a stage line. Two of the four county commissioners—Jasper N. Binkley, a tinner, and Calvin York, a farmer—were nonslaveholders from Tennessee. Gerhard Frels, another nonslaveholding farmer, had come to Texas from Germany. Only Phineas M. Garrett, the fourth commissioner, had a wealthy planter's background, having paid taxes on thirty-three slaves in 1860. He, like Good, Binkley, and York, was Tennessee-born. Of these men, only Gillmore had a reputation for undoubted unionism, and yet only he had held public office before, having served as a county commissioner from 1860 to 1862. Some residents may have objected to these interim officials, but there is no evidence that their appointments occasioned any significant complaint.[8]

Hamilton's appointment of George W. Smith as district judge for Colorado and several neighboring counties also brought no objections. A native of Kentucky, Smith had come to Texas in 1843 and eventually settled in Columbus. Like so many Whig Unionists from the Upper South, he opposed secession but then supported the South once the war came, serving as a district judge while Texas was part of the Confederacy. In an August, 1865, letter thanking Governor Hamilton for the appointment, Smith promised to protect "the civil rights of the people against all unlawful invasions." He also observed that the residents of Colorado County were highly pleased at the quick return of civil authority.[9]

The commissioners' court began to handle county business in August,

8. Election Registers, 1860–1865, have the names of Hamilton's appointees and their previous service, if any. Identifying information on these men is from the Eighth Census, 1860, Schedules 1 and 2.

9. Dallas *Herald*, October 15, 1873; George W. Smith to A. J. Hamilton, August 21, 1865, Governors' Papers: AJH.

and Smith held a regular session of the district court in October. Both were uneventful. The commissioners chose a panel of grand jurors for the district court that included Andrew M. Campbell, the county judge at the time of secession. Campbell had owned forty-one slaves in 1860 and reported wealth amounting to ninety thousand dollars. His selection, and subsequent service as foreman of the grand jury, symbolized the limited extent of change brought by the first few months of Reconstruction.[10]

Of course, one change that began to unfold in June, 1865—the movement of African Americans from slavery to freedom—could not be limited by any measure as simple as restoring civil government. Emancipation created more than four thousand freedmen in Colorado County, the vast majority of whom had no property and no place to go. Most, after a brief testing of their freedom to move, wound up working on plantations in the county for wages or a share of the crop. The commanders of federal troops generally gave no assistance to freedmen beyond advising them to work hard, but help came in October, 1865, in the form of the Freedmen's Bureau. Capt. Eli W. Green of the 29th Illinois, one of the first local agents (subassistant commissioners) appointed in Texas, arrived at Columbus on October 22. He reported optimistically that there would be "little difficulty in making the present system of free labor successful, if properly managed." He also found, however, that some planters were mistreating the freedmen and argued that in such cases the military should intervene. "I am determined," he wrote, "that the Negros *shall not be imposed* upon by this *class of desperadoes.*" Captain Green did not deliver on this promise because his unit left Columbus within the next month. Late in 1865, W. D. Whitall, a special agent of the bureau, visited Alleyton and saw to it that planters in the area paid freedmen for their work since June. He had little difficulty, probably because the bureau required planters to pay only 10 percent of the cotton crop to their workers.[11]

Lt. John T. Raper of the 26th Ohio became the second Bureau agent in

10. Police Court Minutes, 1862–1876, pp. 39–40, County Clerk's Office, Colorado County Courthouse, Columbus, Tex.; District Court Civil Minutes, Book C-2, p. 369, District Clerk's Office, Colorado County Courthouse, Columbus, Tex.; Election Registers, 1860; Eighth Census, 1860, Schedules 1 and 2.

11. Campbell, *Empire for Slavery,* 250–51; Capt. Eli W. Green to Lt. C. C. Morse, October 24, 1865, Records of the Assistant Commissioner for the State of Texas, United States Bureau of Refugees, Freedmen, and Abandoned Lands, 1865–1869, U.S. Department of War, Record Group 105, National Archives, (hereafter cited as BRFAL); Richter, *Overreached on All Sides,* 28–29, 40.

Columbus in November, 1865. He found that "a great many" of the freedmen had gotten the "idea of the division of the lands into their heads" and consequently were unwilling to make labor contracts for the coming year until after Christmas. He tried to dispel the "forty acres and a mule" myth, and the great majority of freedmen signed contracts by January 1, 1866. Some labor agreements called for wages only, but most promised the workers housing, food, fuel, medical attention, and one-third of the crop. Planters grumbled that the freedmen expected too much, but apparently the process went smoothly. "It seems," one Colorado County woman wrote, "that the Freedmen will be more trouble than profit. . . . The hands . . . signed the contract yesterday, and Jim [her brother] went with them to the agent and had it approved. Writing, signing and approving contracts is all the go at present." [12]

Making labor contracts went smoothly for Lieutenant Raper, but his handling of violence against freedmen led to the first major confrontation between military authority and local officials in Colorado County. The agent arrested and fined a citizen of neighboring Fayette County for assaulting a black man in Columbus. The citizen in return swore out warrants against Raper for "swindling" and "false arrest," and the town's mayor, Fred Barnard, asked the post commander to arrest the agent. Raper argued successfully that as an officer of the United States government he could not be arrested. The issue was resolved when Raper requested and received permission from the bureau to leave the service in January, 1866. His replacement did not arrive until April, but at least the freedmen had contracts for the year and, according to one Unionist planter from Eagle Lake, were much encouraged by their prospects. The planter believed, however, that only the military and Unionists protected blacks from the wrath of local whites. [13]

On January 8, 1866, Colorado County took another important step toward completing Presidential Reconstruction by electing a delegate to the constitutional convention scheduled to meet in Austin the next month. Interim district judge George W. Smith, who had opposed secession but then

12. Lt. John T. Raper to Lt. C. C. Morse, November 24, 29, 1865, January 15, 1866, BRFAL, RG 105, NA; Callie Wright to "Dear Sister," November, 1865, January 7, 1866, Wright Papers.

13. Lt. John T. Raper to Lt. C. C. Morse, December 26, 1865, P. H. Webster to Gen. Edgar M. Gregory, February 5, 1866, BRFAL, RG 105, NA; Fred Barnard to A. J. Hamilton, December 26, 1865, Governors' Papers: AJH; Richter, *Overreached on All Sides*, 42–43.

supported the Confederacy, defeated Kidder Walker, the advocate of a more stringent Reconstruction, 130 votes to 99 in a very light turnout. The internal division over secession appeared again in this first election held since the war. Walker received eighty-nine of his ninety-nine votes in the Frelsburg precinct, where Smith received only four. Unionism remained strong among the Germans.[14]

Once the convention created the Constitution of 1866, voters went to the polls again on June 25 to approve the revised fundamental law and elect state and local officials. Statewide the contest pitted Conservative Unionists led by James W. Throckmorton against the Radical Unionists and their gubernatorial candidate Elisha M. Pease. In local races, the *Colorado Citizen* carefully pointed out the military records of those who had fought for the Confederacy and endorsed all conservative candidates (Conservative Unionists such as Throckmorton as well as former secessionists and Confederates). "Our face will blister with shame," editor James D. Baker wrote on May 5, "if the Pease ticket shall receive as many as fifty votes in Colorado County." He was about to be burned badly by German and Radical Unionist voters.[15]

Throckmorton carried Colorado County with 582 votes, but Pease received 329 votes, including 209 from the Frelsburg precinct (Throckmorton had 14) and 40 from the box for Bernardo and Mentz. Voting for other state and district offices followed the same pattern, with the only notable exceptions being the contests for state senator, state representative, and district judge. Colorado County residents Richard V. Cook and Josiah Shaw won the seats in the legislature without real opposition. The district judgeship went to Benjamin Shropshire over John T. Harcourt. In these three elections, however, the winners, all of whom had supported secession and/or served in the Confederate army, received very few votes in the German-dominated precincts. For example, Frelsburg cast 223 votes in the governor's race but only 42 for Cook and 33 for Shaw.[16]

Local elections showed the same regional divisions within Colorado County. The race for county judge proved especially interesting because two conservatives, Richard J. Putney (the last man to hold the county judge

14. Colorado County Election Record, 1854–1866. Frelsburg was precinct three in 1861. It is assumed that it still had that number in 1866.

15. Ramsdell, *Reconstruction in Texas*, 89–112; *Colorado Citizen*, May 5, 1866.

16. *Colorado Citizen*, May 5, 1866; Colorado County Election Record, 1854–1866.

position during the war) and William J. Darden, entered the contest, as did John D. Gillmore, the incumbent appointed by Governor Hamilton. Gill-more won with 416 votes to 345 for Putney and 198 for Darden. The two predominantly German precincts gave the winner two-thirds (275) of his votes. Obviously Putney and Darden split the conservative vote and al-lowed the Unionist minority to keep Gillmore in office. The sheriff's race was decided in largely the same way. In this case, the Hamilton appointee, James B. Good, had the support of the *Colorado Citizen* because he had served in the Confederate army, and he and two other candidates split the conservative vote. Johann Baptist Leyendecker, a German immigrant (and also a Confederate veteran) won the office, receiving 274 of his 363 votes in the two German precincts.[17]

Twelve candidates ran for the four positions on the commissioners' court, making the results difficult to interpret. However, of the four win-ners, only one, Alexander Dunleavy, had owned slaves and held office be-fore or during the war. The other three, Mathias Malsch, William S. Good, and George W. Breeding, definitely did not represent the "aristocracy" of Colorado County. In 1860, Malsch was a merchant in Frelsburg; Good, a stable keeper; and Breeding, a farm renter. Thus Colorado County in 1866, thanks to multiple conservative candidates and Unionist voters (mostly Germans), did not follow the pattern common among former slaveholding, cotton-producing counties in Texas of returning ex-slaveholding, secession-ist leaders to the control of local government. Unionists in the county had relatively few complaints about their situation.[18]

The new commissioners' court met for the first time on October 1, 1866, and resumed normal business such as overseeing county roads. Judge Shropshire began an uneventful session of the district court at the end of that month. Most Colorado County whites, including the Unionists, seem to have been reasonably satisfied with the course of Presidential Recon-struction to that point. Freedmen, however, had played no role in the pro-

17. Colorado County Election Record, 1854–1866; *Colorado Citizen*, May 5, 1866; Eighth Census, 1860, Schedule 1; Index to the Compiled Service Records of Confederate Soldiers Who Served in Organizations from the State of Texas, U.S. Department of War, War Department Collection of Confederate Records, Record Group 109, National Archives.

18. Colorado County Election Record, 1854–1866; Eighth Census, 1860, Schedules 1 and 2. For evidence on the election of ex-slaveholding secessionists across Texas, see Campbell, "Grass Roots Reconstruction," 99–116.

cess. They had no right to vote or serve on juries, and the Eleventh Legislature, which met from August to November, 1866, passed a variety of laws that amounted to a "black code" governing the conduct of former slaves. Moreover, for much of the year of 1866 the Freedmen's Bureau, the agency most likely to assist blacks, did not have strong leadership in Colorado County. Following the mustering out of Sub-assistant Commissioner John T. Raper in January, Lt. George Van De Sande of the 10th United States Colored Infantry assumed the post at Columbus. He served only two months and was replaced in May by Lt. J. Ernest Goodman of the Veteran Reserve Corps. Goodman took an active role at first, trying cases involving assaults on freedmen and forcing whites to uphold labor contracts. In one case he used soldiers to release a freedman who, in his opinion, had been jailed without good reason. By July, however, Goodman apparently tired of his duties. He angered blacks by allowing whites to raise a Confederate flag on Independence Day and by opposing the singing of "The Battle Cry of Freedom" at the freedmen's school. Goodman left Columbus in August, and Enon M. Harris took his place during September. The new agent proved more satisfactory to blacks, especially for his work at enforcing labor contracts. He had problems with townspeople over the ownership of the building in which his office was located and with one of the bureau's schoolteachers, a Miss Hartnett, concerning her "unamiable temper," but remained at his post for the remainder of 1866 and through 1867.[19]

Blacks in Colorado County thus had no political rights and inconsistent support from the Freedmen's Bureau during the first year of Reconstruction. They also suffered to some extent the violence from whites so common across Texas at that time. E. M. Harris reported four blacks murdered by whites in early 1867 when the Freedmen's Bureau began compiling a record of violence. A register of complaints from freedmen kept by Harris from April, 1867, into February, 1868, had 133 entries, many for threatening vio-

19. Police Court Minutes, 1862–1876, pp. 63–72; District Court Civil Minutes, Book D, 34; Crouch, "'All the Vile Passions,'" 13–34; Richter, *Overreached on All Sides*, 40–41, 107–108, 267–70; Lt. J. Ernest Goodman to William H. Sinclair, May 22, 30, 1866, Lt. Goodman to Caswell Coats, May 16, 1866, Lt. Goodman to Mrs. Elizabeth Turner, May 17, 1866, Enon M. Harris to Gen. Charles C. Griffin, February 15, 1867, Records of the Subordinate Field Officers of the Bureau of Freedmen, Refugees, and Abandoned Lands, Sub-assistant Commissioner, Columbus, Tex., U.S. Department of War, Record Group 105, National Archives (hereafter cited as BRFAL, Columbus, Tex.), Robert P. Tendick to Gen. Charles C. Griffin, March 1, 1867, Enon M. Harris to Joel T. Kirkman, March 18, 1867, BRFAL, RG 105, NA.

lence. For example, King Thompson protested to Harris on July 30 that J. N. Wall had vowed to cut his throat "from ear to ear."[20]

In spite of homicides, assaults, and intimidation, Colorado County's blacks appear to have suffered relatively less violence than befell former slaves in many other areas of Texas from 1865 through 1867. More than likely, freedmen benefited from strength in numbers and the fact that their labor was badly needed. One planter commented in 1866 that another, who had a reputation for cruelty to his slaves, could not get freedmen to work for him. Harris noted in June, 1867, that the "better class" of whites seemed to be more accepting of blacks than were the "poorer classes" who found themselves in competition with the former slaves. Freedmen may have benefited also from having a significant portion of the white population, the Germans, who did not have the same views as a majority of southern-born residents. In any case, whatever their treatment and the reasons for it during 1865–1866, the role of freedmen in Reconstruction changed dramatically in 1867 following congressional takeover of the process. They became participants rather than simply subjects.[21]

State representative Josiah Shaw warned Colorado County's conservative whites as early as October, 1866, that Radical Republicans in the North threatened to take Reconstruction away from President Johnson. "Our future," he wrote, "is dark indeed." The Radicals are "maddened with vengeful fury," and if they carry the entire North, "their arrogance, beastly daring and brutal outrage will be without limit." Shaw's rhetoric was overwrought, but his fears soon came true. Radical Republicans took control of Congress in the mid-term elections of November, 1866, and, beginning in March, 1867, passed a series of acts that in effect began Reconstruction anew.[22]

Registration of eligible voters was the first major step in Congressional Reconstruction. Colorado County became part of the Third Registration District supervised by Musgrove Evans, a resident of Fayette County, and Benjamin F. Williams, a fifty-five-year-old African American who lived in

20. "Records of Criminal Offenses Committed in the State of Texas," BRFAL, Vols. 11–13, pp. 57–58; Register of Complaints, April, 1867–December, 1868, BRFAL, Columbus, Tex., RG 105, NA.

21. "Records of Criminal Offenses," Vols. 11–13, report many cases of violence in other Texas counties. P. H. Webster to Gen. E. M. Gregory, February 5, 1866, E. M. Harris to Lt. Joel T. Kirkman, June 4, 1867, BRFAL, RG 105, NA.

22. *Colorado Citizen*, October 20, 1866; Ramsdell, *Reconstruction in Texas*, 145–49.

Columbus. A minister in the Methodist Episcopal Church (Colored), Williams would become the most important black leader in the county during the next few years. "The character that he bears with his former owners," Enon M. Harris wrote of Williams, "and all those who have known him when a slave, & now as a freeman is irreproachable." Williams found that his main responsibility, traveling through his seven-county district and encouraging freedmen to register, proved difficult and dangerous. "Rebels," as he called them, told blacks that those who registered would be sent to Mexico to fight the French there, and they threatened to kill the registration supervisor as a lesson to all others. Williams traveled at night for safety and acted, he wrote, "as wise as a surpent and as harmless as a dove."[23]

A three-man board of registrars—Enon M. Harris, Robert P. Tendick, and Isaac Yates—handled the actual enrollment of voters in Colorado County. Harris, a native of New York, served in his capacity as Freedmen's Bureau agent. Tendick, a native of Germany and former lieutenant in the 30th Missouri Infantry, had come to Columbus with the United States Army in July, 1865. After being discharged, he married the daughter of Charles Schmidt, a local merchant, and began a long political career. Yates was a young black farmer born in North Carolina and brought to Texas as a slave. Thus none of the registrars represented the traditional leadership of the county, and they took to heart the advice from Gen. Charles C. Griffin, commander of the District of Texas, that they could not be "too cautious" in judging the qualifications of those who came before them.[24]

When enrollment began on July 11, the board of registrars rejected whites on the slightest pretext of their being unqualified. For example, they refused to register R. V. Cook, the county's state representative, because he had been a lawyer before the war. The registrars denied County Judge John D. Gillmore, who was generally regarded as a Unionist, because he had served as a county commissioner and justice of the peace before and during

23. Circular No. 16 issued by Gen. Charles C. Griffin, May 16, 1867, Governors' Papers: JWT; Musgrove Evans to Lt. Col. N. Prine, July 8, 1867, Benjamin F. Williams to Prine, November 7, 1867, Records of the Office of Civil Affairs for the Department of Texas and the Fifth Military District, 1865–1870, U.S. Department of War, Records of the United States Army Continental Commands, Record Group 393, National Archives (hereafter cited as OCA); Enon M. Harris to Lt. Joel T. Kirkman, March 2, 1867, BRFAL, Columbus, Tex., RG 105, NA.

24. Musgrove Evans to Lt. Col. N. Prine, July 8, 1867, Lt. Col. N. Prine to J. E. Wheeler, August 3, 1867, OCA, RG 393, NA; Bill Stein, ed., "The Slave Narratives of Colorado County," *Nesbitt Memorial Library Journal: A Journal of Colorado County History*, III (January, 1993), 7; Ninth Census of the United States, 1870, Schedule 1—Inhabitants, NA.

the war. They also turned down at first another Unionist, Daniel D. Claiborne, who was serving at the time as a collector of internal revenue for the U.S. government, because he had been a postmaster in Alabama and then voted for secession in 1861. In the meantime, freedmen, who were eager in the words of Green Harris of Eagle Lake "to do anything to advance or protect the Union," rushed to enroll.[25]

Registration continued until August 31, reopened for a week in late September, and then closed after five more days of enrollment from January 27 to January 31, 1868. By that time the total number of voters stood at 1,847. Of these, 1,141, or 62 percent, were black. It is impossible to say how many whites refused to register or were rejected when they tried, but the number was significant. In spite of the county's many Unionist Germans, registration reduced whites, who were about 55 percent of the population, to a 38-percent minority of qualified voters.[26]

The first opportunity for Colorado County's newly registered voters to go to the polls came February 10–14, 1868, with the election of delegates to a convention that would write a new constitution for Texas. In the meantime, unlike the situation in numerous other counties, Congressional Reconstruction had only limited impact on local government in Columbus. Across Texas, beginning in July, 1867, commanders of the military district of Texas removed hundreds of officials, including Governor Throckmorton, from positions in state and local government. Many counties had all their major officeholders removed by the end of 1867, but Colorado County did not. The men elected there in 1866 remained in office due to their reputations for unionism and the fact that their conduct had not drawn significant complaints from local Unionists or the Freedmen's Bureau agents. Only District Judge Benjamin Shropshire was removed. Isaac B. McFarland, a native of Tennessee whose unionism had led him to leave Texas during the war, took Shropshire's place on September 11, 1867.[27]

Colorado County thus largely escaped one of the most unsettling aspects

25. E. M. Harris to Lt. Joel T. Kirkman, July 15, 1867, Daniel D. Claiborne to Gen. Charles C. Griffin, September 3, 1867, OCA, RG 393, NA; Green Harris to Gen. Charles C. Griffin, July 12, 1867, BRFAL, RG 105, NA.

26. List of Registered Voters in Texas, 1869.

27. Ramsdell, *Reconstruction in Texas*, 168–70, 195–99; Campbell, "Grass Roots Reconstruction," 99–101; Campbell, "District Judges of Texas in 1866–1867," 361–62, 375; James Alex Baggett, "The Rise and Fall of the Texas Radicals, 1867–1883" (Ph.D. dissertation, North Texas State University, 1972), 8, 26.

of Congressional Reconstruction during 1867. However, the February, 1868, election of delegates to the constitutional convention notably stirred partisan feelings. Republicans had begun to campaign, working primarily through Enon M. Harris, the Freedmen's Bureau agent, as early as July of the previous year. Harris received a package containing copies of the Houston *Journal*, a new Republican newspaper, sent by E. M. Wheelock, the bureau's superintendent of education for Texas, with a request to have local Unionists subscribe. "I need not enlarge upon the manifest duty of every Union man," Wheelock wrote, "and especially every government official, aiding to the extent of his ability, the circulation of papers that inculcate firmly and discreetly, national ideas during the coming canvass." Harris obviously agreed and worked actively for Radical Republican candidates, even to the point of ordering printed ballots to distribute to voters. The printer's bill went to George T. Ruby, one of the infant Republican party's most important black leaders, in Houston.[28]

Conservatives attempted to counter the Republicans by appealing to moderates and supporting German candidates. George M. McCormick, a Virginia-born, ex-Confederate lawyer in Columbus, urged Johann Friedrich "Fritz" Leyendecker of Frelsburg to run in order to prevent the election of "ignorant negroes" who would adopt vindictive policies. As the election neared, the public became excited—or at least Harris thought so. On February 7, he asked General Reynolds for troops, claiming that his life was not safe.[29]

H. H. Foster, a Texas-born small farmer, and Ben F. Williams ran as Republicans against Fritz Leyendecker and Frederick W. Boettcher, who represented moderates and conservatives, in the contest for Colorado County's two seats (one shared with Austin County) in the constitutional convention. Nearly 1,000 of the 1,141 registered blacks voted, as opposed to only about 150 of the 706 enrolled whites. Foster and Williams won overwhelmingly with 1,001 and 924 votes respectively, although each received fewer than 10 white votes. Leyendecker showed some strength among freedmen,

28. E. M. Wheelock to E. M. Harris, July 8, 1867, George T. Ruby to Harris, November 1, 1867, *Flake's Bulletin* to Harris, January 19, 1868, Ruby to Harris, January 21, 1868, BRFAL, Columbus, Tex., RG 105, NA.

29. George McCormick to J. F. Leyendecker, January 20, 1868, Leyendecker Family Papers, Eugene C. Barker Texas History Center, University of Texas, Austin; Webb, Carroll, and Branda, eds., *Handbook of Texas*, II, 104; E. M. Harris to 2nd Lt. J. P. Richardson, February 7, 1868, BRFAL, RG 105, NA.

getting 77 black votes, but Boettcher received only 5. The Columbus *Weekly Times* indicated just how much these results displeased conservatives with the following comment on June 6, 1868: "On Monday last . . . the convention met at Austin, composed (with a few exceptions) of carpet baggers, thieves and negroes, to form a constitution for the State. We presume it will be a rich *document,* if the negroes and carpet baggers are in the majority, particularly if the negroes have as little sense as *Parson* Ben, and the carpet baggers are as dishonest and destitute of honor as foster. Old Colorado don't claim Ben and *foster.*" "Ben," of course, referred to B. F. Williams, the black minister who had served as a supervisor of registrars, and "foster" to the other delegate. He was a young native of Texas, so the *Times* could only compare him with the "carpet baggers," not call him one.[30]

The convention met on June 1, 1868, and completed its work on February 6, 1869. Meanwhile, relations between Colorado County's whites and blacks remained relatively calm. The new Freedmen's Bureau agent, Louis M. Stevenson, who replaced E. M. Harris in February, 1868, complained at first about the attitudes of local whites. He reported six cases of attacks by whites on blacks during his first three months of service, and wrote in May: "There is no man so bad but that the best men as a rule will bail him for an outrage on a freedman." William M. Smith, the military appointee as mayor of Columbus, echoed Stevenson's views later that month in a letter to Governor Pease, concluding that "the Bureau is the greatest and almost the only protection the colored people of this vicinity have." However, Stevenson reported only three assaults on blacks by whites for the remainder of 1868 and usually commented that few problems existed and that troops need not be stationed in the county. The outcome of several potentially serious racial incidents bore out the agent's optimistic assessment. In September, after a white storekeeper in Columbus stabbed a freedman, a group of blacks beat and cut the attacker. Local whites reacted by preparing for a "race war," but after talking to Stevenson, they calmed down and committed no violent acts. In December a black man was executed for the rape of a German woman. District Judge McFarland and others feared violence, but nothing happened.[31]

30. Records of the Secretary of State, Election Returns, 1868, Archives Division, Texas State Library, Austin; Columbus *Weekly Times,* June 6, 1868; H. H. Foster can be identified in Eighth Census, 1860, Schedule 1.

31. L. W. Stevenson to 2nd Lt. Charles A. Vernon, May 31, June 30, July 31, August 31, September 21, September 30, October 31, November 30, December 31, 1868, BRFAL, RG 105,

Unlike his view of race relations, Stevenson's attitude toward local civil officeholders became steadily more negative during 1868. In May, he reported that county officials were "efficient and obedient," but within a few months he began to complain about their inefficiency. His greatest difficulty, the agent wrote in November, was the "unreliability of civil officers." District Judge McFarland made the same sort of objections to Governor Pease, aiming his charges especially at County Judge John D. Gillmore and Sheriff J. B. Leyendecker, while William M. Smith added the extreme accusation that most local officials were either members of the Ku Klux Klan or intimidated by it. In early 1869 Robert P. Tendick and the commander of federal troops at Columbus demanded the replacement of Leyendecker with Charles Schmidt, a merchant born in Germany.[32]

These complaints did not lead to any removals by the governor, but the act of Congress in February, 1869, requiring all government officials in Texas to take the test oath that they had never voluntarily supported the Confederacy had the same effect. Most Colorado County officeholders could not meet this requirement when it became effective in April and had to vacate their positions. Daniel D. Claiborne, a one-time large slaveholder who had opposed the war and become a Republican, replaced Gillmore as county judge. Schmidt received, but declined, the nomination to replace Leyendecker in the sheriff's office. Jesse H. Johnson, a young native of Virginia, took the position in May. On the commissioners' court, only German-born Mathias Malsch remained in office. William T. Wilkinson, formerly lieutenant colonel of the 30th Missouri Infantry, native German Henry Boedecker of Columbus, and Andrew S. Wirtz, a carpenter from Virginia, replaced the other three commissioners. Boedecker could not qualify, and eventually in January, 1870, Isaac Yates took his place, thus becoming the first black officeholder in Colorado County. Ironically, District Judge McFarland also could not swear the test oath and lost his place on the bench. His replacement was Tilson C. Barden, a New Yorker who had come to Texas as an officer in the U.S. army after the war.[33]

NA; William M. Smith to E. M. Pease, May 25, 1868, I. B. McFarland to Pease, December 4, 1868, Governors' Papers: E. M. Pease, Archives Division, Texas State Library, Austin (hereafter cited as Governors' Papers: EMP).

32. L. W. Stevenson to 2nd Lt. Charles A. Vernon, May 31, November 30, 1868, BRFAL, RG 105, NA; Stevenson to Pease, July 13, 1868, McFarland to Pease, December 4, 1868, William M. Smith to Pease, December 7, 1868, Governors' Papers: EMP; Robert P. Tendick to I. W. McFarland, February 19, 1869, 2nd Lt. James W. Tanfield to Lt. W. H. W. Krebbs, March 19, 1869, OCA, RG 393, NA.

33. *United States Statutes at Large*, XX, 40th Congress, 3rd Sess., 344; Election Registers,

White conservatives reacted predictably. "Once more the tottering civil power falls to the dust," one wrote. "Alas, when shall we get quit of this unhappy state of things—this periodic thrusting of the sword into the midst of our social and political affairs?" The answer, of course, was that military Reconstruction would end once voters went to the polls November 30–December 3, 1869, and approved the new constitution and chose state and local officers under its terms.[34]

In preparation for this election, General Reynolds ordered the reopening of voter registration from November 16 to November 26, 1869, and appointed John C. Miller, Charles A. Dittman, and Isaac Yates to handle the process. Yates had served previously as the black member of the board of registrars. Miller, a Unionist Scotsman, had been appointed county clerk by A. J. Hamilton in 1865, and Dittman was a German immigrant. They enrolled 422 whites and 246 blacks, bringing the totals to 1,128 and 1,387 respectively. Freedmen, although 45 percent of the total population in 1870, constituted 55 percent of all voters.[35]

The contest for state-level offices in 1869 was essentially between the Radical Republicans led by E. J. Davis and moderate Republicans supporting A. J. Hamilton. In Colorado County, Hamilton drew endorsements from both the *Colorado Citizen* and the Columbus *Weekly Times,* indicating that most conservatives, if they intended to vote, would support him, probably as the lesser of two evils. Both papers strongly endorsed Wells Thompson, a young Alabama-born lawyer who had recently arrived in Columbus, for lieutenant governor. Thompson issued a public statement telling voters to recognize that the Confederacy, for which he had fought in the East, had lost and that it was time to accept a constitution and return to the Union. Moderate Republican candidates for Congress and the state legislature also drew the support of conservatives. The combination of moder-

---

1869; Eighth Census, 1860, Schedule 1; Ninth Census, 1870, Schedule 1; Stein, ed., "Slave Narratives of Colorado County," 8; Hobart Huson, *District Judges of Refugio County* (Refugio, Tex., 1941), 94–97.

34. Letter signed "Clio" in the Austin *Tri-Weekly State Gazette,* April 28, 1869. Also see the *Colorado Citizen,* May 6, 1869.

35. General Orders, No. 179, by Gen. Joseph J. Reynolds, October 8, 1869, OCA, RG 393, NA; Ninth Census, 1870, Schedule 1; Election Registers, 1865; List of Registered Voters in Texas, 1869. The total population of Colorado County in 1870 was 8,326, with 4,625 whites and 3,701 blacks. U.S. Bureau of the Census, *The Statistics of the Population of the United States; Compiled from the Original Returns of the Ninth Census (June 1, 1870)* (Washington, D.C., 1872), 63–65.

ates and conservatives infuriated local Radicals such as County Judge Daniel D. Claiborne. He spoke out as an advocate of Davis because, in his words, "I regard it as the duty of all good *Administration* Republicans to do so, in opposition to sham Hamiltonian Republicanism—alias Ku Klux Democracy."[36]

Curiously, in light of the attention usually given to county government, neither newspaper mentioned candidates for local office or their partisan affiliations. The new constitution replaced the county judge and commissioners' court with a five-man county court composed of justices of the peace elected in separate precincts. The justice representing the precinct containing the county seat would take the position formerly held by the county judge as presiding officer. Obviously, the five justices of the peace and the sheriff would be the most important local officials, and there were numerous candidates for those positions. The local newspapers, however, concentrated on statewide races, giving no indication of the nature of the contest for county offices.[37]

The campaign heated up on November 25 when E. J. Davis spoke in Columbus to a crowd of mostly black listeners. "His speech," commented the *Colorado Citizen*, "was well suited to the audience, and a stereotyped effort for the campaign, and doubtless convinced many that he was no orator, and stood a poor chance to be governor." Once again, however, as in 1866 when he had predicted only fifty votes in the county for Pease, the editor of the *Colorado Citizen* proved a poor prophet. Davis won the governorship and in the process carried Colorado County by a vote of 1,175 to 728 for Hamilton. Radicals swept all the other races in the county as well. J. W. Flanagan defeated Thompson for lieutenant governor, 1,163 to 698, and Edward Degener had a similar margin over John L. Haynes in the race for Congress. Degener had migrated to Sisterdale in Kendall County from Germany after the Revolution of 1848 and had become known for his antislavery views. The state senate seat for the Twenty-fifth District (Colorado and Lavaca

36. *Colorado Citizen*, December 2, 1869; Columbus *Weekly Times*, October 30, November 27, 1869; Galveston *Daily News*, August 2, 1869; Daniel D. Claiborne to editor of the San Antonio *Express*, November 17, 1869, in James P. Newcomb Papers, Eugene C. Barker Texas History Center, University of Texas, Austin.

37. *Colorado Citizen*, December 2, 1869; Columbus *Weekly Times*, October 30, November 27, 1869. A WPA publication, *Inventory of the County Archives of Texas, No. 94: Guadalupe County* (San Antonio, 1939), 105–13, 225–28, 251–53, contains a convenient summary of the powers and duties of county judges, county commissioners, and sheriffs during the Reconstruction years.

Counties) went to A. K. Foster, a Republican from Lavaca County, who defeated John D. Gillmore, the former county judge and a moderate Republican. W. T. Wilkinson, Ben F. Williams, and H. C. Youngkin won the district's three seats in the lower house. Wilkinson, former county commissioner, and Williams, the most important black leader in Colorado County, had strong credentials as Radicals. Youngkin, a native of Ohio, was a Lavaca County Republican.[38]

Clearly, the victors, who generally received about 1,150 votes in Colorado County, owed their success to black voters, 1,160 of whom participated. However, there may have been more white votes for Davis and other Radical candidates than the returns would suggest. Daniel D. Claiborne insisted that fraud—pasting Hamilton tickets on the face of Davis ballots and giving them to "unlettered freedmen"—had reduced the margin of victory for the Radicals and hidden the fact that approximately 150 whites voted for the winner. This charge cannot be proven, especially since precinct-level returns are not available for this election. Nevertheless, given the number of Unionists in the county, the Davis ticket probably did receive significant white support.[39]

Radical Republicans won all countywide elections for local government offices as easily as they won the contests for state positions. R. P. Tendick, the German-born officer from the 30th Missouri, defeated Alex Lookup by a vote of 1,192 to 678 in the race for district clerk, and William M. Smith won the sheriff's office with 1,129 votes to 740 for J. B. Leyendecker. The Radical sweep ended, however, in electing justices of the peace, probably because voting in those contests was by precinct. Camillus Jones, a native of Virginia who belonged to the Union League and supported Davis, bested three opponents in the Columbus precinct, and became the presiding justice (county judge). George Ziegler, who like Wilkinson and Tendick had been an officer in the 30th Missouri, easily won in the Eagle Lake precinct. But the other three winners—Daniel W. Jackson in the Oakland precinct (western Colorado County), Fritz Leyendecker in the Frelsburg precinct, and

38. *Colorado Citizen,* December 2, 1869; election returns for 1869 are found in *Senate Miscellaneous Documents,* 41st Cong., 2nd Sess., No. 77, pp. 38–79. The unsuccessful candidates for the lower house included John Zweigel and George McCormick of Colorado County and M. V. Kinneson of Lavaca County. Demographic information on the candidates is from the Eighth Census, 1860, Schedule 1, and Ninth Census, 1870, Schedule 1. Degener's career is sketched in Webb, Carroll, and Branda, eds., *Handbook of Texas,* I, 482.

39. Claiborne to Gen. Joseph J. Reynolds, December 8, 1869, OCA, RG 393, NA.

Henry C. Everett in the Alleyton precinct—were moderates. Fritz Leyendecker, the older brother of J. B. Leyendecker, who had been elected sheriff in 1866 and then defeated by Smith in 1869, would become one of the central figures in Colorado County politics over the remaining years of Reconstruction. A native of Germany, he served in the 17th Texas Infantry from 1862 to 1865, apparently without enthusiasm or distinction, and then joined the Republican party soon after its founding, serving as a judicial district committeeman in 1868. He supported the Hamilton wing of the party, however, and differences with the Radicals eventually led him to join the Democrats.[40]

The new officials took office in May, 1870, and dissension arose almost immediately over the bond of Sheriff Smith. Presiding justice Camillus Jones concluded that, although Smith's bond was adequate, the three "Democrats" on the court would not approve it. Therefore, he and Ziegler walked out with the intent of preventing any action. Leyendecker, Jackson, and Everett then continued in session and declared the sheriff's office vacant. Jones appealed to Governor Davis, who told him that he could not adjourn court without the approval of a majority, but that the three remaining justices could only refuse to accept the bond, not declare the office vacant. The dispute became even more complicated when District Clerk R. P. Tendick, a Radical, sided with the three moderate justices against Jones and Smith. He praised Leyendecker and the other two as loyal Unionists, saying "each one of them have selected from their respective precincts good colored men as Grand Jurymen." Sheriff Smith, Tendick told Governor Davis, did indeed deserve to be removed and replaced with one "who is not only a good republican but also a terror to evil doers."[41]

Davis did not act quickly to settle this dispute, and for the next year deputies and constables handled the duties of the sheriff's office. The whole

40. *Senate Miscellaneous Documents*, 41st Cong., 2nd Sess., No. 77, pp. 38–79; Stein, ed., "Slave Narratives of Colorado County," 8; Camillus Jones *et al.* to E. J. Davis, December 27, 1869, Governors' Papers: Edmund J. Davis, Archives Division, Texas State Library, Austin (hereafter cited as Governors' Papers: EJD); Camillus Jones to J. P. Newcomb, June 28, 1871, Newcomb Papers; Eighth Census, 1860, Schedule 1; John L. Haynes to J. F. Leyendecker, September 18, 1868, Leyendecker Family Papers. Biographical information on Fritz Leyendecker and other members of the family is summarized in this collection.

41. Camillus Jones to E. J. Davis, July 6, 1870, R. P. Tendick to E. J. Davis, July 6, 1870, Governors' Papers: EJD; E. J. Davis to Camillus Jones, July 9, 1870, Executive Record Books: E. J. Davis, Vol. 1, p. 207, Archives Division, Texas State Library, Austin (hereafter cited as Executive Record Books: EJD).

affair was symptomatic of the factionalism that occupied the time and energy of Republicans across Texas during the early 1870s. Party leaders such as Governor Davis and Secretary of State James P. Newcomb must have shaken their heads in disbelief when, first, in December, 1869, they received letters signed jointly by Tendick, Smith, Jones, and Daniel D. Claiborne, and then, by the next summer, had complaints from Tendick against Smith and Jones and from Claiborne against Tendick. Meanwhile Tendick insisted that he remained a good Radical, opposing what he called the "unfortunate mixture of all shades of democrates [sic] and moderate Hamilton Republicans (so called)." William Sinclair, a former Freedmen's Bureau inspector and Radical himself, saw it largely as a matter of office seeking. "I believe the majority of the *professed* new converts will go back on us," he wrote Davis in July 1870, "as soon as they get fixed for their share of the spoils as have the Jones, Smiths, etc. in Colorado Co."[42]

Fortunately for Colorado County Republicans, factional disputes did not destroy their ability to win elections. They controlled the electoral machinery set up in 1870, thanks especially to the appointment by Governor Davis of George Ziegler as registrar of voters.[43] More important, they kept the support of blacks, who constituted nearly a majority of voters even after virtually all whites were re-enfranchised by the new constitution. Also, Republican candidates, regardless of the suggestion that only blacks voted for them in 1869, could still win votes from whites, especially Germans. Tendick proved this when he ran in December, 1870, for the state senate seat left open by the death of A. K. Foster. Early reports from Columbus claimed that Tendick's opponent, Wells Thompson, was certain to win because white voters were more numerous than black, but the Republican candidate prevailed by 140 votes. At the same election, H. M. Shoemaker, a carpetbagger who had settled in Lavaca County, won the seat in the state

42. R. P. Tendick, William M. Smith, Daniel D. Claiborne, and Camillus Jones to E. J. Davis, December 27, 1869, Tendick to Davis, July 6, 1870, William Sinclair to Davis, July 11, 1870, Governors' Papers: EJD; R. P. Tendick to James P. Newcomb, August 26, 1870, Daniel D. Claiborne to E. J. Davis, Newcomb Papers.

43. Election Registers, 1870. Republicans did not have to elect a district judge. Under the Constitution of 1869 the governor appointed all district judges. Davis appointed J. Livingston Lindsay, a Republican originally from Virginia, to the bench in the Twenty-first District, and he served without serious incident until 1876. See Campbell, "Scalawag District Judges," 80, and the approval of Judge Lindsay expressed in the Columbus *Colorado Citizen*, November 2, 1871.

house of representatives vacated by the death of W. T. Wilkinson of Colorado County.[44]

Thus, in spite of factionalism, those Republicans identified with E. J. Davis controlled Colorado County through 1870. During that year, however, the Twelfth Legislature enacted the governor's program for Texas, and that gave conservatives the focus for a much stronger attack on radicalism. The state police force and state militia, both of which enrolled blacks, and a highly centralized public school system all cost money and meant increased levels of taxation. In Colorado County, local property taxes, which had not been higher than 25 cents per $100 assessed value since the war, jumped to $1.125 on $100 in 1871. State property taxes added another 55 cents on $100. These new policies and taxes attracted outraged editorials in the conservative press. The *Colorado Citizen* of February 2, 1871, called on Texans to rescue the state from bankruptcy and ruin. "The welfare of every white man, woman and child in the State," the editor wrote, "demands the expulsion of radicalism from power and the repeal of all the laws passed by the present legislature that are detrimental to the best interests of the people and the State." Four months later, the *Citizen* took an even uglier tone: "We have received from Mr. R. P. Tendick . . . a copy of the tax law, enacted by the nigger conclave at Austin, to rob the people of the fruits of their industry, for the benefit of the Radical party." The public schools, it went on, are interested primarily in teaching "negroes to be impudent to the white race," and, the newspaper concluded, Governor Davis is the "most corrupt, vindictive and proscriptive man in Texas."[45]

Increasingly vocal conservatives put Republican strength to the test in the election of a United States Congressman in October, 1871. A printed circular headed "Anti-Radical" announced a meeting at the courthouse on August 10 to consider candidates. Signed by Fritz Leyendecker, H. C. Everett, Mathias Malsch, and others, the circular promised support for the Democratic party or any candidate—moderate Republicans included—who would op-

44. Galveston *Daily News*, December 1, 2, 3, 1870; E. M. Glenn to E. J. Davis, October 29, 1870, Governors' Papers: EJD; Ninth Census, 1870, Schedule 1; *Journal of the House of Representatives, 12th Legislature* (Austin, 1870), 197–98.

45. Moneyhon, *Republicanism in Reconstruction Texas*, 134–48; Records of the Comptroller of Public Accounts, Ad Valorem Tax Division, Real and Personal Property Tax Rolls, Colorado County, 1865–1871, Genealogy Division, Texas State Library, Austin; *Colorado Citizen*, February 2, May 11, 1871.

pose the incumbent, Edward Degener. Radicals, it warned, are destroying Texas with taxes and aggrandizing blacks, carpetbaggers, and thieves. The signatures of Leyendecker and Malsch, both of whom were Germans known for unionism, were especially significant indicators that the Republicans' main source of white votes was weakening. Malsch, the Frelsburg merchant who had served as a county commissioner throughout Congressional Reconstruction, provided another sign of growing conservatism when he attended the taxpayers' convention in Austin held September 22–25. He returned to make speeches (in German) reporting the convention's attack on virtually every policy favored by the Davis administration.[46]

Colorado County conservatives endorsed John Hancock, a Unionist-turned-Democrat, in the race against Degener, but Republicans still had all the black votes and enough white support to win by 109 out of well over 1,000 tickets cast in the county. The *Colorado Citizen* commented after the second day of the election that the vote was generally along racial lines, although a few "nondescripts" with "pale skins" were "putting in their ballots against us and for a continuance of Radical rule." Although losing in the county vote, Hancock defeated Degener districtwide, and conservatives in Colorado County, in spite of their failure at home, held a celebration. They illuminated Columbus (except for the businesses owned by "Rads"), held a torchlight parade, heard speeches, and "all retired to dream sweet dreams of Texas Freedom and Radical defeat."[47]

After their setback in losing the congressional election, county conservatives stepped up their appeals to German voters. The *Colorado Citizen,* under the editorship of Wells Thompson and George McCormick from October, 1871, to April, 1872, insisted that "the foreigner will never forget that the ignorant negro has been elevated above him, and given privileges under the Constitution that have been denied to sons of the heroes of Blenheim, Waterloo, Sadowa, and Sedan." The editors also claimed that Republicans had criticized the Catholic Church as a way of attacking the foreign-born and that the Republican party was nothing more than the anti-foreign Know-Nothing party in disguise. Democrats killed the Know-Nothings, the paper said, and they came back as Republicans.[48]

46. The circular is in the Leyendecker Family Papers. *Colorado Citizen,* October 5, 1871.
47. *Colorado Citizen,* October 5, 19, 1871; Webb, Carroll, and Branda, eds., *Handbook of Texas,* I, 482, 763–64.
48. *Colorado Citizen,* October 5, 19, November 30, 1871.

As the conservative attack continued during 1871, the controlling party suffered further embarrassment over the sheriff's office. Governor Davis finally appointed a replacement for William M. Smith in June, but somehow the new sheriff, Charles Schmidt, the father-in-law of Robert P. Tendick, also had difficulty meeting bonding requirements. A grand jury eventually indicted Tendick for perjuring himself in swearing to a list of property used as security for Schmidt's bond. The state senator escaped when the jury of eight blacks and four whites could not reach a decision, and the *Colorado Citizen* had great fun wondering in print if the accused went into court with a blank pardon from Governor Davis in his pocket. In the meantime, Schmidt left the office, and James B. Good, A. J. Hamilton's appointee as sheriff back in 1865, took over in December.[49]

This rapid turnover doubtless hurt the Republican party, but not enough to keep it from winning a special election in January, 1872, to select a new presiding justice for the county court. Camillus Jones resigned as justice of the Columbus precinct late in 1871, telling Governor Davis that he could do more for the party in private life. The election to replace him turned into a contest between John D. Gillmore, the moderate Republican who had held the office from 1865 to 1869, and Jahu W. Johnson, a Davis Republican whose brother had received a military appointment as sheriff. The *Colorado Citizen* supported Gillmore, but Johnson won the position, opening the way to become one of the county's most important Republican leaders over the next few years.[50]

The general election of 1872 apparently presented a difficult choice to Unionists and Germans in Colorado County. Democratic conservatives statewide generally endorsed Horace Greeley and the Liberal Republicans, whereas Radicals supported President U. S. Grant and the regular Republican party. This left moderates in the middle, and in Colorado County most seemed to come down on the side of Greeley. R. P. Tendick commented in September that "what few white *Grant Republicans* we have in our county have no more political sagacity than the man in the moon." The results bore

49. Election Registers, 1870–1871; Police Court Minutes, 1862–1876, pp. 174–232; *Colorado Citizen*, February 29, 1872.

50. Camillus Jones to James P. Newcomb, November 20, 1871, Newcomb Papers; *Colorado Citizen*, November 23, 1871; Election Registers, 1869, 1872. Returns of this election are found in Executive Record Books: EJD, Vol. 1, p. 753. Johnson received 404 votes to 234 for Gillmore, and a third candidate, L. M. Newsom, a native of Tennessee, received 189 votes. A two-man contest would likely have been very close.

out his comment on how few whites supported Grant when the regular Republicans carried the county by only 25 votes, 1,175 to 1,150. It seems certain that Grant won almost exclusively due to black ballots.[51]

The same was true in the election of three state representatives from the district composed of Colorado and Lavaca Counties. Republican candidates Benjamin F. Williams, John Zwiegel, and Eugene L. Overbay narrowly carried the county over George W. Smith, Thomas A. Hester, and Fritz Leyendecker. Leyendecker, for example, received 1,154 votes to Williams' 1,162. Because they came close in Colorado and won easily in Lavaca, the three Democrats went to Austin, helping "redeem" the state legislature from Republican control.[52]

The 1872 election also resulted in narrower than expected Republican victories in contests for local office. In the race for sheriff, both candidates—James B. Good, the incumbent, and John R. Brooks, the challenger—were Republicans, but Brooks, who was more closely identified with the Radicals, won by 1,197 to 1,107. Not surprisingly, these "greatly reduced majorities," as a Colorado County correspondent to the Galveston Daily News referred to the Radicals' margin of victory, encouraged conservatives to believe that they would soon unify the white vote and regain control of county government.[53]

The next general election of state and local officeholders on December 2, 1873, found Democratic conservatives poised to complete the "redemption" of Texas from Radical government by electing Richard Coke to replace E. J. Davis as governor. At the same time, the election of new county courts provided an opportunity to reclaim county governments as well. Coke won statewide, and many counties were indeed "redeemed," but Colorado County Radicals strongly endorsed Davis and strengthened their hold on local offices. Their success depended on continuing control of the black vote and regaining some of the support from Germans apparently lost during 1871–1872. Davis carried the county over Coke by a vote of 1,348 to 801, winning four of the five justice precincts. His margins were much larger in the heavily black Eagle Lake precinct and in the Columbus precinct, but he prevailed in the Frelsburg precinct, 236 to 190. Davis lost

51. R. P. Tendick to J. P. Newcomb, September 12, 1872, Newcomb Papers; Kingston, Attlesey, and Crawford, Political History of Texas, 72.
52. Galveston Daily News, November 12, 1872.
53. Ibid.

only the Content precinct which was located in the western part of the county just south of Weimar, a town created by German immigrants arriving largely after 1865 and possibly less familiar with the issues of the Civil War.[54]

The returns in other state and local elections followed almost the same pattern. Frederic W. Fahrenthold, candidate for the Twenty-fifth District's state senate seat, defeated Olinthus Ellis of Lavaca County by 1,321 to 828. Benjamin F. Williams and W. P. Ballard, a young Lavaca County farmer, carried Colorado County in the races for the district's two seats in the house of representatives by similar margins over two local Democrats, Mathias Malsch and William S. Delaney. In these legislative races, Fahrenthold, Williams, and Ballard carried neither the Felsburg nor Content precincts, but in both they received enough votes to combine with large margins of victory in the other three precincts and ensure carrying the county. Farenthold, for example, lost the Content precinct by thirty votes (267 to 237) and Frelsburg by only five (213 to 208). Probably the sole consolation that Colorado County Democrats could take in the outcome was that a strong conservative vote in Lavaca County gave districtwide victories to Ellis and Delaney.[55]

The Radicals' most impressive success came in the election of justices for the county court. Three incumbents—D. W. Jackson (Content precinct), J. F. Leyendecker (Frelsburg precinct), and H. C. Everett (Alleyton precinct)—who were moderates leaning toward the Democrats lost to Radical challengers. A. Schrimscher defeated Jackson; Eugene Himley won over Leyendecker; and Ernst Louis Theuman beat Everett. These Radical successes were possible largely because Governor Davis' interpretation of constitutional provisions concerning elections permitted countywide contests for justices of the peace rather than having each chosen by the voters in a single precinct. All three incumbents carried their home precincts but lost badly at the Eagle Lake and Columbus boxes. On the other hand, the challengers did gain significant support in the home precincts of the incumbents. Theuman, for example, lost to Everett in the Alleyton precinct by

54. Moneyhon, *Republicanism in Reconstruction Texas*, 181–94; Colorado County Election Returns, 1873. On the arrival of German immigrants at Weimar, see especially Terry G. Jordan, "The German Settlement of Texas After 1865," *Southwestern Historical Quarterly*, LXXVIII (1969), 197.

55. Colorado County Election Returns, 1873; Ninth Census, 1870, Schedule 1; *Members of the Texas Legislature, 1846–1980* (Austin, 1980), 75–78.

only ten votes, 147 to 157. Perhaps this was because the precinct included Bernardo and Mentz, the homes of Germans like Theuman. Even Leyendecker had a margin of less than one hundred votes over Himley in their home precinct, winning by 252 to 164. Himley, however, was also a German. He had served in the United States Army during the war, but had ties to Colorado County, his uncle, Alexander Himley, having lived there since the late 1840s. The Radicals completed their sweep by reelecting George S. Ziegler from the Eagle Lake precinct and placing a longtime resident immigrant from Germany, Leopold Steiner, in the position of presiding justice. Steiner died of yellow fever on December 6, 1873, and therefore never took office, but a special election on March 7, 1874, resulted in victory for the Republican, James A. Toliver, who carried every precinct against the Democratic activist, Basil G. Ijams.[56]

Republicans thus solidified their control of Colorado County just as the inauguration of Governor Coke in January, 1874, signaled the end of their party's control statewide. The county's Democrats worked hard in opposition during the next two years by organizing, supporting their party's candidates in state and national elections, having the *Colorado Citizen* constantly criticize all things Republican, and endorsing the call for a new state constitution to replace the one written during Reconstruction. When the legislature called an election in early August, 1875, to choose delegates to a constitutional convention, Democrats of Colorado and Lavaca Counties nominated George McCormick, the ex-Confederate lawyer and party activist from Columbus, Gen. J. W. Whitfield of Lavaca, and Julius E. Arnim of Lavaca. These candidates undertook an intensive speaking campaign throughout the two counties and spared no effort in opposing the Republican nominees—J. W. Johnson and E. L. Theuman of Colorado County and state representative W. P. Ballard of Lavaca.[57]

The results of the election, however, were very similar to those in 1873. Johnson, Ballard, and Theuman all received more than 1,075 votes in Colorado County, whereas only McCormick among the Democratic candidates received as many as 825 votes there. Again, German precincts favored the Democrats by narrow margins, but these precincts provided a significant

56. Colorado County Election Returns, 1873, 1874; Election Registers, 1873–1874. Biographical information on Himley is in Eugene Himley to Joel Kirkman, May 24, 1867, BRFAL, RG 105, NA; Police Court Minutes, 1862–1876.

57. *Colorado Citizen*, July 30, August 6, 1874, April 8, July 1, 8, 15, 1875.

minority vote that combined with overwhelming black support to give victory to the Republicans. McCormick, Whitfield, and Arnim won convincingly enough in Lavaca County to overcome their defeat in Colorado and go to Austin. Nevertheless, Republicans had demonstrated their continuing mastery of Colorado County.[58]

When the new constitution was submitted to voters on February 15, 1876, both parties in Colorado County held conventions to endorse nominees in state-level races and choose candidates for positions in county government. The Democrats supported Richard Coke for reelection as governor, Wells Thompson of Columbus for state senator, and M. V. Kinnison and Ibzan W. Middlebrook of Lavaca for state representatives. The Republicans endorsed William M. Chambers for governor, E. H. Anderson for state senator, and Andrew Carroll and M. Schuetterle for state representatives. Anderson, a teacher in Columbus, and Carroll, a farmer from Lavaca, were black, while Scheutterle was a German immigrant. Key races at the county level involved the election of a county judge and four county commissioners, those positions having been restored by the new constitution, and a sheriff.[59]

On February 15, 1876, Republicans won most of the races in Colorado County, but they generally received less support among Germans than in 1873 and had very narrow margins of victory. Chambers, for example, carried the county over Coke by 65 votes, 1,441 to 1,376. His margin of victory was 150 votes in Eagle Lake (232 to 82) and 155 in Columbus (478 to 323), but he lost Frelsburg by 150 votes (204 to 54) and Weimar by 130 (316 to 186). E. H. Anderson defeated Wells Thompson in the state senate race by a vote of 1,401 to 1,043 in Colorado County, but Thompson's total was reduced by another Democratic candidate, S. C. Patton, who received 347 votes. Thompson received enough votes in the other counties in the district, Lavaca and Gonzales, to win the seat. In the race for the two seats in the state house of representatives, M. V. Kinnison and I. W. Middlebrook reversed the pattern of Republican success, receiving 1,338 and 1,230 votes respectively to defeat Carroll (1,080 votes) and Schuetterle (1,118 votes). These Democratic victories, the only countywide successes enjoyed by conservatives, can be explained by the fact that Carroll and Schuetterle had not

58. *Ibid.*, August 12, 1875.

59. *Ibid.*, November 18, December 2, 23, 30, 1875, January 13, 1876; Ninth Census, 1870, Schedule 1; Tenth Census of the United States, 1880, Schedule 1 (Population), NA.

been notably active in local politics and were last-minute nominees of their party. Less than a month before the election, Republicans had offered the nominations unsuccessfully to W. P. Ballard, the incumbent, and to Josiah Shaw.[60]

County races followed the same pattern as most state-level contests. The Republican, Jahu W. Johnson, defeated former state representative W. S. Delaney by a vote of 1,432 to 1,365 in the race for county judge, and James A. Toliver won the sheriff's office over Thomas J. Grace by a similar margin. Contests for each of the four seats on the reconstituted commissioners' court attracted multiple candidates, and Republicans won three of the four. Alex F. Kinnerson, a black resident of Columbus, Christian Heydorn, a teacher from the Weimar area, and Williamson Daniels, a farmer from the Eagle Lake region, defeated their Democratic challengers. The only Democratic winner was Mike Muckleroy, a farmer from Tennessee and longtime resident of the northern part of the county dominated by German voters in Frelsburg. Republicans also won all the county's administrative positions including district clerk, county clerk, treasurer, and tax assessor/collector. The contest for county clerk was especially interesting in that Fritz Leyendecker, the perennial Democratic activist and former state representative, lost to a relative unknown, Henry Wagenfuhr. One local conservative interpreted the election as a rescue "in part from the black pall which had settled over [the county]," and concluded that "only a little time and considerable patience is necessary to entirely redeem the people from their thralldom."[61]

Once again, however, conservative predictions of success proved overly optimistic. Colorado County remained under Republican control into the 1880s as political life became concerned with the problems of farmers and "Redemption" lost its Reconstruction-era importance. Republican candidates won the office of county judge and all other important countywide positions in 1878 and 1880. They momentarily lost their majority on the commissioners' court in 1878 by having too many candidates competing against each other in several races and allowing Democrats to win three of the four positions. However, another important black leader, Cicero How-

60. Colorado County Election Returns, 1876; *Colorado Citizen*, February 3, 10, 24, 1876. The Republicans did not have a candidate for district judge in 1876. That position went to Everett Lewis, a Democrat from Gonzales County.

61. *Colorado Citizen*, February 24, March 2, 1876; Colorado County Election Returns, 1876; Ninth Census, 1870, Schedule 1; Tenth Census, 1880, Schedule 1.

ard, emerged that year by winning the seat on the court for the southern part of the county that included Eagle Lake. Howard, who had come to Colorado County after the war with the Union veterans Wilkinson and Ziegler, would serve four consecutive terms on the court, lose in 1886, and then serve three more terms beginning in 1888. He would be joined on the court in 1880 by another black, James Shepard, as Republicans regained control after their 1878 defeat. Colorado County did not elect a Democrat as county judge until W. S. Delaney won the office in November, 1890. The county voted Democratic for the first time in a gubernatorial race in 1888 when it narrowly supported L. S. "Sul" Ross against Marion Martin who ran as an independent rather than a Republican. It also went Democratic for the first time in a presidential election in 1888, supporting Grover Cleveland over the colorless Benjamin Harrison. Cleveland carried the county again in 1892, but four years later it went back to the Republican fold when William McKinley bested the Democrat William Jennings Bryan.[62]

Thus Reconstruction in Colorado County did not end with a specific election that Democratic conservatives could hail as "redemption." Republicans maintained control well beyond the dates usually associated with the problem of restoring the defeated Confederate states to the Union. Their successes depended primarily on the fact that from 1865 into the 1880s freedmen constituted more than 40 percent of the population and Germans accounted for at least another 20 percent. Black voters provided most of the party's strength, but help from the Germans and a handful of white southern Unionists such as Daniel D. Claiborne, Camillus Jones, and the Johnson brothers proved vital. German support weakened once the issues at stake shifted in 1869 and 1870 from unionism to the expensive policies of the Davis administration, but the areas around Freslburg and Weimar still provided enough votes to give the Republicans a majority in most elections. On the occasions when Democrats were successful politically, they won with men such as Fritz Leyendecker who were moderates rather than diehard Confederates. Unlike many counties in the cotton-producing region of Texas, Colorado never returned to the control of former slaveholding secessionists.[63]

62. *Colorado Citizen*, November 21, 1878, November 18, 1880; Election Registers, 1876–1892; Tenth Census, 1880, Schedule 1; Stein, ed., "Slave Narratives of Colorado County," 8–9; Kingston, Attlesey, and Crawford, *Political History of Texas*, 62, 76.

63. U.S. Bureau of the Census, *Statistics of the Population of the United States (1870)*, 372–

Blacks in Colorado County during Reconstruction attempted to take full advantage of the opportunities provided by Federal policies and by the willingness of many Germans and some southern whites to cooperate with them politically. Obviously, the results were far from ideal—equality in any respect remained a dream—but freedmen nevertheless made important progress after 1865. Blacks gained the franchise in 1867 and immediately became enthusiastic participants in political life, both as voters and officeholders. The county's best-known African-American leader, Benjamin F. Williams, served in the constitutional convention of 1868–1869 and the state house of representatives. Isaac Yates acted as a registrar of voters during 1867–1869 and became the first black county commissioner in 1870. Alex Kinnerson's election in 1876, followed by those of Cicero Howard in 1878 and James Shepard in 1880, assured blacks representation on the commissioners' court for well over a decade after Texas was returned to the control of white conservatives. Freedmen also held numerous lesser offices. For example, from 1870 to 1874, Edmund Eason and Granville Norman served as appointees by Governor Davis on the three-man board that heard appeals concerning voter registration in Colorado County. African Americans began to participate in the justice system beginning in 1870 by serving on the grand jury and trial juries for each session of the district court. They did not have representation in proportion to their numbers in the population, but the presence of even four or five blacks with the Germans and southern whites was a step forward.[64]

Socially during Reconstruction, Colorado County's freedmen showed strength in two important areas—the family and education. In 1880, families composed of a husband, wife, and children made up three-quarters (73 percent) of all black households in the county. Like other former slaves across Texas, members of these families wanted education and did what they could to take advantage of the schools provided by the Freedmen's Bureau during the late 1860s and by the state during the early 1870s. Efforts to educate blacks were plagued by indifference or opposition on the part of

73; U.S. Bureau of the Census, *Statistics of the Population of the United States at the Tenth Census (June 1, 1880)* (Washington, D.C., 1883), 528–31. Natives of Germany made up only about 10 percent of Colorado County's population in 1870 and 1880, but their children, who were reported as native-born, were also thoroughly German.

64. Election Registers, 1870–1880; Ninth Census, 1870, Schedule 1; Tenth Census, 1880, Schedule 1; District Court Civil Minutes, Book D, 303, Book F, 250, Book G, 1; *Colorado Citizen*, October 8, 1874, February 4, June 10, July 15, October 7, 1875.

many whites, by the poverty of the families of would-be students, and by the need for children to work rather than go to classes. Nevertheless, many received some education, and as late as 1880, 41 percent of black families with children aged six to sixteen had at least one of those children attend school.[65]

As would be expected, freedmen depended overwhelmingly on agricultural occupations throughout the Reconstruction era. A little more than one-third of household heads (38 percent) reported farming as their occupation in 1880, and about the same proportion (37 percent) worked as farm laborers. Of those who called themselves farmers and appeared on the agricultural census, nearly half (47 percent) worked for shares of their crops, and more than a quarter (29 percent) rented land for cash. Most of these nonlandowners at least had livestock of their own, especially horses or mules. The remaining 24 percent of farmers owned the land that they worked—averaging about sixty-five acres each. They produced corn and cotton and virtually all owned livestock.[66]

From one perspective, then, Colorado County blacks lived in destitution in 1880 with only a minority able to call themselves farmers and an even smaller number actually owning land. It should be remembered, however, that most had emerged from slavery fifteen years earlier with virtually no property and had received no assistance in acquiring any. Indeed, one observer in 1870 commented that freedmen could not buy land even if they had the means because whites would not sell to them, preferring to rent instead. Emigration was not an option either, the observer went on, because "they have no transportation, next a great many have a few hoggs & cattle & cant very well move them; again a great many of them are afraid to go away from the neighborhood where they have always lived." Under these circumstances the ownership of property by even a small minority should be considered significant progress.[67]

Certainly the county's blacks valued above all the freedom that they had gained at the onset of Reconstruction. "Juneteenth" called for the largest

65. Demographic information on the black population of Colorado County in 1880 was drawn from a random sample of 250 African American households from the Tenth Census, 1880, Schedule 1.

66. Information on the occupations and agricultural production of the random sample of 250 black households from the census of 1880 was drawn from Tenth Census, 1880, Schedule 1 and Schedule 2 (Productions of Agriculture).

67. S. T. Burney to E. J. Davis, June 22, 1870, Governors' Papers: EJD.

celebration of the year, although at first freedmen celebrated June 22, the day word of emancipation reached Columbus, rather than the nineteenth when it was announced at Galveston. The celebration in 1867 included a parade, barbecue, and speeches to a crowd estimated at two thousand people in Columbus. By 1875, a baseball game and dance had been added to the usual events.[68]

Colorado County's blacks also stood ready to fight for their safety as demonstrated by an incident known as the Eagle Lake Riot in October, 1873. Already upset by the forcible arrest of a freedman accused of theft, blacks in the Eagle Lake area reacted furiously when two others disappeared the next night. A party of seventy-five to one hundred freedmen armed themselves and searched for the missing men, and engaged in what one newspaper called "riotous demonstrations." Sheriff John R. Brooks attempted unsuccessfully to talk the freedmen into dispersing and, that failing, decided not to use armed force because of the bloodshed that would follow. The next day a boy led him to the bodies of the two men, and although the murderers were not found, the tension eased. A deputy United States marshall investigated the incident and found that no one, white or black, would swear to any charges arising from the "riot." Colorado County's freedmen had the numbers, weapons, and willingness to defend themselves aggressively. Reconstruction did not bring equal opportunity or prosperity to freedmen in Colorado County, but the participation and accomplishments of at least one generation of African Americans during that era should not be minimized. Regardless of what happened in the age of segregation and disfranchisement, the promise of Reconstruction remained.[69]

The white population of Colorado County did not put up the same sort of near-unified front as was common in many areas of Texas. Many German immigrants apparently blamed white slaveholders for the disaster of secession and accepted Congressional Reconstruction as necessary and deserved. This left white southerners in a minority position as they faced occupation by the military, regulation by the Freedmen's Bureau, disfranchisement of former leaders, enfranchisement of blacks, and participation by freedmen in local government and the justice system.

68. Galveston Daily News, June 30, 1867; Colorado Citizen, June 24, 1875.
69. Hallettsville (Tex.) Herald and Planter, October 23, 1873; Galveston Daily News, October 19, 22, 28, November 5, 6, 7, 11, 19, 1873.

Colorado County's economy did not expand notably during Reconstruction. The total assessed value of taxable property rose only from $2,100,568 to $2,144,640 between 1865 and 1876, an increase of 2 percent. State and county property taxes, however, rose to unprecedented levels during the early 1870s and remained high throughout the decade, even after white conservatives reclaimed control statewide. The county's economic elite, defined as the wealthiest 5 percent of all taxpayers in 1865, appear to have suffered more than did their counterparts in counties that were "redeemed" before or by 1873. In Colorado County, only 33 percent of the economic elite in 1865 remained in that class in 1880, whereas in Dallas and McLennan Counties at least one-half stayed in the top 5 percent of taxpayers during that fifteen-year period. Many factors, of course, explain rising and declining fortunes at any particular time, but in this era those who suffered reversals could easily blame Radical policies.[70]

Understandably, then, conservative Democrats in Colorado County saw Reconstruction as negative in every respect. However, their worst fears such as redistribution of property and violence by the former slaves were not realized, and the county grew in some ways once it recovered from the immediate impact of the war. Aided especially by the completion of a bridge across the Colorado River in 1867 and the extension of the Buffalo Bayou, Brazos, and Colorado Railway (renamed the Galveston, Harrisburg, and San Antonio Railway in 1870) to San Antonio by 1877, the county's population increased from 8,326 in 1870 to 16,673 in 1880. Columbus had nearly two thousand people by the end of the 1870s, and Weimar, the new town in the western part of the county, had 626. Cotton production surpassed antebellum levels, reaching 15,552 bales in 1879.[71]

Reconstruction had a greater and more lasting impact on Colorado County than on most localities in Texas. Thanks to the county's multiethnic population, Republicans maintained control through the 1870s and beyond. This gave freedmen opportunities much greater than those generally enjoyed by blacks across the state and caused conservative

70. Real and Personal Property Tax Rolls, Colorado, Dallas, and McLennan Counties, 1865, 1876, and 1880.

71. Colorado County Chronicles, I, 144, 159; Webb, Carroll, and Branda, eds., Handbook of Texas, I, 240, 665; U.S. Bureau of the Census, Statistics of the Population of the United States (1880), 342, 409, 443; U.S. Bureau of the Census, Report on the Productions of Agriculture as Returned at the Tenth Census, 1880 (Washington, D.C., 1883), 242.

whites to view the period as one of corruption and ruin. From the perspective of the late twentieth century, *radical* seems too strong a term for the changes that came to Colorado County after 1865, but to contemporaries, especially blacks, the changes were dramatic enough to affect an entire generation.

# 3

## DALLAS COUNTY

$D$allas County did not belong to the Cotton Kingdom of the Old South. Located on the Trinity River in north-central Texas, the county reported no cotton production in the census of 1860—not because of soil or climate but because it lacked transportation outlets. The region's blackland prairie soil was ideal for cotton, but the river did not provide reliable navigation, and arrival of the railroad lay more than a decade in the future. Since they could not market cotton efficiently, antebellum Dallas County farmers concentrated on subsistence and the production of small grains and therefore had limited use for slaves. In 1860, the county had 1,074 black bondsmen, 12 percent of the total population of 8,665. Most of the 228 slaveholders, representing 17 percent of all households, owned just a few slaves. Only three owned at least twenty slaves and could be called planters.[1]

Eight north-central Texas counties that, like Dallas, grew relatively little cotton and had small numbers of slaveholders and slaves opposed secession in 1860 and 1861. For example, voters in Collin County, located immediately north of Dallas, cast 70 percent of their ballots in favor of the Union.

1. Brief descriptions of Dallas County and Dallas are found in Webb, Carroll, and Branda, eds., *Handbook of Texas,* I, 456–60. Only a tiny proportion (2 percent) of Dallas County's population was foreign-born in 1860. Population statistics are from U.S. Bureau of the Census, *Population of the United States in 1860,* 484, 487–89. Statistics on slaveholders and cotton production are from U.S. Bureau of the Census, *Agriculture of the United States in 1860,* 140–41, 240.

## Map 3

## Dallas County

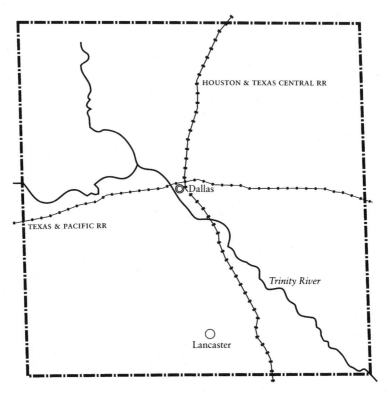

HOUSTON & TEXAS CENTRAL RR

Dallas

TEXAS & PACIFIC RR

*Trinity River*

Lancaster

Adapted, with permission, from the Dallas County map in the *Texas Almanac* for 1996–1997.

Dallas County residents, however, being influenced by the pro-secession stance of local leaders such as John J. Good, the ultrasouthern editorials of Charles R. Pryor's Dallas *Herald,* and a supposedly abolitionist-inspired plot that resulted in the burning of the town square of Dallas in July, 1860, supported disunion by a vote of 741 to 237.[2]

Unionists in Dallas County constituted a small but apparently consistent group of voters. The 237 negative votes on secession represented 24 percent of the total, exactly the same percentage who had supported the Constitutional Unionist John Bell in the presidential election of 1860. John C. Breckinridge, the Southern Democratic party candidate won that contest in Dallas County by a vote of 868 to 274. The Unionists thus voted their convictions under difficult circumstances. The minority had some strong leaders such as A. Bledsoe of Lancaster in the southern part of the county. Bledsoe, a native of Kentucky who came to Texas in 1847, stood six feet, four inches tall and weighed 260 pounds. An imposing man always carrying a cedar cane so large that it amounted to a staff, he stood courageously for the Union during and after the war. However, without a large black population to free and enfranchise, Bledsoe and other local Unionists faced an uphill battle in any attempt to control county government at the close of the conflict.[3]

Dallas County's relative isolation assured protection against invading armies during the Civil War, but its people nevertheless were heavily involved in the southern military effort. Men from the county filled or helped fill the ranks of at least nine companies of cavalry. John J. Good organized local men into a light artillery battery that fought at the Battle of Pea Ridge (Elkhorn Tavern) in 1862. Good gave up command of the battery after his health failed later in 1862 and, with the rank of colonel, served as the judge of a military court in Louisiana, Mississippi, and Alabama until the end of the war. In addition to supplying men, Dallas County served the Confederacy as a regional supply, recruiting, and transportation center. Small arms

2. Timmons, "Referendum in Texas on the Ordinance of Secession," 15–16; Buenger, *Secession and the Union in Texas,* 174–75; Donald E. Reynolds, *Editors Make War: Southern Newspapers in the Secession Crisis* (Nashville, 1966), 98–110.

3. Kingston, Attlesey, and Crawford, *Political History of Texas,* 72; A. B. Rawlins [Bledsoe's grandson], "My Memories of A. Bledsoe," A. B. Rawlins Papers, Dallas Historical Society Archives, Dallas, Tex. According to Rawlins, Bledsoe had no first name other than "A" because when he was born a neighbor remarked, "Well, whatever his name is to be, he is a Bledsoe."

were manufactured and repaired at Lancaster, and three mills in the county produced flour for the army.[4]

Dallas County residents began to think about Reconstruction during June and July, 1865, when the *Herald* carried news of the Confederacy's final surrender, the arrival of Federal troops at Galveston, and the appointment of Andrew J. Hamilton as provisional governor of Texas. Announcement of the Emancipation Proclamation on June 19 occasioned little comment, probably because of the relatively small number of slaves in the county. However, there was much concern over the restoration of state and local government and the possibility of occupation by Federal soldiers. On June 15, the *Herald* expressed the fear that until "thorough Union organizations" could be created, "the people of the rebel States will be without local government." Two weeks later, editor John W. Swindells pointed out that, regardless of rumors, federal troops had not been sent to Dallas and possibly would never be sent unless necessary to suppress "resistance to the Federal authority . . . which we see no indication of at the present."[5]

Developments during the remaining months of 1865 doubtless reassured those in the county who had supported secession and the Confederacy. In early August, Governor Hamilton appointed officials to run the county government on an interim basis until the impending constitutional convention could complete its work. Appointees to key governmental positions in most counties had Unionist credentials of some sort, but in the case of Dallas, the sheriff (N. O. McAdams) and three of the county commissioners (Isaac B. Webb, James H. Holloway, and Henry K. Brotherton) had been elected to those positions in 1864 while Texas was part of the Confederacy. Moreover, William H. Hord, Hamilton's choice as county judge, had held that position from 1848 through 1850 and was a strong secessionist. The remaining county commissioner, George W. Barton, had not held office before and did not have a reputation as a disunionist, but he had served in the Confederate army.[6]

---

4. Winsor, *Texas in the Confederacy*, 13–16, 42–43, 45, 55–56; John H. Cochran, *Dallas County: A Record of Its Pioneers and Progress, Being a Supplement to John Henry Brown's History of Dallas County (1887)* (Dallas, 1928), 87–111. A useful sketch of the life of John J. Good is found in the *Biographical Encyclopedia of Texas* (New York, 1880), 116–18.

5. Dallas *Herald*, June 15, July 1, 29, 1865.

6. Election Registers, 1848–1865, have the names of Hamilton's appointees and their previous service, if any. Barton's military service is found in the Index to Compiled Service Records of Confederate Soldiers, RG 109, NA.

Perhaps Governor Hamilton failed to appoint Unionists because he was rushed and had many other responsibilities. Certainly, he could have found qualified Unionists among the 25 percent of voters who had opposed secession in Dallas County—as some of them quickly pointed out. Within a month of the appointment of Hord, Samuel S. Jones and G. A. Kilbourn complained to Hamilton that he had made a mistake. Jones, a merchant from Tennessee who quickly became one of the most active Unionist/ Republicans in the county, pointed out that Hord was a rabid secessionist. Kilbourn, a doctor born in Ohio, called the county judge "one of the first mobocrats of the county" and argued that loyalists could expect no justice from him. Hamilton responded by replacing Hord with A. Bledsoe, the county's best-known Unionist, on September 22, 1865. Hord's removal did not occasion any protest from former secessionists, and Bledsoe held a routine session of the commissioners' court in November.[7]

In the meantime, another Unionist had filled a position of key importance to local government in Dallas. On August 18, Governor Hamilton appointed R. W. Scott of Johnson County as judge of the state's Sixteenth District, which included Dallas and six other north-central counties. Scott, a forty-four-year-old native of New York, had lived in Texas since the early 1850s and owned at least one slave during the war, but his known unionism earned him the appointment. He held court in Dallas for the first time in October and November, 1865, and the session went smoothly. The *Herald* informed its readers that a speech made by the judge at the courthouse was considered "sensible" by those in attendance, and when the session ended, members of the bar passed resolutions praising him for his "kind, courteous, and upright manner."[8]

Another of Hamilton's Unionist appointees, county clerk W. K. Masten of Ohio, also provided evidence that the white majority in Dallas County

7. Samuel S. Jones to A. J. Hamilton, August 26, 1865, G. A. Kilbourn to A. J. Hamilton, September 1865, Governors' Papers: AJH; Eighth Census, 1860, Schedule 1; Election Registers, 1865; Commissioners' Court Minutes, Book C, 235, Dallas County Commissioners' Court Office, Dallas, Texas. The Dallas *Herald* had no comment in September or October concerning Hord's removal.

8. Campbell, "District Judges of Texas in 1866–1867," 359; Election Registers, 1865; Eighth Census, 1860, Schedule 1; Ninth Census, 1870, Schedule 1; Real and Personal Property Tax Rolls, Falls and Johnson Counties, 1860–1870. Scott lived in Falls County at least until 1864, when the tax records show him as the owner of one slave, but was in Johnson County by 1870. District Court Minutes, Book C, 370–428, Book D, 1–20, Dallas Public Library, Dallas; Dallas *Herald,* October 28, November 1, 11, 1865.

was encouraged by the governor's first steps in local Reconstruction. Here, Masten wrote Hamilton in October, "the best citizens are coming forward and cheerfully taking the amnesty oath, and . . . your course is sustained by the thinking portion of the county." When questions arose about Masten's appointment because he had served briefly in the Confederate army, Nathaniel M. Burford, a district judge before the war and colonel of the 19th Texas Cavalry (C.S.A.), came to his defense. Masten voted against secession, Burford informed Hamilton, but he is a "Conservative" whose appointment will "do much to produce harmony and concord in the county."[9]

One major reason for the "harmony" in Dallas County during the first months of Reconstruction was the federal government's apparent willingness to do little or nothing for the minority who were former slaves. Having few if any financial resources, most of the freedmen remained with their former masters or other local whites, working for small wages or a portion of the crops. Their labor was not in great demand at first, since the area did not have a highly developed cotton economy, and they did not have the protection of written contracts as most agreements were simply verbal. Also, in spite of their relatively small numbers, freedmen began to suffer some of the violence that would typify North Texas during Reconstruction. In July, 1867, Samuel S. Jones would report five murders of blacks and numerous cases of assault during the previous two and one-half years.[10]

Editor Swindells of the *Herald* argued in November, 1865, that freedmen should have protection for rights of person and property but should not expect equality in any other respect. Public policy, he wrote, should "forbid that the negro should ever be entrusted with the exercise of any political rights, or that he should ever be endowed with any rights tending to make him politically and socially the equal of the whites." It must be made clear, he concluded, that "Texas is a white man's country, and that none but white men shall ever vote, sit in the jury box, or hold office in Texas." Swindells professed satisfaction and amusement at the treatment accorded local freedmen when the first federal troops, a detachment of 250 cavalry heading for Sherman, finally reached Dallas on December 6, 1865. "The poor foolish negroes," he wrote, "believed that [the troops] had come to Dallas for

9. W. K. Masten to A. J. Hamilton, October 4, 1865, Nathaniel M. Burford to A. J. Hamilton, October 20, 1865, Governors' Papers: AJH.

10. William H. Horton to Joel T. Kirkman, July 30, 1867, Samuel S. Jones to William H. Horton, July 22, 1867, in BRFAL, RG 105, NA.

the purpose of dividing among them, the property of the whites, and many were the long faces and rueful countenances to be seen among them, when they were told that the government did not intend to take the property of the whites and give it to the negroes; upon the whole most of our *unbleached* population were disappointed at the treatment they received at the hands of the Federal troops." Dallas' blacks would have no help from the government until the arrival of a Freedmen's Bureau agent in the spring of 1867.[11]

Dallas County voters went to the polls on January 8, 1866, to elect two delegates to the upcoming constitutional convention. Two Unionists, A. Bledsoe and James K. P. Record, announced as candidates in early December, 1865, and scheduled eleven speaking engagements across the county, concluding in Dallas on January 5. Bledsoe had consistently opposed disunion and would side with the Radical Republicans. Record, a Tennessean by birth who came to Dallas County in 1860, served in the Confederate army but would join the moderate Republicans by 1868. Shortly before the election, Alexander Harwood and J. P. McKnight also announced as candidates, apparently to oppose Bledsoe and Record. Little is known of McKnight except that he was a native of Tennessee. Harwood had served in the Confederate army, but had not played an important role during the secession crisis. On January 8, Record and Harwood won the two seats in the convention. This result appears consistent with the tone of moderation that had generally marked Reconstruction in Dallas County to that point, as neither delegate was a die-hard secessionist nor would either become a Radical Republican.[12]

The constitutional convention completed its work in April, 1866, and voters went to the polls again on June 25 to approve the amended constitution and elect state and local officers. In the governor's race, the *Herald* endorsed James W. Throckmorton, the Conservative Unionist who had opposed secession and then become a general in the Confederate army, and

---

11. Dallas *Herald*, November 25, December 9, 1865; Thomas H. Smith, "Conflict and Corruption: The Dallas Establishment vs. the Freedmen's Bureau Agent," *Legacies: A History Journal for Dallas and North Central Texas*, I (Fall, 1989), 24.

12. Returns for this election are unavailable. Information on the campaign and winners is from the Dallas *Herald*, December 10, 1865, January 6, February 3, 1866. Identifying information on the candidates is from the Eighth Census, 1860, Schedule 1; Ninth Census, 1870, Schedule 1; and Berry A. Cobb, *A History of Dallas Lawyers, 1840 to 1890* (Dallas, 1934), 71–72.

criticized his opponent, Elisha M. Pease, for leading what Swindells called the "Texas Radicals." The newspaper did not make endorsements in district or local contests, generally limiting itself to positive comments on the candidates. For example, when R. W. Scott, Governor Hamilton's appointee as district judge, became a candidate to remain on the bench, Swindells noted that he had given "very general satisfaction" during his tenure in 1865–1866. Scott's two opponents were John J. Good, the county's best known secessionist and a popular ex-Confederate, and Justus W. Ferris of Ellis County, who had held the position in 1864 and 1865.[13]

Election returns convincingly demonstrated that conservative voters controlled Dallas County in 1866. Throckmorton defeated Pease 921 to 267; Good won the district judgeship with 656 votes to 375 for Scott and 172 for Ferris; and Col. N. M. Burford took the county's seat in the Texas House of Representatives. James Record, who had joined Conservative Unionists in the constitutional convention in supporting Throckmorton, ran successfully for the state senate seat representing Dallas, Henderson, and Kaufman Counties. In local elections, Z. Ellis Coombes, a young lawyer from Kentucky and former captain in the Confederate army, defeated A. Bledsoe in the race for county judge by a margin of 783 to 308. Jeremiah M. Brown, a native of Kentucky and former slaveholder, won the sheriff's office over John C. Chapman, a young farmer from Iowa, by a vote of 900 to 254. Bledsoe and Chapman received nearly one hundred votes each in the Lancaster precinct, their home district, but lost overwhelmingly in the town of Dallas. Two of Governor Hamilton's interim appointees, Isaac B. Webb and George W. Barton, remained on the commissioners' court. They were joined by Joshua P. Stratton and James R. Clements, both farmers from Kentucky who had no notable records on public issues.[14]

The commissioners' court held a special meeting in July, and the district court met in regular session on October 22. County Judge Coombes and District Judge Good presided over their respective courts without any apparent difficulty. Some of Dallas County's Unionists were unhappy with the course of Presidential Reconstruction, but they had no hope of successful opposition unless Republicans in Congress took control from the president.

13. Dallas *Herald*, April 21, May 5, 19, June 23, 1866; Election Registers, 1864–1865; Eighth Census, 1860, Schedule 1.

14. Dallas *Herald*, June 30, 1866; Election Registers, 1865–1866; Eighth Census, 1860, Schedules 1 and 2; Winkler, ed., *Platforms of Political Parties in Texas*, 98.

By mid-summer of 1866, local conservatives saw that possibility as a serious threat. A meeting on July 18 attended by Hord, Good, and Burford expressed support for President Johnson and his National Union movement. Swindells commented in the *Herald*: "The people of Dallas County are now in the fullest sense of the term a united people—united in the earnest support of President Johnson and his Reconstruction policy." He spoke accurately of the majority, but events would soon prove that some of "the people" did not share in that unity.[15]

The *Herald* kept interested citizens of Dallas well informed of developments in Washington and Austin as Congress took Reconstruction away from President Johnson during late 1866 and early 1867. The "Jacobins" have assembled in Washington, Swindells wrote on December 8, and will engage in "wilder and more unreasonable displays of fanaticism than any the country has yet seen." The South will be ruined, he continued, "And yet there are men in the South, some even in our midst, who . . . are ready to extend to these fell destroyers of a nation's peace and prosperity, the right hand of fellowship—for the sake of office they would assist in forging chains for the further degradation and enslavement of their own people." Swindells followed this admission (his first) that some in the county opposed conservative control with a warning that their sins would not be forgotten once the government returned to "its former purity."[16]

In general, however, the *Herald* advocated moderation. For example, in March, 1867, when the first Reconstruction act in effect destroyed everything done under President Johnson and renewed the process under congressional directives implemented by the United States army, Swindells urged local citizens to "acquiesce" and do nothing that would "tend to justify the harsh measures which they have adopted toward us." Yielding to conquerors, he wrote in early April, is the "only sensible conclusion to which all reasonable men must come." Nothing should suggest "hostility or disloyalty." Even the enfranchisement of blacks, which he had denounced so strongly in 1865, brought a measured response from the editor. Whites have to accept black suffrage, he said, so they should do everything possible to register and maintain their own voice at the polls. In mid-April, Swindells expressed pleasure at the "prudence and equanimity of temper" shown

15. Commissioners' Court Minutes, Book C, 300–28; District Court Minutes, Book C, 109–248; Dallas *Herald*, July 21, 1866.

16. *Ibid.*, December 8, 1866.

by the people of Dallas in accepting the new laws and promised that this reaction would "work its own salvation."[17]

Although he never explained his motivation explicitly, Swindells' moderation probably arose from two considerations. First, he recognized that the conservative white majority in Dallas County could simply outvote Unionists and blacks at the first opportunity. Thus, while black suffrage was wrong, he reasoned, it was not ruinous. Second, he saw stirrings of growth and prosperity and wanted nothing to interfere with Dallas' future. In 1866, the county, and especially the town, began to profit from an influx of immigrants from the Upper South and a major economic expansion began. The McKinney *Enquirer,* published in neighboring Collin County, commented in March, 1867, on the "great improvements made since last fall" in Dallas. "The people of that county," the editor wrote, "seem to have forgotten Congress, confiscation, territorial government, equal government, equal suffrage and the *devil,* remembering only their individual interests and looking forward to the welfare of their children. Like sensible and enterprising citizens, the people of Dallas improve and beautify their city, thereby pleasing and catching immigrants who pass that way." Swindells regularly reported on new buildings and new businesses and reminded his readers not to allow opposition to Congressional Reconstruction to interfere with growth. All citizens, he wrote on June 29, 1867, in urging compliance with the laws, "have the same interests at stake: all are to be benefited alike; and all have the same interest in the speedy restoration of peace and prosperity to the country."[18]

Of course, Swindells' talk of unity had never included Unionists, at least not politically, and they meant to make the most of opportunities provided by Congressional Reconstruction. In April, 1867, Jesse A. Asberry wrote to Gen. Philip Sheridan, commander of the Fifth Military District, complaining that many of the county officials elected on June 25, 1866, were "rebels of the deepest dye" who allowed murderers to "run at large unapprehended by the civil authorities." Many competent loyalists including himself, Asberry wrote, stood ready to run county government, if they were appointed and protected. Two months later a group of approximately twenty-five Unionists, including Asberry and Samuel S. Jones, asked military authorities to station a company of troops in Dallas to protect the civil and political rights of local loyalists. There is still so much intimidation, they com-

17. *Ibid.,* March 30, April 6, 20, 1867.
18. *Ibid.,* March 30, June 29, August 3, 1867.

plained, that Union men are reluctant to express their opinions publicly.[19]

Unionists found an ally in their attack on local officials in early May, 1867, with the arrival of Lt. William H. Horton, a U.S. Army veteran who had lost an arm at the Battle of Chancellorsville, to serve as the first sub-assistant commissioner of the Freedmen's Bureau in Dallas County. In an interview with Swindells, Horton promised not to interfere with the administration of justice locally. "He urgently desires to have the utmost harmony in his intercourse with all," the *Herald* reported, "and says it shall not be his fault if the reverse is the case." The comment about "fault" hinted that Horton expected disharmony; if so, he was correct. He reported to bureau headquarters that freedmen were not treated fairly in labor contracts, had no schools, and did not receive equal justice. Civil authorities, he wrote in June, acted so slowly in cases involving crimes against freedmen that perpetrators always had time to escape. Local officials, Horton reported, knew that white criminals frequently threatened blacks with death if they complained about offenses, but the practice continued. Moreover, Union men received the same treatment. "They are no better than a Negro," he concluded.[20]

During the spring of 1867, Unionists and Horton concentrated their complaints on District Judge John J. Good, the former Confederate officer elected in 1866. They were especially upset with the judge's reaction to the so-called jury order issued by Gen. Charles C. Griffin on April 27, 1867, requiring all jurors to swear the test oath of 1862. General Griffin issued this order in response to objections that judges such as Good were not treating Unionists and freedmen fairly, and he combined it with a section of the Civil Rights Act of 1866 that prohibited actions denying any citizen equal rights. Judge Good and others wondered if the general meant to force the seating of freedmen on juries, a proposal that would be difficult since prospective jurors were chosen by the commissioners' court well in advance of district court sessions, and state law prohibited blacks from serving in that capacity. Griffin left the final interpretation up to "the local authorities whose duties it is to impanel juries."[21]

19. Jesse A. Asberry to Gen. Philip Sheridan, April 10, 1867, OCA, RG 393, NA; Unionists of Dallas County to Gen. Charles Griffin, June 9, 1867, BRFAL, RG 105, NA.

20. Dallas *Herald*, May 18, 1867; William H. Horton to Lt. Joel T. Kirkman, June 29, 1867, BRFAL, RG 105, NA. Horton's story is told in detail in Smith, "Conflict and Corruption," 24–30.

21. The origins of the jury order controversy are detailed in Campbell, "District Judges of Texas in 1866–1867," 368–69.

Judge Good protested angrily to Governor Throckmorton that the jury order would "pollute the channels of justice" and stir up feelings that should have been buried with the war. The test-oath requirement could not possibly be the sole qualification for jurors, he argued in a fine bit of *reductio ad absurdum,* because that would mean the inclusion of women, children, and idiots on juries since they had not voluntarily supported the Confederacy. Instead, he concluded, the oath had to be an additional qualification, meaning that freedmen, who were otherwise disqualified, could not serve. Having decided on an interpretation, Good attempted to obey the order. However, according to Horton, he could not entirely disguise his anger when he opened court in Dallas on June 3. The judge, Horton reported, was "insulting and intimidating" to Union men and commented on the jury order in a way that was "unpleasant to hear." [22]

Regardless of his displeasure, Judge Good attempted to impanel grand and petit juries. When the group of men selected originally by the commissioners' court had only one who qualified, Good ordered Sheriff Brown to call more than one hundred additional prospective jurors and by June 24 succeeded in assembling the two juries from what the *Herald* called "the 'loyal' white men of the county." Samuel S. Jones and Jesse A. Asberry, two of the county's most noted Unionists, served as grand jurors. Judge Good would not place blacks on juries, but he did not, like some of the state's district judges, stop the operation of his court in response to the test oath directive. [23]

Editor Swindells praised Judge Good's "honest, earnest effort to get through the mass of business crowding both the state and civil docket." When the court session closed in late July, however, Horton called it a "farce." "The civil law is dead," he wrote, "except in instances when it can be enforced against Union men and Freedmen. It is a shame that such men as Judge Good . . . should be allowed to hold positions that permit them to protect their own sort and crush Union men and blacks." Jones complained to Horton that the placement of loyalists such as himself on the grand jury had meant nothing because Judge Good had permitted the court's bailiffs and deputies to warn those indicted for murdering Unionists during the

22. John J. Good to James W. Throckmorton, May 14, 21, 1867, Governors' Papers: JWT; William H. Horton to Lt. Joel T. Kirkman, June 3, 1867, BRFAL, RG 105, NA.
23. District Court Minutes, Book D, 250–81; Dallas *Herald,* June 29, 1867; Campbell, "District Judges of Texas in 1866–1867," 371–73.

war, giving the criminals time to flee the county. In mid-August the "Loyal Citizens of Dallas County" wrote to Elisha M. Pease, who had recently become governor upon the removal of Throckmorton by the military, making similar charges in the case of men accused of murdering a freedman. As long as Good is judge, the letter said, "no Union man has any show whatever." The precise truth of these accusations is impossible to determine. Good at least placed Unionists on juries, but there must have been some basis for the allegations that certain criminals were not prosecuted aggressively.[24]

Judge Good was not the only local officeholder who upset Unionists in Dallas County during the summer of 1867. On August 22, they complained to Governor Pease that other "impediments" remained in the way as well. "In this county," they contended, "every office is now filled with ex-rebels or their sympathizers." They sought the replacement of County Judge Coombes and all four county commissioners. On November 1, Gen. Joseph J. Reynolds removed virtually all the officials elected in June, 1866, and appointed Unionists to take their places. A. Bledsoe replaced Coombes as county judge, and Norvell R. Winniford, a farmer from Kentucky, took over the sheriff's office from J. M. Brown. During the war, Winniford had hidden out in the brush for weeks to avoid conscription by the Confederacy and then appeased authorities by hauling cotton to Mexico. Samuel S. Jones became county clerk. All four of the new county commissioners had been nonslaveholding farmers in 1860, three came from the Upper South and one from Ohio. The *Herald* had little to say about these removals and appointments except for a few sarcastic remarks about better luck next time for those displaced. Several weeks later Reynolds discharged Good and replaced him with D. O. Norton of Parker County, a Unionist who had come to Texas from Tennessee during the 1840s. Swindells simply reported Good's ouster without making any editorial comment.[25]

During the summer of 1867, while pressure was mounting for the replacement of local officeholders, another major step in Congressional Re-

24. Dallas *Herald*, June 29, 1867; William H. Horton to Lt. Joel T. Kirkman, July 31, 1867, Samuel S. Jones to Horton, July 22, 1867, BRFAL, RG 105, NA; Loyal Citizens of Dallas to E. M. Pease, August 17, 1867, Governors' Papers: EMP.

25. Loyal Citizens of Dallas to E. M. Pease, August 22, 1867, Governors' Papers: EMP; Election Registers, 1867; Melinda D. C. Smith, "Congressional Reconstruction in Dallas County, Texas: Was It Radical?" (M.A. thesis, University of North Texas, 1992), 24–28; Dallas *Herald*, November 16, 30, 1867.

construction—voter registration—began in Dallas County. Some conservative whites indicated an unwillingness to participate in the process, but the *Herald* appealed to all men to register. Swindells argued that apathy or hostility would "give over the State to the tender mercies of men, who will labor to inaugurate a system of proscription and disfranchisement." It will be far better, he contended, to unify in opposition to radicalism. "Let this be the great conservative heart of the State," he editorialized on June 29, "and let the old devotion of loyalty and attachment to the Federal Union that burned so brightly in the hearts of the people here be aroused with renewed energy and vigor."[26]

Apparently a majority of whites accepted these arguments. Shortly before registration opened, Samuel S. Jones, the Unionist, expressed the opinion that Congressional Reconstruction had brought a "very perceptible and salutary change" to political views in the area. Whereas most whites were "arrogant and domineering" in June of 1866, Jones reported, they had now accepted the new rules and were working in good faith for the completion of Reconstruction. Thus as voter registration began in Dallas County, moderation still seemed the rule, probably because white conservatives expected to have a majority and continue their control of local politics.[27]

Unionists Jones and Asberry, and Melvin Wade, a young black man from Tennessee who was destined to become the most important African-American leader in Dallas, served on the board of registrars that went to work on July 30. They opened registration in Dallas, traveled during early August to Scyene, east of the county seat, and to Lancaster in the southern part of the county, and returned to Dallas from mid-August until early September. Registration reopened for six days later that month and concluded on September 28, with a total of 1,205 voters, 837 whites and 368 blacks. The board disqualified nearly one-quarter (255) of the whites who attempted to register. The rejection of these men plus the refusal of other whites to attempt to register meant that blacks constituted twice as large a percentage of voters (31 percent) as they did in the population as a whole (16 percent).[28]

26. Dallas *Herald,* June 29, July 6, 1867.
27. Samuel S. Jones to William H. Horton, July 22, 1867, BRFAL, RG 105, NA.
28. Dallas *Herald,* August 3, September 14, October 5, 1867; List of Registered Voters in Texas, 1869. Melvin Wade is identified in the Ninth Census, 1870, Schedule 1. Curiously, the

Voter registration alarmed Swindells of the *Herald* far more than did other policies of Congressional Reconstruction, including the removal of local officials. Racial prejudice fueled his concern, which was for the state as a whole rather than Dallas County alone. Texas, the *Herald* began to tell its readers during the fall of 1867, is to be "Africanized." "It has been but a few brief months since the struggle first began in this State for black supremacy," Swindells wrote on October 5. "Since then, it has made fearful progress." As he watched the progress of voter registration, he became convinced that the convention would enfranchise blacks and disfranchise whites in order to place Texas "completely under Negro rule." Therefore, he concluded, the convention must be defeated. To this end, the *Herald* by mid-November began to advocate registering to vote but then refusing to participate in the election to approve calling the convention and select delegates. This strategy, generally endorsed by conservatives across Texas at that time, was meant to block the convention because the Reconstruction acts required participation by at least half of all the voters registered at the time of the election. Swindells wrote on November 23, "If we desire to defeat a convention—and we believe that to be the wish of every genuine conservative in Texas—we must not vote against a convention, for that may bring one upon us; *we must not vote at all.*" For once conservatives in Dallas County received advice to act in an extreme rather than moderate manner.[29]

In mid-December, 1867, Gen. Winfield S. Hancock, commander of the Fifth Military District, scheduled the election for February 10–14, 1868. The board of registrars in Dallas County reopened their books for five days in late January. A total of 102 additional voters registered, 80 whites and 22 blacks, but at the same time, 66 whites who had enrolled earlier were struck from the rolls. Final registration by February 1, 1868, amounted to 851 whites and 390 blacks (31 percent of the total). Approximately 300 whites had attempted unsuccessfully to register (the 255 who were denied registra-

---

*Herald* never commented on the fact that Wade was an African American. According to the census of 1870, Dallas County had a population of 13,314, including 11,197 whites, 2,109 blacks (16 percent of the total), and 8 Indians. U.S. Bureau of the Census, *Statistics of the Population of the United States (1870)*, 63–66.

29. Dallas *Herald*, October 5, 26, November 23, 1867. The fourth Reconstruction act in March, 1868, ended the possibility of this conservative strategy by requiring approval only of a majority of those participating in the election rather than of those registered.

tion and most of the 66 who were struck from the rolls in January), and others had refused to try. Even then, regardless of the presence of at least one hundred Unionists on the rolls and the fact that the percentage of black voters was nearly double in proportion to their numbers in the general population, conservative whites had a strong majority in Dallas County. They would have no difficulty in controlling the election, providing that they rejected the *Herald*'s conservative strategy and participated.[30]

At the last moment in January, 1868, conservatives statewide decided that refusing to participate was a mistake and decided to vote no on the convention but then vote for their candidates in case the meeting won approval. That way, they might block the convention, and that failing, they would have some representation in it. This change in strategy, however, came too late for general publication. In Dallas County only 381 whites voted, 138 for the convention and 243 against. Virtually every registered black voted, 383 of 390, and their support of the convention was unanimous. A. Bledsoe, the county's best-known Unionist, defeated the conservative N. O. McAdams 518 to 245 and became Dallas' delegate to the convention. Bledsoe received 135 votes from whites and unanimous support from the blacks. Swindells did not recant the strategy that had cost local conservatives a voice in writing the new constitution, but he did point out that the non-participants could easily have created a different outcome. He would not make the mistake again of urging Dallas County's conservatives not to take advantage of their power at the ballot box.[31]

Election of the constitutional convention still left Texas more than two years away from returning to the Union and restoring control to elected officials. For the remainder of 1868 and throughout 1869, local government in Dallas County continued as it had since November, 1867, under officers appointed by military authorities. District Judge D. O. Norton, who had replaced John J. Good in mid-November, 1867, died on March 25, 1868, and was in turn replaced by Anthony Banning Norton, a man with unimpeachable Unionist credentials. County Judge Bledsoe and Sheriff Winniford served throughout the period, but there was some turnover on the commissioners' court. Two of the four men appointed in November, 1867,

30. List of Registered Voters in Texas, 1869. The estimate of approximately 100 white Unionists is based on the fact that 138 whites voted for the constitutional convention in February. Dallas *Herald*, February 15, 1868.

31. Ramsdell, *Reconstruction in Texas,* 197–99; Dallas *Herald*, February 15, 1868.

refused to qualify, and another died before he could take office. Thus three more county commissioners had to be appointed in 1868. One of them, John M. Rawlins, was in reality a conservative. According to family tradition, Rawlins, who had not served the Confederacy because of a physical disability, took the appointment at the request of other conservatives who told him that they needed someone they "could trust" in county government.[32]

The Freedmen's Bureau maintained a presence in Dallas County during most of 1868, but its agents did relatively little to protect the interests of local blacks. Problems began when William H. Horton, the county's first sub-assistant commissioner, abused his power and discredited himself as an agent of the bureau. After his arrival in the spring of 1867, Horton, having no faith in local civil authorities, set up his own court and assessed heavy fines on whites who committed offenses against blacks. From this probably necessary and certainly defensible beginning, however, the agent became involved in actions that opened him to the charge of taking bribes. For example, in September, 1867, he arrested Daniel Murry for the murder of a freedwoman and, some alleged, allowed the accused to leave Dallas only after making an arrangement whereby the bureau agent received $350. Horton's enemies pounced on these accusations. In April, 1868, former district judge John J. Good and former governor James W. Throckmorton brought suit against Horton, charging him with false imprisonment of Daniel Murry. That same month, bureau headquarters responded to a request from Horton for reassignment elsewhere in Texas because of threats to his life and "embarrassments" in Dallas and transferred him to Bastrop. The bureau then investigated the complaints in Dallas and in September, 1868, dishonorably discharged Horton for taking a bribe. Four years later Good and Throckmorton dropped their suit.[33]

Horton's reassignment ended any significant presence by the Freedmen's Bureau in Dallas County. His replacement, George F. Eben, was murdered on April 8 in Kaufman County while traveling to Dallas. Unionists assumed that politics motivated the killing, but nothing could be proven. In June,

32. Election Registers, 1867–1869; Smith, "Congressional Reconstruction in Dallas County," 28; Randolph B. Campbell, "A Moderate Response: The District Judges of Dallas County During Reconstruction, 1865–1876," *Legacies: A History Journal for Dallas and North Central Texas*, V (Fall, 1993), 7–8.
33. Smith, "Conflict and Corruption," 25–29.

Willis A. Bledsoe, the son of County Judge A. Bledsoe, took over as bureau agent. He set up his office in Lancaster, citing fear for his life in Dallas, but the *Herald* suggested that he could expect at least toleration. The new agent is a "clever gentleman," the newspaper said on June 8, "and we doubt not will be as well thought of as any man could be in *that* position." Bledsoe served without incident until mid-July, when Lt. Henry Norton of the 17th United States Infantry took his place. Norton and his command of about forty infantrymen remained in Dallas until late October, 1868, and seemingly won full approval from the white majority. The *Herald* expressed the community's regret when the troops left and praised the company for not stepping "beyond its line to disgust, annoy or oppress the people." There is no indication of what blacks thought of federal troops and a bureau agent who won so much praise from local whites, but in any case neither soldiers nor the bureau would return during Reconstruction.[34]

Dallas County's freedmen thus had no active advocate during most of 1868 and none in 1869, and without doubt suffered, along with white Unionists, many of the threats and a large part of the violence that characterized those years. At the beginning of 1868, William Horton reported that feelings toward Unionists and blacks were just as bad as before the removals of local officials. Dallas County is in a "perfect state of terrorism," he wrote in a mid-February letter appealing for troops—both infantry and cavalry. (Horton had a small detachment of troops at his disposal during the summer of 1867, but they were removed by the end of the year.) Dallas loyalists attached a petition to the agent's February report claiming that his life was in danger. To back up his complaints, Horton on March 4, 1868, submitted a list of forty-two cases of violence by whites against blacks in Dallas County, many of them murders. These incidents had occurred over a period of nearly three years since emancipation, and some had been described earlier by the agent in monthly reports. Now, however, they were combined into a single indictment of conditions in the county. In April, Jesse A. Asberry added his voice to the protests in a letter to General Reynolds. "I cannot stay at home any more unless I am protected by soldiers," he wrote, because the rebels are organizing to drive all government officials out of the county. Judge A. B. Norton reported the same month that "assas-

34. *Ibid.*, 29–30; Smith, "Congressional Reconstruction in Dallas County," 68–75; Dallas *Herald*, June 8, November 14, 1868.

sination, murder, robbery, and larceny are heard of on all sides" in North Texas, and in August, 1868, he asked for a military escort, saying that he could not open court in Ellis County without one.[35]

Horton and local Unionists may have exaggerated to some extent when they complained of threats and violence against themselves and freedmen, but the *Herald* contained evidence to support the charges. In August, 1867, Swindells published an editorial criticizing what he called "a disposition manifested by some persons in some parts of this county" to speak harshly to and threaten the freedmen. He urged everyone to be "circumspect and just" in their dealings with blacks and to "turn their faces against" anyone who behaved otherwise. During the spring of 1868, someone posted handbills in Dallas warning that the Ku Klux Klan had arrived to reap a "harvest of Death." The *Herald* tended to dismiss the notices as the work of pranksters and argued that concern over the Klan arose from the fevered imaginations of radicals. There is no proof that the Klan organized in Dallas County, and no particular act of violence can be traced to it. Nevertheless, the threat was there.[36]

Violence and general lawlessness continued into 1869. Judge Norton reported to General Reynolds in July that murders and robberies occurred regularly and again requested troops. County Judge Bledsoe made similar appeals. "Anarchy and misrule is the order of the day in this county," he wrote on September 4, "and has been for some time past." By the summer of 1869, however, conservatives joined Unionists in denouncing lawlessness. John J. Good wrote Reynolds on July 21 asking the general to place two squads of cavalry under the command of Capt. C. H. Campbell, who had been in charge of Judge Norton's escort. The captain was familiar with the country, according to Good, and well respected by local citizens. A public meeting at Scyene considered ways to deal with the "bands of desperadoes" in the area. Judge Norton expressed his gratification that "some of the citizens are waking up to the necessity of themselves acting to put a stop to robberies, horse stealing, murder, etc." The "waking up" may have taken

35. William H. Horton to Lt. J. P. Richardson, February 12, March 4, 1868, BRFAL, RG 105, NA; Jesse A. Asberry to Gen. J. J. Reynolds, April 18, 1868, OCA, RG 393, NA; A. B. Norton to Elisha M. Pease, April 20, 1868, Governors' Papers: EMP.

36. Dallas *Herald*, August 17, 1867, April 11, 1868; Smith, "Congressional Reconstruction in Dallas County," 124–28.

the form of vigilante action in some cases. For example, six white men were found hanged near the Trinity River in August, probably in retaliation for stealing horses and cattle.[37]

Thus threats and violence—often of a racial or political nature—plagued Dallas County during 1868 and 1869. The perpetrators, however, apparently did not have even the tacit approval of conservative leaders. Instead, the *Herald* opposed violence, generally urged moderation, and focused even more than in 1867 on the county's and city's rapid economic expansion. An editorial of June 6, 1868, for example, commented that "the live town of Dallas seems determined to do all it can in the way of improvement. Several large, substantial, tastefully designed buildings are steadily going up, others in contract, and in almost every direction is heard the inspiring music of trowel, saw, forge, foundry and mill." The paper filled its columns with calls for improving navigation on the Trinity River, encouraging railroads to reach Dallas, building telegraph connections to the east and to Houston, and constructing an iron bridge across the Trinity. Nothing except "stinginess and false notions of economy," said the same June 6 editorial, prevents Dallas from having all the facilities necessary "for transacting the immense business that nature and the law of demand and supply indicates she should have in charge. Think of it, speak of it, write of it, do it. Everything earthly is possible to indomitable energy and iron will." In May, 1869, the *Herald* again sounded a call to action for economic development, saying that "a little nerve on the part of capitalists would make a large, populous and beautiful city of Dallas in four or five years, and its name would rank with that of Houston and Galveston on the records of the world." At the beginning of 1870, the paper proclaimed that the city's population had nearly doubled during the previous two years.[38]

The civic career of A. B. Norton, the military appointee as district judge in 1868, demonstrates the good luck and success Dallas conservatives had with their emphasis on economic expansion. Norton—a lawyer, newspaper editor, and Whig politician in his native state of Ohio—came to Texas during the 1850s and settled in Austin where he served three terms in the state house of representatives and supported the political career of Sam Houston.

37. A. B. Norton to Gen. J. J. Reynolds, July 16, August 21, 1869, A. Bledsoe to Reynolds, September 4, 1869, John J. Good to Reynolds, July 21, 1869, OCA, RG 393, NA; Smith, "Congressional Reconstruction in Dallas County," 129–30.
38. Dallas *Herald*, June 6, 1868, May 15, 1869, January 27, 1870.

A Unionist of more than ordinary courage and conviction, he left the state after secession and spent the war years in Ohio before returning to Texas and establishing a newspaper called the *Union Intelligencer* at Jefferson. A mob destroyed his press there and forced him to seek refuge in Van Zandt County. Obviously, then, in 1868 when Norton received the appointment as judge of the district that included Dallas he was both a colorful and controversial Unionist.[39]

Judge Norton had enough difficulty holding court in some counties that he requested a military escort, but his first session in Dallas during late 1868 and early 1869 seems to have gone smoothly. A few days after it began, the *Herald* editorialized about "the fine impression Judge Norton is making by his urbanity as a man and genuine dignity and ability as a judge." Later in December, Col. Nathaniel M. Burford introduced the judge to the crowd assembled for the launching on the Trinity River of a Dallas-built steamboat called the *Sallie Haynes.* Norton congratulated local businessmen on building the boat, forecast a great future for transportation on the Trinity, and predicted that Dallas would grow into "a large city which would be the emporium of North and Central Texas." The *Herald* commented that the speech was "happy, timely, pertinent, and was received with most hearty applause by the audience." Norton, of course, was incorrect about commerce on the Trinity, but in 1869 he involved himself in the movement to obtain a railroad, the kind of transportation that would work for Dallas. He and another prominent Republican, James K. P. Record, were among the speakers at a citizens' meeting concerning a railroad for their town. The meeting resolved to have the county issue three hundred thousand dollars in bonds to pay for stock in the first railroad company that would build to Dallas and erect a depot there. A special tax would be levied to pay for the bonds. Thus Judge Norton played a leading role in emphasizing economic growth rather than political partisanship. He remained on the bench until June, 1870, and the last grand jury to serve before his retirement adopted a report expressing their "high regard and appreciation" for his "untiring energy and indefatigable efforts" to "preserve order, enforce law, and develop the resources of the country."[40]

Regardless of their general moderation and focus on economic expan-

39. Campbell, "A Moderate Response," 7–8.
40. Dallas *Herald,* December 5, 19, 1868, January 30, 1869, June 18, 1870; Campbell, "A Moderate Response," 8.

sion in 1868–1869, however, Dallas County conservatives had no intention of accepting political control by Republicans at either the state or local level. When the constitutional convention assembled on June 1, 1868, in Austin, the *Herald* furiously denounced the delegates as a group of "Yankee adventurers, non-residents, and Southern Benedict Arnolds" who would give "negro suffrage, negro equality, negro supremacy over the Caucasian race of Texas." The Democratic party must lead, the editor wrote, in defeating any constitution that they write.[41]

In February, 1869, however, when the convention finished its work, the *Herald* changed its position. The editor found some aspects of the new constitution such as black suffrage and the governor's centralized powers objectionable, but concluded that the time had come to accept change and end Reconstruction. Texans, he wrote, "are worn out with delay. They are weary of the anomalous condition of affairs. Military rule, however mild and wise, cannot be acceptable." Thus he urged Democrats to accept the constitution and organize for the election that would endorse the new fundamental law and choose state and local officials. In fact the county's conservatives had organized thoroughly during 1868, and by 1869 the Dallas Democratic Association stood ready to marshal opposition to Republicans at the polls.[42]

When the elections were held November 30–December 3, 1869, the *Herald* joined most other conservatives across Texas in endorsing the moderate Republican candidate for governor, A. J. Hamilton, against the Radical Republican Edmund J. Davis. Davis, Swindells' paper said early in the campaign, is a "man of great pretensions and contemptible merit [who] if all the wind were pumped out of him would not be larger than a young hummingbird." The *Herald* also supported the candidacies of James K. P. Record, the local Republican moderate, for the state senate and John C. Conner for the United States House of Representatives. Conner was a carpetbagger and former Union army officer, but he ran as a Democrat and was the most conservative candidate in the race. Ten days before the election the *Herald* told its readers that every voter should do his duty because the election would be "the most important ever held in this state."[43]

41. Dallas *Herald*, June 6, 1868.
42. *Ibid.*, February 27, 1869; Smith, "Congressional Reconstruction in Dallas County," 150–51.
43. Dallas *Herald*, March 13, November 20, 1869; Moneyhon, *Republicanism in Reconstruction Texas*, 122, 153.

Swindells and Dallas County conservatives knew that to win they had only to get a reasonable percentage of their voters to the polls. In voting on the constitutional convention in February, 1868, they had wasted their majority position by refusing to participate. By November, 1869, they had even greater numbers and did not intend to lose another opportunity to gain control. General Reynolds ordered the reopening of voter registration from November 16 to November 26, and appointed Daniel Madden, William Fleming, and Melvin Wade as registrars. Madden was a captain in the 6th United States Cavalry; Fleming was a native of Pennsylvania who had been in Texas before the war; and Wade was the young black man who had served as a registrar in 1867 and 1868. Only 13 more blacks registered, bringing the total to 403, whereas 428 whites were added to the poll lists, bringing their numbers to 1,279, or 76 percent of all voters. Blacks, who were only 16 percent of the total population, were slightly overrepresented even at 24 percent of the voters, but they and the white Unionists were definitely in a minority position.[44]

The four-day election from November 30 to December 3 brought 893 of Dallas County's 1,279 registered voters to the polls and resulted in a total victory for the more conservative candidates. In the race for governor, A. J. Hamilton defeated E. J. Davis by a vote of 592 to 289. Other statewide contests had similar results—even the race for state comptroller in which A. Bledsoe, Dallas County's best-known Republican activist, lost to Armistead T. Monroe, a moderate Republican from Houston, 591 to 250. Bledsoe, however, gained enough support across Texas to win the election. The Democratic carpetbagger John C. Conner carried the county (550 to 272 for his nearest competitor) in the process of winning a seat in the United States House of Representatives. James K. P. Record, the popular moderate Republican from Dallas who ran for the state senate from the district comprising Dallas, Tarrant, and Collin Counties, came close to defeating a more conservative opponent, but he lost to the Democrat Samuel Evans by a vote of 457 to 426 in Dallas and by an even wider margin in the other two counties of the Twenty-first District. Three Democrats—John W. Lane of Dallas, B. S. Shelburne of Collin County, and A. F. Leonard of Tarrant County— won the same district's seats in the Texas House of Representatives. A. M.

44. General Orders No. 179 by Gen. Joseph J. Reynolds, October 8, 1869, OCA, RG 393, NA; List of Registered Voters in Texas, 1869; Dallas *Herald,* January 12, 1868; Ninth Census, 1870, Schedule 1.

Cochran, also a local moderate Republican, had 440 votes to Leonard's 444 in Dallas County, but lost badly districtwide.[45]

Democratic conservatives also won all of the important county elections. John D. Kerfoot, a thirty-four-year-old lawyer who had moved to Dallas County in the mid-1850s and then returned to his native Virginia to fight with a Confederate unit there during the Civil War, won the position of presiding justice of the county court by a vote of 172 to 125 against John C. Seydel, a Pennsylvania-born Republican who had come to Texas before the war. Kerfoot had not registered until November 16, 1869, just before the election. The other four justices—Benjamin F. Ricketts, Meredith Myers, William J. Halsell, and Thomas L. Franks—were natives of Kentucky who had lived in Texas since before the war. Ricketts, who represented the justice precinct encompassing the Lancaster area, defeated Norvell R. Winniford, the military appointee as sheriff of Dallas County and the best-known Republican to run for justice of the peace, by a vote of 69 to 40. The race for sheriff between Jeremiah M. Brown and Ben Long was especially interesting. Brown, who had won the sheriff's office in June, 1866, and then had been removed by military order in November, 1867, received 592 votes to 291 for Long, a native of Switzerland who had served as the military appointee-mayor of Dallas in 1868. The margin matched almost exactly those in other races such as the contests for governor and comptroller that represented clear choices between conservatives and Republicans.[46]

The *Herald* commented that the election results in Dallas County "surprised and chagrined the Radicals not a little" and claimed that Democrats had manipulated the blacks and "prevailed upon quite a number of them to smuggle in Democratic tickets." It is difficult to imagine that many Republicans, if they had looked at the list of registered voters, were surprised at the outcome. And, although perhaps it happened, there was no need in Dallas County to manipulate black voters. On that point Swindells' paper may have been engaging in the practice, common among racist editors during Reconstruction, of laughing about how easily the supposedly unintelligent blacks were duped into voting conservative.[47]

45. Election returns for 1869 are found in *Senate Miscellaneous Documents,* 41st Cong., 2nd Sess., No. 77, pp. 38–79.

46. *Ibid.*; Smith, "Congressional Reconstruction in Dallas County," 156–59; Election Registers, 1869; Ninth Census, 1870, Schedule 1.

47. Dallas *Herald,* December 18, 1869.

The newspaper did not exaggerate, however, the chagrin of some leading Republicans in the county. On January 20, 1870, Samuel S. Jones wrote Edmund J. Davis, who had won the governorship and been appointed to that office in anticipation of his inauguration in April, to complain about conditions in Dallas. "In this county," he claimed, "every officer elected from District Clerk down to Justice of the Peace are of the most extreme, unrelenting and unrepentant rebels in the country. . . . Something ought to be done to help loyalty out in this section of the State. Gen we look to you to inaugurate that which will relieve not only this section of the State, but every other where Loyalty is under the heavy yoke of rebeldom." Jones concluded by recommending a solution to get rid of Rebels and protect Unionists: "Apply the test oath throughout the State." Unfortunately for men like Jones, Governor Davis could not require new officeholders to swear the ultimate oath of loyalty to the Union, and on May 2, 1870, the new officials took over the government of Dallas County. Jones, the outgoing county clerk, described the event for the *Herald* in words that probably masked his true view. "The utmost good feeling prevailed among the parties, throughout the entire proceedings," he wrote, "after which the old officers bowed themselves into retirement." Dallas County never had an elective government by Republicans during Reconstruction and thus never had to be "redeemed."[48]

After the spring of 1870, local Republicans knew that the state district court provided their primary hope for maintaining influence and power. The new constitution and laws passed in 1870 allowed Governor Davis to appoint thirty-five district judges, all of whom presumably would be Republicans. Samuel S. Jones saw the possibilities clearly. "All quiet in the county," he wrote Davis on July 14, 1870. "We desire a good *radical* judge."[49]

Robert H. Taylor of Fannin County, Davis' first appointee as judge of the Fourteenth District, could not qualify for the position, probably because af-

48. Samuel S. Jones to E. J. Davis, January 20, 1870, Governors' Papers: EJD; Dallas *Herald*, May 7, 1870.

49. Samuel S. Jones to E. J. Davis, July 14, 1870, Governors' Papers: EJD. Republicans had one other political foothold locally during the Davis administration because a new voter registration law allowed the governor to appoint a registrar and three-man board of appeal for each county. Davis made James Bentley the registrar in Dallas County and named John C. Seydel to the board of appeal; Election Registers, 1871. Seydel was the unsuccessful candidate for presiding justice in 1869, and Bentley was committed to Davis. See Bentley to Davis, May 17, 1870, Governors' Papers: EJD.

ter unsuccessfully opposing secession he had become a colonel in the Confederate army. With Taylor failing to qualify, it appeared that court would not be held in Dallas during 1870. On the appointed first Monday in October no judge arrived, and most of the men called for jury duty went home. Then, unexpectedly, Judge C. T. Garland arrived and opened the session. Garland had built a reputation as a Republican radical in Jefferson, Texas, during Congressional Reconstruction. He attended the Radical Republican state convention in 1869, established a paper called the Jefferson *Radical* that same year, and served as a military-appointee judge of the Eighth District in 1869–1870. Finding only two of the twenty-two men called for grand jury service present, Garland ordered the absentees fined and directed Sheriff J. M. Brown to summons more prospective jurors, black as well as white. The judge then impaneled a grand jury of sixteen whites and four blacks, including Melvin Wade, the voter registrar from 1867 to 1869. Wade and the other blacks were the first African Americans to serve on a jury in Dallas County.[50]

Judge Garland represented the radicalism that conservatives such as Swindells of the *Herald* despised, at least at the state and national levels. For example, in April, 1870, Swindells' paper described the Radical party as "rotten to the core" and called it "the chief cause of all our woes, our national crimes and national disgrace." This attack on radicals did not, however, extend to Garland, even when the judge put blacks on the grand jury. Two weeks into the session, the *Herald* reported: "Judge Garland, we are informed, in his rulings upon all questions of law, has given universal satisfaction to the members of the bar." In late October the judge attended a dinner given by the businessmen of Dallas in honor of a surveyor for the Missouri, Kansas, and Texas Railway Company, the first such railroad official to arrive in the town. A toast was offered to "the Judiciary," and Garland responded with a brief speech in which he praised lawyers for their support of railroads and commercial improvements in general. His remarks, observed Swindells, "were well received and heartily approved." Judge Garland, for all his radicalism, seems to have met with the same sort of reception given A. B. Norton in 1868.[51]

50. Campbell, "A Moderate Response," 8–9; Election Registers, 1869; Dallas *Herald*, August 21, 1869, October 8, 1870; Winkler, ed., *Platforms of Political Parties in Texas*, 121; District Court Minutes, Book E, 580, Book F, 84.

51. Campbell, "A Moderate Response," 9; Dallas *Herald*, April 4, October 15, November 5, 1870.

C. T. Garland held only one session of the district court in Dallas because the state senate, for unspecified reasons, refused to confirm his nomination. No judge appeared for the next scheduled court term in February, 1871, but on June 5 court opened with Hardin Hart from Greenville in Hunt County presiding. Dallas conservatives had managed to be positive about A. B. Norton and C. T. Garland, but Hart constituted a much more difficult challenge.[52]

Hardin Hart was born in Hardy County, Virginia (now West Virginia), in 1814 and moved to Texas during the 1830s. He had no formal education but learned enough law to be admitted to the bar. He and his brother, Martin D. Hart, opened a law practice in Greenville in the mid-1840s. They enjoyed enough success that Hart even owned a few slaves, but both Harts supported the Union during the Civil War. Martin D. Hart led a force of irregulars from Texas who fought on the side of Federal troops in Arkansas; Confederates there captured and executed him for treason. Hardin Hart managed to survive the war in Hunt County, although as one local historian later wrote, he was "severely abused and roughly handled while the war was in progress." After the war, Hart continued to take unpopular positions, serving as county judge in 1865–1866 under appointment from A. J. Hamilton and as Freedmen's Bureau agent in Greenville in 1867.[53]

Hardin Hart began a controversy-filled career as a district judge in November, 1867, when he received a military appointment to serve on the bench of the Seventh District in northeast Texas. The noted Unionist Albert H. Latimer of Red River County endorsed Hart's nomination, telling General Griffin: "He is a most reliable man, not polished, but possessing strong native intellect and firmness. He is the man for the times and the place." The Clarksville *Standard* thought that Hart needed no endorsement. "Hardin . . . is six feet four in his stockings," the editor wrote, "staunch built and positive in character, and able to maintain his own qualifications." As a radical judge serving in a district noted for violence, Hart lived with constant danger during Congressional Reconstruction. He sought and obtained a military escort in 1868, but even the squad of seven soldiers could not protect him from an ambush on the road from Bonham to Greenville on September 4, 1869. Wounded several times, the judge had to have one

52. Campbell, "A Moderate Response," 9; Election Registers, 1870; District Court Minutes, Book F, 85, 88.
53. Campbell, "A Moderate Response," 9.

arm amputated, but he recovered and continued to serve on the bench of the Seventh District until 1870.[54]

Governor Davis appointed Hart judge of the Fourteenth District in February, 1871, and he held court in Dallas for the first time in June of that year. In this case conservatives reacted by saying nothing—either positive or negative—about a radical judge. The *Herald* noted that the district court was in session, but virtually never mentioned Hart's name. The judge continued the practice of having African Americans serve on grand and petit juries and apparently did nothing to ingratiate himself with conservatives such as endorsing transportation and commercial developments. The *Herald* continued its rule of silence.[55]

In the fall of 1871, as they tolerated Hardin Hart's tenure on the bench, Dallas conservatives demonstrated again that they had total control of the county and would easily do their part to eliminate Republican government, and judges, in Texas. The Texas legislature called a special election in October to choose U.S. Representatives for the Congress scheduled to meet in December of that year. In the Second Congressional District, which included Dallas and the north Texas area, John C. Conner, the carpetbagger Democrat elected in 1869, ran for reelection. His opponent was Anthony M. Bryant, a Republican leader from Grayson County. The *Herald* urged voters to get to the polls early and vote for Conner. Yes, the editor said, Conner was a Union soldier, but he is now a friend of the South who will help rid us of radical rule. The incumbent won by a vote of 1,071 to 340. At the same election, conservative voters showed their strength in selecting two new justices of the peace to the county court. Thanks to a ruling by Governor Davis, justices of the peace in 1871 were elected countywide rather than by precinct as was the case in 1870. Robert S. Guy, a Democratic lawyer from Virginia, defeated Willis A. Bledsoe, son of A. Bledsoe and former Freedmen's Bureau agent, 1,016 to 353 for one position, and C. C. Husted, a Democrat born in Illinois, won the other over two opponents.[56]

During 1872 Dallas finally gained the transportation outlet necessary to

54. *Ibid.*, 9–10; A. H. Latimer to Gen. Charles Griffin, August 12, 1867, Governors' Papers: EMP; Clarksville (Tex.) *Standard*, quoted in Dallas *Herald*, February 8, 1868.

55. Campbell, "A Moderate Response," 10.

56. Dallas *Herald*, September 23, 30, October 7, 1871; Election Registers, 1871; Ninth Census, 1870, Schedule 1.

make the *Herald*'s optimistic predictions come true. Navigation of the Trinity had failed. One steamboat actually navigated the river from the coast to Dallas in 1867 and 1868, but it required 369 days for the trip. The *Sallie Haynes,* launched at Dallas in December, 1868, never reached Galveston. Pleas for a railroad, however, paid off on July 16, 1872, when the Houston and Texas Central began service to Dallas. In 1873, it met the Missouri, Kansas, and Texas Railroad at Denison, and the Texas and Pacific extended to Dallas from the east. At that point the town had rail transportation to the Gulf Coast, the Midwest, and the Mississippi River.[57]

No major obstacles stood in the way of the commercial expansion envisioned by Dallas' leaders since shortly after the end of the war. Even newly arrived Dallas dwellers such as John Henry Brown, a member of the secession convention and former Confederate officer who moved to the city in 1871, quickly embraced an optimistic vision of the area's future. Brown wrote his brother and sister on January 2, 1872:

> The great Texas Central R. R. will be here by May, & next fall will meet the Kansas & St. Louis RR. at R. R. [Red River]. Then the National Texas Pacific or latitude 32 will pass here for California in 12 or 15 months. Then the Transcontinental from Memphis will unite with the Texas Pacific here at the same time. Then we have the new Dallas & Wichita to run from here on the route to Denver northwest. At 120 miles it reaches inexhaustible coal and copper mines. So, with the magnificent forests of East Texas brought to our doors & iron from both east & west in 100 miles & coal in 120, Dallas will rapidly become a great manufacturing centre in the heart of a first class cotton, wheat & corn country.[58]

Results of the presidential, congressional, and state legislative races in November, 1872, were a foregone conclusion in Dallas County. Horace Greeley, the Liberal Republican candidate who had the support of Democrats as well, was endorsed by the *Herald* and carried the county over President Grant by a vote of 1,097 to 403. William P. McLean, a Mississippi-born former major in the Confederate army, defeated Republican Fred W.

57. Christopher LaPlante, "Reconstruction in Dallas County, 1865–1873" (M.A. thesis, University of Texas at Arlington, 1974), 43–45, 49–58.

58. John Henry Brown to "Dear Bro. & Sister," January 2, 1872, in John Henry Brown Papers, Eugene C. Barker Texas History Center, University of Texas, Austin, Tex. For a sketch of Brown's life, see Webb, Carroll, and Branda, eds., *Handbook of Texas,* I, 225–26.

Miner by 1,152 to 404 in the race for the Second District seat in Congress. Three new Democratic state representatives, two of whom were especially well known for pro-southern and conservative views, won seats in the legislature without any opposition from Republican candidates. John Henry Brown of Dallas and Khleber M. Van Zandt of Tarrant County both had supported secession and served in the Confederate army. The third new representative was Edward Chambers of Collin County. These men went to Austin in January, 1873, as part of the Democratic majority that reclaimed the state legislature from Republican control.[59]

By the time of the next state and local general election on December 2, 1873, Democrats in Dallas County found that their complete control created a problem—too many Democratic candidates for the same offices. Without unified nominations, a group of leaders said in a front-page letter to the *Herald*, "the Radical faction of this noble Democratic county (a few white men and nine-tenths of their dupes the poor, ignorant black men), will elect our county officers." Responding to this argument, Democrats held a county primary election on October 11 and selected candidates behind whom all were expected to unite. Swindells' paper endorsed all the primary winners as well as the party's state ticket led by Richard Coke of McLennan County who was seeking to regain the governor's office from E. J. Davis. Throughout November the *Herald* urged Dallas' voters to play a major part in "the glorious redemption of Texas from bondage" by casting the largest majority for Coke of any county in the state.[60]

Coke carried Dallas County over Davis by a vote of 2,028 to 336, but even an 86 percent majority placed the county only fourth in the state among margins of victory for the Democratic candidate. "Shame! Oh! Shame!" cried the *Herald*. All the Democratic primary nominees, led by incumbent presiding justice John D. Kerfoot, easily won election, although three of the five justices of the peace drew opposition from other candidates claiming to be Democrats. The sheriff's race was the closest contest, with Maj. James E. Barkley, the primary nominee, defeating Jeremiah M. Brown, the incumbent Democrat, by a vote of 1,301 to 830. By 1874, when Coke took office and marked the end of Republican government in Austin, Dallas

59. Dallas *Herald,* November 2, 16, 23, 1872; Webb, Carroll, and Branda, eds., *Handbook of Texas,* I, 225–26, II, 120, 832.
60. Dallas *Herald,* August 16, 30, October 18, November 22, 1873.

County conservatives only had to worry about fighting among themselves.[61]

The last vestige of Republican power in Dallas was removed when District Judge Hardin Hart resigned on February 18, 1874, his sixtieth birthday. The *Herald* continued its rule of silence to the end, saying nothing about Hart as he left the bench. As Hart's replacement, Governor Coke appointed Hickerson Barksdale, a Confederate veteran from Tennessee who had come to Dallas in 1870. Politically, Barksdale was a Democrat of the John C. Calhoun states' rights school. He served without controversy until the spring of 1876, and at the end of his tenure the bar of Dallas presented him with a gold-headed ebony cane in appreciation of his "spotless integrity as a Judge, his courtesy and impartiality as a presiding officer, and his learning and ability as a lawyer."[62]

The final step in statewide "redemption" was the writing of a new state constitution in 1875. Three conservative Democrats—John Henry Brown of Dallas, Nicholas H. Darnell of Tarrant County, and Justus W. Ferris of Ellis County—represented Dallas County in the convention. Brown, a former Confederate officer, had served the county in the Thirteenth Legislature. Darnell, after moving from Tennessee to Texas in 1838, held numerous political positions and served in the Confederate army as colonel of the 18th Texas Cavalry. Ferris, a native of New York, sat as a district judge during the Civil War.[63]

The main issue in the election of officials under the new constitution on February 15, 1876, was not if, but which, Democratic candidates would win in Dallas County. Richard Coke showed the full measure of Democratic strength in the race for governor by defeating William Chambers, 4,476 to 601. In district and county contests, however, there were no Republican candidates, and the Democrats, who did not hold a primary as in 1873, wound up dividing their votes among several members of their own party. For example, Robert S. Guy, a former justice of the peace, narrowly defeated the incumbent John Henry Brown for the state senate seat from Dal-

---

61. *Ibid.*, December 6, 20, 1873. Official returns in the governor's race are from Kingston, Attlesey, and Crawford, *Political History of Texas*, 58.

62. Campbell, "A Moderate Response," 10; Dallas *Herald*, March 18, 1876.

63. Dallas *Herald*, August 14, 21, 1875; Webb, Carroll, and Branda, eds., *Handbook of Texas*, I, 465, 593.

las. Both men were former Confederate officers and strong Democrats. Nathaniel M. Burford won the race for district judge, defeating Z. Ellis Coombes and John M. Crockett. Again, all three men had unquestionable records as Democrats and supporters of the Confederacy, Burford and Coombes as officers and Crockett as superintendent of the arms factory at Lancaster. The contest for sheriff involved Jeremiah M. Brown, who won the office in 1869; James E. Barkley, who won in 1873; and William M. Moon, who lost the 1873 primary to Barkley. This time, Moon won. Close races among Democratic candidates may have given Republicans a chance to affect the result if they agreed on a single choice. The *Herald* thought so and grumbled that the "six hundred Republican vote was pretty well united on certain local candidates and may have determined to a considerable extent the outcome."[64] Even if true, this probably gave little comfort to the minority party in that nothing indicated any appreciable difference in commitment to the Democratic party among the various candidates.[65]

The era of Reconstruction thus closed in Dallas County with hardly a ripple to disturb the control enjoyed by Democrats since the restoration of civilian government in 1870. Overall, the period was one of rapid expansion and notable prosperity. The total population increased 54 percent between 1860 and 1870 (from 8,665 to 13,314) and then zoomed upward by more than 150 percent during the next decade to a total of 33,488. Dallas grew from a town of about 3,000 people in 1870 to a near-city (by nineteenth-century Texas standards) of 10,358 in 1880. Its population more than doubled in 1872 and 1873 when the Houston and Texas Central and the Texas and Pacific railways arrived. The total assessed value of taxable property in the county rose from $1,814,464 in 1865 to $7,695,584 in 1876, an increase of 324 percent. During the same period, the overall value of town lots in the county, most of which were in Dallas, rose from $77,655 to $1,800,732. Cotton production, which was virtually nonexistent in 1860, reached 3,834 bales in 1869 and 21,469 bales in 1879. Higher state and local

64. Dallas *Herald*, February 12, 26, 1876; Election Registers, 1876; Kingston, Attlesey, and Crawford, *Political History of Texas*, 58; Webb, Carroll, and Branda, eds., *Handbook of Texas*, I, 436.

65. There was one probable exception to this generalization. Fleming G. Bledsoe, one of A. Bledsoe's sons, ran successfully for the position of county commissioner. The *Herald* did not give returns on commissioners' races and made no comment about Bledsoe. Nevertheless, given A. Bledsoe's politics, it seems almost certain that his son would have been a Republican. F. G. Bledsoe's victory is shown in the Election Registers, 1876; and that he was A. Bledsoe's son in the Eighth Census, 1860, Schedule 1.

property taxes, which jumped from less than 50 cents on $100 of assessed value prior to 1871 to $1.50 on $100 that year and remained around $1 through 1876, apparently did nothing to retard economic growth.[66]

Dallas County's expansion in the late 1860s and 1870s depended heavily on new arrivals, but it did not leave older economic leaders ruined in the wake of defeat and harsh congressional policies. An examination of the wealthiest 5 percent of taxpayers in 1865 and in 1880 reveals that exactly half of the same individuals or members of the same families remained in this elite class through the period of Reconstruction and beyond. One-quarter of the wealthiest 5 percent in 1865 had left the county by 1880, and only one-quarter of those individuals or their surviving family members had fallen from the elite class. Neither Reconstruction nor rapid population growth greatly affected the wealthiest people of Dallas County.[67]

Blacks in Dallas County received relatively little help in adjusting from slavery to freedom. The Freedmen's Bureau maintained an office there only from May, 1867, to December, 1868. William H. Horton, the sub-assistant commissioner for most of that time, reported that the county's black population suffered a great deal from the racial violence that typified northeast Texas during Reconstruction. He offered some protection to freedmen but became involved in what appeared to be efforts to use his position for personal gain and eventually, after leaving Dallas, was given a dishonorable discharge for corruption. Dallas' black population remained stable as a proportion of the total during the era—constituting 12 percent in 1860, 16 percent in 1870, and 15 percent in 1880—and made only limited economic progress during the fifteen years following freedom. A random sample of 250 black households from the census of 1880 shows that of 163 men who called themselves farmers, farm laborers, or simply laborers, only eleven (7 percent) actually owned farm land. Two rented for cash, twelve were share-croppers, and the remainder were in fact day laborers on farms or in town. Thus only a handful of Dallas County blacks had achieved the most com-

66. U.S. Bureau of the Census, *Population of the United States in 1860*, 484; U.S. Bureau of the Census, *Statistics of the Population of the United States (1870)*, 63–66; U.S. Bureau of the Census, *Statistics of the Population of the United States (1880)*, 343, 409; LaPlante, "Reconstruction in Dallas County," 58; Real and Personal Property Tax Rolls, Dallas County, 1865–1876; U.S. Bureau of the Census, *Agriculture of the United States in 1860*, 141; U.S. Bureau of the Census, *The Statistics of Wealth and Industry of the United States . . . from the Original Returns of the Ninth Census (1870)* (Washington, D.C., 1872), 252; U.S. Bureau of the Census, *Report on the Productions of Agriculture (1880)*, 242.

67. Real and Personal Property Tax Rolls, Dallas County, 1865 and 1880.

mon goal among freedmen, ownership of their own plot of land. Limited economic progress, however, did not prevent significant social stability. Nearly three-quarters (74 percent) of the 250 sample households were headed by nuclear families—a man with his wife and children. Widows, divorcees, and single women headed only 18 percent of all households. Of the 140 households in the sample that had children aged six through sixteen, sixty-two (44 percent) had at least one of those children attend school within the past year.[68]

Blacks did not have the numbers to play a major role in political life. They and their Unionist/Republican allies were a minority from the outset, and no black held an elective county office between 1865 and 1876. Nevertheless, the Reconstruction generation of freedmen clearly valued the opportunity to participate in politics and public life. They registered and voted at the first opportunity and served on juries when that right became available. At least one black man, Melvin Wade, emerged as a leader, serving as an appointive member of the board of registrars from 1867 to 1869, and on the grand jury as early as 1870. Wade remained active in public life and became one of the most important black Populists in North Texas during the 1890s.[69]

In summary, the Reconstruction era marked dramatic change in Dallas County, but Reconstruction itself did not cause the change. Congressional intervention bothered white conservatives for a few years, but given the county's small percentage of blacks and loyalist whites, Republicans of any sort, let alone "Radicals," had no chance of holding power against the Democrats once constitutional government was restored. Conservatives resumed control in 1870, and within a few years Republican candidates were nonexistent. The extremely limited nature of political change brought by Reconstruction is symbolized by the presence of Judge Nathaniel M. Burford in 1876 on the same district court bench that he had occupied in 1860.[70]

Throughout the era, conservative spokesmen, especially John W. Swin-

68. U.S. Bureau of the Census, *Population of the United States in 1860*, 484; U.S. Bureau of the Census, *Statistics of the Population of the United States (1870)*, 63–66; U.S. Bureau of the Census, *Statistics of the Population of the United States (1880)*, 343. Information on the occupations and agricultural production of the random sample of 250 black households from the census of 1880 was drawn from the Tenth Census, 1880, Schedules 1 and 2.

69. Gregg Cantrell, *Kenneth and John B. Rayner and the Limits of Southern Dissent* (Urbana, Ill., 1993), 203, 212–13, 215.

70. Campbell, "A Moderate Response," 11–12.

dells of the Dallas *Herald,* generally maintained a tone of relative moderation concerning local affairs. They railed at the idea of black suffrage and
at the "tyrannical" state government of E. J. Davis, but did not condone
violence against freedmen or loyalists and spoke against the general lawlessness that characterized the region in 1868 and 1869. They urged voters
to do what was necessary to return to the Union as quickly as possible.

Conservatives preached moderation for at least two reasons. First, they
could afford moderation because they had numbers on their side. Second,
Dallas County during the late 1860s entered a period of rapid growth and
economic development that put the locality well on the way to becoming
the commercial center of North Texas. The promise of prosperity doubtless
encouraged conservative leaders to emphasize a moderate course in politics
in order to enjoy the benefits of economic expansion. Dallas County
changed dramatically between 1865 and 1876, but agricultural and commercial growth coupled with transportation improvements, rather than the
policies of Reconstruction, made the difference.

# 4

## HARRISON COUNTY

A visitor from the black belt of Alabama would likely have felt perfectly at home in late-antebellum Harrison County. Located on the Louisiana border in northeast Texas, Harrison was among the most southern of all the state's counties. Natives of the South headed more than 90 percent of its households in 1860, and nearly two-thirds (61 percent) of the heads of households owned slaves. Harrison's 8,784 slaves, the largest number living in any Texas county on the eve of the Civil War, constituted 59 percent of the total population. Only one man, William T. Scott, owned more than one hundred bondsmen, but 145 held twenty or more and could therefore call themselves planters. By 1859 nearly 85 percent of the county's farmers produced cotton, and the crop amounted to 21,440 bales, the second largest in the state.[1] Harrison County cotton was exported to Shreveport, Louisiana, and thence to New Orleans by way of Caddo Lake (a natural lake on the county's northeastern border), the Red River, and the Mississippi. To move cotton to this relatively reliable and inexpensive water route, planters sponsored the building of a railroad that in 1858 began transportation from Marshall, the county seat, to Swan-

---

1. A detailed account of antebellum Harrison County is presented in Randolph B. Campbell, *A Southern Community in Crisis: Harrison County, Texas, 1850–1880* (Austin, 1983), 17–179. Statistical information on the population and slaveholding is from the Eighth Census, 1860, Schedules 1 and 2. Statistics on cotton production are from U.S. Bureau of the Census, *Agriculture of the United States in 1860*, 140–49.

# Map 4

## Harrison County

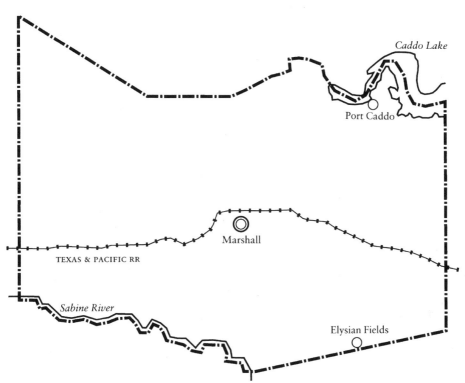

*Caddo Lake*

Port Caddo

Marshall

TEXAS & PACIFIC RR

*Sabine River*

Elysian Fields

Adapted, with permission, from the Harrison County map in the *Texas Almanac* for 1996–1997.

son's Landing on the lake. The twenty-five-mile-long Southern Pacific Railroad hardly matched its name, but it was one of only two in antebellum Texas outside the Houston area and greatly aided planters east of Marshall, the region that produced most of the county's cotton.[2]

Political life in antebellum Harrison County naturally reflected its overwhelmingly southern economy and society. Slaveholders dominated officeholding at all levels, and protection of the South's peculiar institution against northern abolitionism and antislavery sentiment was always a major concern. The *Texas Republican* of Marshall, Texas, edited by Robert W. Loughery, consistently took an ultrasouthern position on all sectional issues, insisting that any compromise or concession was "submissionist," and a sizable majority of the county's voters agreed. Nevertheless, Unionists constituted a significant minority throughout the 1850s (at least one-third of the voters) and had their own newspaper voices, the Whig-oriented *Star State Patriot* early in the decade and then the *Harrison Flag,* which supported the Know-Nothing and Constitutional Union parties. Leading ultrasoutherners and Unionists, however, were very similar in terms of demographic and economic characteristics—virtually all were relatively wealthy southern-born slaveholders—and differed only in their views on the best way to protect southern interests.[3]

In the presidential election of 1860, Loughery's *Texas Republican* warned that the nomination of Stephen A. Douglas by the Democratic party would be "the first step to a final surrender to the demands of Black Republicanism" and cheered when southern delegates left the party rather than accept the Little Giant. Ultrasoutherners in Harrison County supported John C. Breckinridge, the Southern Democratic candidate. Unionists formed a fusion ticket promising to support either John Bell, the Constitutional Union party candidate; or Douglas, the northern Democratic nominee; or even Breckinridge, if necessary to defeat Lincoln. "This is a union for the sake of the Union," the *Harrison Flag* explained. Breckinridge easily carried the county by 681 to 366 over Bell, but the fusion ticket drew 36 percent of the vote, notably greater support than Unionists had statewide.[4]

2. Campbell, *Southern Community in Crisis,* 85–95.
3. *Ibid.,* 147–67, 173; *Texas Republican* (Marshall), September 23, 1851. For evidence that the Whigs had greater strength in Harrison than in most Texas counties in 1848 and 1852, see Randolph B. Campbell, "The Whig Party of Texas in the Elections of 1848 and 1852," *Southwestern Historical Quarterly,* LXXIII (1969), 17–34.
4. *Texas Republican,* April 21, June 2, July 7, 28, September 8, 15, 1860; Marshall *Harrison*

Once it became clear that Lincoln had won the presidency, a movement for secession developed immediately and spontaneously in Harrison County. Mass meetings called for a state convention to consider disunion and swept away nearly all opposition. On February 23, 1861, the county's voters endorsed secession by a vote of 866 to 44. Unionism seemed to have disappeared except for a handful of votes from the northwestern part of the county where slaveholding was somewhat less prevalent. Voter turnout, however, was 159 less than in the 1860 presidential election, suggesting that some Unionists stayed at home rather than risk the wrath of their neighbors in a hopeless cause. In Texas counties less dominated by slaveholders and ultrasouthern spokesmen such as Loughery, the minority who opposed secession apparently found it easier to express their convictions in 1861. This circumstance indicated that Harrison County residents who tended to support the Union would face inordinate difficulties when Reconstruction began in 1865.[5]

When news of the firing on Fort Sumter reached Marshall on April 17, 1861, the town resounded with cannon fire and patriotic speeches, and young men rushed to serve the Confederacy. During the first two years of the war, one-third to one-half of the county's men aged fifteen through forty-nine joined the army. Most remained in the Trans-Mississippi Department throughout the war, but the "Marshall Guards" became part of Hood's Texas brigade and fought in thirty-eight battles and skirmishes including Antietam, Gettysburg, and the Wilderness. More than half of those who served in the company were killed, wounded, or captured. As the war progressed, Marshall became increasingly important as a center for Confederate military operations. A powder mill and ordnance works moved there from Arkansas in 1863, and once Union forces split the Confederacy along the Mississippi in July of that year, Gen. Edmund Kirby Smith, commander of the Trans-Mississippi Department, located many of his operations near and in Harrison County. For example, paperwork for the quartermaster bureau based in Shreveport was handled in Marshall.[6]

Harrison County narrowly escaped Federal invasion during the spring of

*Flag*, September 22, October 13, 20, 1860; Kingston, Attlesey, and Crawford, *Political History of Texas*, 72–75.

5. Timmons, "Referendum in Texas on the Ordinance of Secession," 15–16; Campbell, *Southern Community in Crisis*, 183–93.

6. Campbell, *Southern Community in Crisis*, 199–219.

1864. General Kirby Smith's command operations in northwest Louisiana and northeast Texas, as well as the agricultural resources of that region, made it such an inviting target that a twenty-five-thousand-man Union army commanded by Gen. Nathaniel P. Banks and supported by a flotilla of gunboats under Adm. David D. Porter moved up Red River and nearly reached Shreveport. Confederate forces commanded by Gen. Richard Taylor defeated Banks's army at Mansfield, Louisiana, on April 8, 1864, safeguarding Harrison County from invasion for the remainder of the war.[7]

Nevertheless, the threatened attack brought additional defensive troops to Marshall who lost discipline as the Confederacy collapsed in the spring of 1865. In April, Gen. Thomas J. Churchill ordered those under his command to stop "committing depredations upon and otherwise annoying the citizens in the vicinity of Marshall." Within a month, Churchill's soldiers simply quit and went home, leaving the ordnance works and powder mill open for pillage. A Federal officer reported: "This property was plundered to a great extent by disorganized commands. The officials of the city [Marshall] deeming it necessary to protect the property and lives of the inhabitants, placed a guard upon the workshops, store-houses, magazines, etc., and so far as I was enabled to learn the property was rigidly cared for."[8]

Loughery of the *Texas Republican* remained both defiant and optimistic as Harrison County entered the era of Reconstruction during the spring and summer of 1865. He warned against radical policies such as military rule, property confiscations, or anything that would "elevate" blacks. "Our armies, it is true, are destroyed," he wrote on May 26, "but the spirits of the people are unbroken. . . . They are not yet fit for slaves." He thought it "useless to send a single company of soldiers to garrison any portion of the territory" and expressed the hope that slavery would continue in spite of the Emancipation Proclamation and the proposed Thirteenth Amendment. Some masters have freed their bondsmen, he wrote on June 16, but most "continue to support and control their Negroes as formerly." In his opinion, this was best because blacks were "naturally idle and migratory."[9]

7. *Ibid.*, 213–14.
8. *The War of the Rebellion: A Compilation of the Official Records of the Union and Confederate Armies* (130 vols.; Washington, D.C., 1880–1901), Ser. I, Vol. XLVIII, Pt. 2, pp. 1282, 965; hereafter cited as *OR*. Unless otherwise indicated, all citations are to Series I.
9. *Texas Republican*, May 26, June 16, 1865.

Loughery's defiant optimism, which was seconded by a public meeting later in June, proved groundless, of course. On June 17, 1865, two days before Gen. Gordon Granger arrived at Galveston to take formal possession of Texas for the United States, federal troops—the 8th Illinois Infantry and a company of cavalry—under the command of Lt. Col. Loyd Wheaton reached Marshall from Shreveport. Military authority replaced civilian government, and the Emancipation Proclamation became operative. Harrison County then awaited Presidential Reconstruction under the direction of provisional governor A. J. Hamilton.[10]

Hamilton arrived in Texas on July 21, and residents of Marshall, like those in other towns across the state, wasted no time in giving advice and making requests concerning the appointment of local officeholders. Some emphasized their unionism and ability to accept the changes brought by the end of slavery. For example, Isaac W. Johnston described himself as a conservative who "preferred a settlement of all national questions between the State and the United States government by compromising of mutual concessions" rather than war. N. H. Wilson, an Ohio-born lawyer, sought the position of district judge. "Having been born and educated in a free state," he wrote, "I know something of the free labor system, and believe it can be . . . inaugurated in the South." By contrast, Hamilton also received appeals from local leaders who could not possibly deny their records as defenders of slavery and the Confederacy. Asa H. Willie, a Marshall attorney, former slaveholder, and ex-Confederate army officer, wrote at least four letters in July and August asking the provisional governor to appoint longtime county residents to key positions. For example, his recommendation for sheriff, Solomon R. Perry, had won that office four times since 1850. William T. Scott and Montreville J. Hall, both large slaveholders who had served in the state legislature during the 1850s, took the offensive by going to Austin to visit Hamilton. After his return Hall wrote the governor: "There is no disloyalty here; many are sore about the emancipation of the slaves, but they all intend honestly and faithfully to submit to the government as it is." Those who claimed unionism and accused men such as himself of disloyalty, Hall contended, had never been faithful to any government. Do not be misled, he said, by "*little petty lying pretended union*

10. *Ibid.*, June 23, 1865. Federal troops hurried to Marshall because of Confederate quartermaster operations there. *OR*, Vol. XLVIII, Pt. 2, p. 903.

*men.*" Clearly, Harrison County's antebellum leaders did not intend to give way to those who had opposed secession and war.[11]

Hamilton's appointments to the key offices in local government on August 7, 1865, did not entirely please either Unionists or secessionists. He made J. B. Williamson interim district judge and named Davis B. Bonfoey to act as county judge. Both men were northerners by birth, and neither had held public office during the antebellum years or supported secession. However, both were longtime residents of the county. Williamson had participated in Democratic party activities during the 1850s, and Bonfoey had owned slaves. Following the advice of Willie and others, Hamilton appointed Solomon R. Perry to the sheriff's office. Perry, the owner of twenty-four slaves at the end of the war, had been elected to that position in 1862 and 1864. The four county commissioners were all natives of the South and former slaveholders, although two, Nicholas V. Board and Silas D. Wood, were former Whigs who had strong records of unionism. Board, for example, had resigned as a commissioner in 1861 rather than take the oath of loyalty to the Confederacy. The other two commissioners—John S. Powell and Elijah B. Blalock—had planter-size slaveholdings and were in effect incumbents, having been elected to the county court in 1862 and 1864.[12]

Trouble developed immediately over the appointment of S. R. Perry. District Judge Williamson refused to administer the oath of office to the sheriff because the latter had used dogs to chase Union soldiers who escaped in Harrison County while on their way to the prisoner-of-war camp (Camp Ford) at Tyler, Texas. Williamson asked Governor Hamilton to appoint John F. Womack to the office, but the position went to Isaac W. Johnston in early September. In an angry letter of protest, Womack blamed his rejection

11. Isaac W. Johnston to A. J. Hamilton, July 20, 1865, N. H. Wilson to A. J. Hamilton, August 3, 1865, Asa H. Willie to A. J. Hamilton, July 20, 21, August 1, 4, 1865, John F. Womack to A. J. Hamilton, September 18, 1865, M. J. Hall to A. J. Hamilton, September 24, 1865, Governors' Papers: AJH. For Perry's service as sheriff, see Election Registers, 1850–1864. Biographical information on Willie is from Webb, Carroll, and Branda, eds., *Handbook of Texas,* II, 918.

12. Hamilton's appointments and previous offices held by his appointees are found in the Election Registers, 1850–1865. Demographic and economic information on the appointees is from the Seventh Census, 1850, Schedules 1 and 2, and Eighth Census, 1860, Schedules 1 and 2. Information on slaveholding is also from Real and Personal Property Tax Rolls, Harrison County, 1850–1864. Williamson's participation in Democratic politics during the 1850s is seen in the *Texas Republican,* November 22, 1856.

on the influence of Scott and Hall and told the governor that he had been "imposed upon and deceived." Johnston, however, kept the office.[13]

Other key positions in local government also changed hands shortly after Reconstruction began. Bonfoey resigned as county judge in November, 1865, to become a collector of internal revenue for the federal government, and soon thereafter S. D. Wood moved from the commissioners' court to Bonfoey's former office. Two of Hamilton's appointees as county commissioners, Powell and Board, refused to serve, necessitating new appointments in the fall of 1865. Almost immediately both new commissioners moved from the county, and in February, 1866, Hamilton had to select yet another two men as well as fill the spot vacated by Wood. This frequently shifting version of county officeholding must have provoked comment, but nothing negative appeared publicly—probably because all the appointees were men familiar to the local citizenry.[14]

Civil government resumed during September, 1865, when Judge Williamson held a district court session and Bonfoey convened the commissioners' court. Both handled their affairs routinely, and by the end of the month, even Loughery of the *Texas Republican* expressed reassurance about the progress of Reconstruction. The Unionist, Bonfoey, also indicated that affairs were going smoothly in a letter to Governor Hamilton in November. Residents of Harrison County were finding the oath of loyalty to the United States "bitter to their tastes," he commented, but most desire "to become good and law abiding citizens." The next step would come in January, 1866, with the election of a delegate to the constitutional convention.[15]

While Harrison County's whites learned the meaning of defeat and occupation, the black majority, nearly nine thousand in all, had an even larger adjustment to make. For the first time in their lives, they owned their own bodies and did not have to endure as someone else's property. One remembered a fellow ex-slave saying, "we is free—no more whippings and beatings." Another, however, recalled that many slaves found freedom fright-

13. J. B. Williamson to A. J. Hamilton, August 29, 1865, John F. Womack to A. J. Hamilton, September 18, 1865, Governors' Papers: AJH.

14. Election Registers, 1865–1866.

15. District Court Civil Minutes, Book H, 297–99, District Clerk's Office, Harrison County Courthouse, Marshall; Commissioners' Court Minutes, County Clerk's Office, Harrison County Courthouse, Marshall; *Texas Republican,* August 18, September 29, 1865; Davis B. Bonfoey to A. J. Hamilton, November 11, 1865, Governors' Papers: AJH.

ening because "they knowed nothing and had nowhere to go." Planters and farmers generally urged their former bondsmen to remain with them and work for wages, and apparently a majority of freedmen chose that option, at least for a while. There was no difficulty in finding labor to pick the 1865 cotton crop. On the other hand, enough freedmen left their former owners that in late June the *Texas Republican* complained about hundreds of idle blacks roaming the countryside. Some ladies, Loughery complained, have been "reduced to the necessity of doing their own housework without assistance."[16]

Blacks might reasonably have expected some assistance in the transition from slavery to freedom, but the great majority received none from their former masters and very little from the national government. Local whites and federal officials alike agreed with the advice Governor Hamilton gave the former slaves: "You are free—free to work for yourselves and to do right. No man is free to do wrong and to live upon the labor of others." The first general order issued by Lt. Col. Wheaton after the arrival of his troops in Marshall stated that "Negroes will not be allowed to collect about the city or camps and all Freedmen must have passes from their employers or they will be arrested and punished as vagrants." Even the first representative of the Freedmen's Bureau to arrive in Harrison County, Col. H. Seymour Hall, indicated that African Americans could expect little more than simply not being enslaved any longer. Soon after reaching Marshall in November, 1865, Hall published a circular urging freedmen to uphold their labor contracts, be responsible, and earn a living for themselves.[17]

In spite of repeated statements from Governor Hamilton and federal officials, blacks in Harrison County persisted in believing that the government intended to divide the property of slaveowners among their former bondsmen. This rumored redistribution was to take place at Christmastime 1865. Colonel Hall denied the rumor in a speech to fifteen hundred freedmen in mid-November. Soon, however, a story began to circulate to the effect that the agent did not speak for the government, and he had to refute that before another large crowd. In December, Governor Hamilton's ad-

16. George P. Rawick, ed., *The American Slave: A Composite Autobiography* (19 vols.; Westport, Conn., 1972–79), Vol. IV, Pt. 3, pp. 265–67, Pt. 1, pp. 1–3; Campbell, *Southern Community in Crisis*, 249–51; *Texas Republican*, June 23, 1865.

17. *Texas Republican*, June 23, December 8, 1865.

dress recommending work and doing "right" was read to one more meeting of freedmen in Marshall.[18]

Presidential Reconstruction thus brought virtually no material assistance to Harrison County's former slaves as they adjusted to freedom. In fact, it did not even bring equality before the law in 1865 and 1866. The arrival of the Freedmen's Bureau brought special courts that offered fair treatment in matters such as disputes involving labor contracts, but any case that went to the state district court put blacks at a disadvantage. When District Judge J. B. Williamson held a session of his court in September, 1865, he instructed the grand jury that, although the slave codes had died with slavery, restrictions on the testimony of blacks against whites would have to stand until the legislature altered them. These laws, Williamson said, derived from the mental and moral inferiority of blacks as well as their condition of servitude. Loughery of the *Texas Republican* applauded the judge's comments.[19]

Finally, and worst of all, Harrison County freedmen faced constant intimidation that often turned to violence. In November, 1865, bureau agent Hall reported that the interests of blacks had to be protected by troops, but then a month later, he told headquarters that the troops of the 26th Illinois Volunteers stationed at Marshall had the "greatest hatred for the negroes." These soldiers, Hall wrote, commit offenses daily against the freedmen, including even one murder, and set a terrible example for "the evil disposed among the citizens." He recommended correcting this seemingly ironic situation by posting black troops at Marshall. Thus most whites, including agents of the federal government as well as southerners, placed severe restrictions on the meaning of freedom for blacks during the first months of Presidential Reconstruction in 1865.[20]

The registration of voters pursuant to electing a convention that would bring Texas back into its proper constitutional relationship with the Union began on August 19, 1865. Residents of Harrison County, many of whom had shown reluctance to take the oath of loyalty, did not rush to register. Editors Loughery of the *Texas Republican* and S. D. Wood of the *Harrison Flag*, although far apart in their political views, both urged men to register

18. *Ibid.*, November 17, December 1, 15, 1865.

19. *Ibid.*, September 29, 1865.

20. Col. H. S. Hall to Gen. Edgar M. Gregory, November 4, 1865, Hall to Gregory, December 26, 1865, BRFAL, RG 105, NA; Richter, *Overreached on All Sides*, 46–47.

and vote, but large numbers remained apathetic, even after Governor Hamilton set the election date for January 8, 1866.[21]

The election of a delegate to the constitutional convention demonstrated that the antebellum division between ultrasoutherners and Unionists had not disappeared in Harrison County. The *Flag* argued that secession should be declared null and void and that conservative men rather than disunionists should direct the process of Reconstruction. County Judge Bonfoey, a former Whig, encouraged voters to choose someone who had been "conservative in the past." Henry Ware, a large slaveholder who had recommended ending the war in 1864, came forward as a conservative candidate, declaring publicly that secession had been wrong and that freedmen deserved fair treatment and education. Perhaps in a generation, he said, blacks will be ready to vote. Col. John Burke, a war hero who had served with Hood's Texas brigade, represented the views of secessionist Democrats. He admitted that slavery was dead but opposed the Thirteenth Amendment and wanted the revised state constitution to bar freedmen from voting or holding office. "It is impossible," he said, "for me to vote for any measure which makes the negro the equal of the white man." Loughery backed Burke and attacked Ware for not admitting "that the negro can never become the political equal of a the white man, and whether it is this year, or twenty, or a hundred years from now, the negro will still be a negro, and remain in the subordinate position in which nature has placed him."[22]

Only 313 voters cast ballots on January 8, 1866, and Burke narrowly defeated Ware, 162 to 146. Five votes went to two other candidates. Ware's support was impressive, although it may have been a testimonial to his personal stature rather than to the strength of the conservative-Unionist position. This suggestion is borne out by the election to choose a second delegate who was to represent Harrison and neighboring Panola County jointly. That contest involved Lemuel D. Evans, a noted Unionist who had served a term in the United States Congress during the 1850s, and Charles A. Frazier, an ardent advocate of slavery and secession. Evans had left Marshall during the war and could be accused of siding with the North. He lost

21. Marshall *Texas Republican,* November 3, 1865; *Harrison Flag* (Marshall), November 15, 1865.

22. *Harrison Flag,* November 22, December 7, 21, 28, 1865; *Texas Republican,* December 29, 1865. Burke's military career is found in Harold B. Simpson, *The Marshall Guards: Harrison County's Contribution to Hood's Texas Brigade* (Marshall, Tex., 1967), 8–10.

to Frazier in Harrison County by a margin of 263 to 11. The *Flag* expressed displeasure at the results, especially the victory by Burke, and complained that "old associations and former partialities and prejudices" had elected men who would behave as obstructionists and bring worse things than Presidential Reconstruction down on the state.[23]

Burke and Frazier attended the constitutional convention in Austin from February 7 to April 2, 1866, but even as they met, Radical Republicans in Congress were moving to take Reconstruction away from the president. As a key step in this process, the Joint Committee on Reconstruction, created in January, 1866, held several months of hearings to collect evidence concerning the unrepentant attitude of ex-Confederates and the unfair treatment of Unionists and freedmen across the South. Harrison County became directly involved in building the indictment of Presidential Reconstruction when, on February 20, 1866, Lieutenant Hall of the Freedmen's Bureau testified in Washington. Leaders in Harrison and the surrounding counties, Hall told the committee, "denounce most bitterly . . . the radical party" in Congress and consider the Freedmen's Bureau "an unmitigated nuisance." Without a military presence, Hall continued, "there would be neither safety of person nor of property for men who had been loyal during the war; and there would be no protection whatever for the negro." Blacks, he concluded, "would be liable to worse treatment than ever before—to assaults in many cases, and even to murder." To prove his point, Hall described how, even with the military present, two "discharged rebel soldiers" had beaten a freedwoman named Lucy Grimes to death and gone free because there were no witnesses except blacks to testify to the murder.[24]

Testimony such as Hall's contributed in a small way to the complex series of events and developments that would enable Congress to take Reconstruction away from President Johnson by the spring of 1867. In the meantime, Harrison County, along with all others in Texas, completed reconstructing itself under presidential direction. When elections were held on June 25, 1866, to approve the new constitution and elect state and local officials under its terms, those candidates who had the least identification with unionism or had held office during the antebellum years, or both, won

23. Election Returns, 1866; Campbell, *Southern Community in Crisis*, 255; *Harrison Flag*, January 11, 1866.

24. *Report of the Joint Committee on Reconstruction at the First Session Thirty-Ninth Congress* (Washington, D. C., 1866), Pt. IV, 46–50.

strong support from voters in Marshall and the surrounding precincts. Local newspapers gave an indication of what was to come well before the election when the Unionist-leaning *Flag* joined the *Texas Republican* in supporting J. W. Throckmorton, the Conservative Unionist candidate, against the Radical Unionist leader, Elisha M. Pease. None of the men who ran for lesser state and county offices openly supported the Republicans in Congress. For example, both candidates for the state senate, E. A. Blanch and C. C. Coppedge, made a point of informing voters of their total support for President Johnson.[25]

On June 25, 1866, Throckmorton defeated Pease in Harrison County by a vote of 796 to 6. Democrats and former Confederates won the elections for seats in the state senate (E. A. Blanch) and house of representatives (Robert C. Garrett for the county's seat and Samuel J. Richardson for a larger "floater" district), although by smaller margins of victory than Throckmorton's. At least eight men ran for county commissioner. The four winners (Lodwick P. Alford, John Munden, George B. Conway, and R. W. Blalock) all had been slaveholding residents of the county in 1860, and Munden had held the same office in 1864–1865.[26]

White Unionists had some strength in the county, however, as the contests for district judge, county judge, and sheriff indicated. In the race for judge of the Sixth Judicial District, Matthew D. Ector, a former Confederate brigadier general, defeated J. B. Williamson, the incumbent appointed by Governor Hamilton in 1865, by a vote of 595 to 216. Obadiah Hendrick, who had served as county judge from 1856 to 1860 and been elected district clerk in 1864, became county judge again with 431 votes to 233 for John F. Williams, who had not supported the war. Solomon R. Perry won the sheriff's office with 659 votes to 168 for Isaac W. Johnston. Perry was the occupant whom Judge Williamson would not allow to serve in 1865, and Johnston was the incumbent appointed by Governor Hamilton. These returns—216 for Williamson, 233 for Williams, and 168 for Johnston (against the very popular Perry)—suggest that Harrison County had about two hundred whites willing to vote for Unionists in 1866, far too few to win an election, but enough to jump into leadership positions if blacks were enfranchised.[27]

25. Marshall *Texas Republican*, April 28, 1866; *Harrison Flag*, May 17, June 7, 14, 1866.
26. Election Returns, 1866; Eighth Census, 1860, Schedules 1 and 2; Election Registers, 1850–1865; Campbell, *Southern Community in Crisis*, 258–59.
27. Election Returns, 1866; Election Registers, 1860–1866; John F. Williams to A. J. Ham-

County Judge Hendrick convened the commissioners' court in July, 1866, and District Judge Ector held a session of his court in Marshall during September. Most of the county's whites believed that Reconstruction was nearing completion and would end as soon as the state's senators and representatives were elected in the fall of 1866 and seated in the second session of the Thirty-ninth Congress, which would assemble in Washington in December. Blacks, however, could only hope that somehow Radical Republicans in Congress would gain power and act to make freedom mean something more than inequality, intimidation, and violence. The first Freedmen's Bureau agent in Harrison County, Colonel Hall, had been relieved in January, 1866. His replacement, Col. Thomas Bayley, announced at the end of February that local planters were generally treating their workers well, and in April a company from the 80th United States Colored Infantry arrived to replace the racist troops of the 26th Illinois. Bayley reported some cases of abuse from the first, however, and a bad crop year soon made matters worse. "Many planters irritated by the loss of their crops," the agent wrote in July, "vent their displeasure upon the helpless Freedmen." Blacks could not expect help from the civil courts, he continued, because of "wicked men resorting to all means, even to force, to prevent any ill treatment becoming known."[28]

Captain Charles F. Rand replaced Bayley as sub-assistant commissioner in December, 1866, and at the end of his first month in Marshall declared that blacks in the area endured truly dismal conditions. "Yesterday," he wrote, "a freedman presented himself with two bullet holes through him for no other cause than by being one of a Christmas jubilee." Blacks, Rand continued, "dare not carry anything to protect themselves with for they would be surrounded and all arms and whatever else they had valuable would be taken away from them. Outrages are committed daily with impunity and all pass unnoticed for lack of assistance." Owen F. Baker, the first Freedmen's Bureau teacher in Marshall, protested on January 1, 1867, that an "enraged rebel mob" had attacked his house, smashed all the windows, and fired numerous bullets into it. In mid-February, Rand informed military headquarters of ten murders of blacks by whites during the past month and

---

ilton, July 23, 1865, Governors' Papers: AJH; Webb, Carroll, and Branda, eds., *Handbook of Texas*, I, 541. Another local Unionist, Elijah Blackwell, received 196 votes in the race for county commissioner.

28. Commissioners' Court Minutes; District Court Civil Minutes, Book H, 196; Richter, *Overreached on All Sides*, 47–48, 112–13; Col. Thomas Bayley to C. C. Morse, February 28, 1866, Bayley to Gen. Joseph Kiddoo, July 31, 1866, BRFAL, RG 105, NA.

a half in Harrison County. Two neighborhood cutthroats, he said, "would kill a f.m. for 75 cents and boast of the action as a laudable one of high minded chivalry." According to the bureau agent, local civil officials took no action in such cases.[29]

Military authorities sent Rand's complaints to Governor Throckmorton, who relayed them to County Judge Hendrick. "As a matter of course," the governor wrote, "I do not believe one word of this," but please investigate and punish all crimes. Two weeks later Hendrick replied that he knew of only three such cases, all of which had been handled promptly by Rand himself. In Harrison County, the judge said, rather than racial violence, there is an "unusual degree of good feeling for the blacks who conduct themselves well and politely." Hendrick asked Rand for a list of the incidents, but the agent refused on the grounds that neither the governor nor judge deserved any reports from him. Rand's irritation is understandable, although his refusal even to discuss problems with civil authorities could not have helped the situation. More than likely, most of the county's black majority were left alone to lead peaceful lives so long as they did not challenge white supremacy; but violent incidents occurred, and the threat was always present.[30]

In April, 1867, General Griffin attempted to ensure greater justice in legal proceedings by issuing the jury order requiring that all members of grand and petit juries be able to swear the test oath. Somewhat surprisingly, when the district court met in June, Judge Ector and Sheriff Perry found forty-nine men who could swear that they had never voluntarily supported the Confederacy. Thus, as was the case in some districts, the court did not simply close in response to the jury order. Fifteen Unionists served on the grand jury, and the others acted as petit jurors for a two-week session of the court. There is no indication that these loyalists brought equal justice to Freedmen, but at least the jury order represented a step in that direction.[31]

---

29. Richter, *Overreached on All Sides,* 113–14; Capt. Charles F. Rand to Gen. Joseph Kiddoo, December 31, 1866, "Records of Criminal Offenses," XI–XIII, 47, BRFAL, RG 105, NA; Owen F. Baker to Gen. E. M. Wheelock, January 1, 1867, Records of the Superintendent of Education for the State of Texas, Bureau of Refugees, Freedmen, and Abandoned Lands, 1865–1869, U.S. Department of War, RG 105, National Archives (hereafter cited as BRFAL-Education).

30. James W. Throckmorton to Gen. Charles Griffin, March 4, 1867 (enclosing a copy of his letter to County Judge Hendrick), in James W. Throckmorton Papers, Eugene C. Barker Texas History Center, University of Texas, Austin; Obadiah Hendrick to J. W. Throckmorton, March 18, 25, 1867 (enclosing a copy of Rand's rely to him), Governors' Papers: JWT.

31. Campbell, "District Judges of Texas in 1866–1867," 368–70, 373; District Court Civil

Of course, by the summer of 1867 the circumstances of freedmen had taken a leap, rather than a step, forward in that Republicans had gained complete control of Congress in the mid-term elections of 1866 and taken over Reconstruction. The Reconstruction act of March, 1867, enfranchised blacks and disfranchised most former white officeholders of the county. Moreover, it soon became clear that the officers elected in 1866, those whom Rand and others blamed for mistreatment of the freedmen, could be removed by military order as impediments to Reconstruction.

The congressional takeover must have brought joy to Harrison County's blacks, although there are no records of such a reaction. Whites responded, at least as the newspapers expressed it, with a mixture of indignation and resignation. For example, the *Harrison Flag* accused Republicans of "subversion of the constitution" and recoiled at the prospect of "all the horrors of social equality." The editor declared that "to exalt the common African, with his thick skin, wooly head, his superstition and silly notions, to a level or perfect state of equality with the proud of Anglo-Saxon blood, is an attempt to place a libel upon the great and original purposes of God himself." On the other hand, both newspapers urged whites to submit quietly to the new rules, register if they could, and vote. The editors also advised their readers to stay on good terms with local blacks, support schools for the newly enfranchised voters, and work to see that they trusted their former masters and were not deceived by outsiders. "Listen to the pratings of no imported political teachers," the *Texas Republican* told blacks, "for their only object is to ride to power on your backs." Southern whites know, he continued, that "as a race you are inferior," but they are your true friends. "Be not deceived." The wisdom of Loughery's telling blacks that they were inferior as he appealed for their loyalty is doubtful at best, but at least he responded to Congressional Reconstruction within a democratic framework, hoping somehow to register enough whites and gain enough black support to win at the ballot box.[32]

Voter registration began in Harrison County on July 24, 1867, and continued until August 28, then reopened for a week in late September and again for one more week in late January, 1868. N. V. Board, Jacob Foster, and Mitchell Kendall served as registrars on appointment by General Grif-

---

Minutes, Book I, 2–75; J. B. Williamson to Gen. Charles Griffin, August 22, 1867, Governors' Papers: EMP.

32. *Harrison Flag,* March 7, May 2, 9, 14, 30, 1867; *Texas Republican,* April 20, June 8, 15, 1867.

fin. Board, although a longtime resident of the community who had served as a county commissioner before the war, could swear the test oath that he had never voluntarily supported the Confederacy. Foster, a native of Pennsylvania, apparently had arrived in the county only recently, and Kendall was a freedman. Registration went quietly, and by the end of January, 1868, the total number of voters came to 3,404, of which 2,521 were blacks (74 percent of the total) and 883, whites.[33]

Although there were some complaints against the board of registrars, white disfranchisement was not extensive in the county. Antebellum office-holders such as Solomon R. Perry who had sworn to uphold the Constitution and then supported the Confederacy were denied registration, but numerous former Confederate soldiers who had never held public office registered without difficulty. Some whites decided to show their disapproval of Congress' plan and black suffrage by refusing to register and stuck with this position even when the *Flag* called it "puerile and womanish." Overall, however, the number of whites who registered amounted to 26 percent of all voters, a percentage not terribly smaller than the approximately 32 percent that whites constituted in the population as a whole at the census of 1870.[34]

Harrison County's new electorate would go to the polls February 10–14, 1868, to vote on the calling of a constitutional convention and to elect delegates to that convention if it won approval. In the meantime, during the summer and fall of 1867, federal troops and the people of Harrison County got along reasonably well. The *Texas Republican* of September 14 heaped praise on Company C of the 20th U.S. Infantry that had replaced the 80th U.S. Colored Infantry in February, 1867. "Here the most complete accord and good feeling exists," Loughery wrote. "A man might remain in Marshall a month without being aware there was a United States command here, unless he met a soldier on the street." Also, the Freedmen's Bureau agent Lt. Adam G. Malloy, although he found numerous minor disputes to adjudicate, generally reported that conditions were satisfactory for blacks. During this same period, however, uncertainty about

33. List of Registered Voters in Texas, 1869; Campbell, *Southern Community in Crisis,* 275–76.

34. List of Registered Voters in Texas, 1869; *Harrison Flag,* June 27, August 1, 1867. The population of Harrison County in 1870 included 4,301 whites and 8,931 blacks (67.5 percent). U.S. Bureau of the Census, *Statistics of the Population of the United States (1870),* 64–65.

the impact of Congressional Reconstruction kept white conservatives on edge.[35]

As early as June, 1867, the *Republican* began to complain of "hireling emissaries" in Harrison County "instilling into the minds of the black population poisonous and dangerous sentiments against the southern whites, and meeting with more success than we are willing to acknowledge, or ready to concede." Loughery did not specify the affiliation of these "emissaries" beyond calling them "radicals," but a few days later he found a familiar target for his wrath—George W. Whitmore. Whitmore, a native of Tennessee who represented Harrison County in the Texas House of Representatives during 1860–1861, had strongly opposed secession at the time and continued to voice disapproval of the Confederacy during the war to the point that he had been imprisoned with federal soldiers at Camp Ford in 1863. On July 4, 1867, he came back to Marshall from Smith County, where he had settled after the war, and spoke to a crowd of blacks gathered to celebrate Independence Day. Addressing the freedmen as "my fellow citizens," Whitmore told them to give their support to white Republicans, the men who had set them free. Loughery responded by calling Whitmore a fifth-rate lawyer, "a low demagogue . . . destitute of principle," and a man known for cruelty to his slaves and meanness in his social relations.[36]

Conservative whites attempted to counter the influence "radicals" such as Whitmore had with freedmen by arguing that the true interests of blacks lay with their former masters. For example, James Turner, the mayor of Marshall, spoke to the same July 4 crowd addressed by Whitmore and urged them to remember that prosperity depended on cooperation between the races. Such words, however, had a hollow ring to men only recently freed from bondage, and everyone knew it.[37]

The anxiety of white conservatives concerning radical appeals to newly enfranchised blacks increased in the fall of 1867 when Gen. Joseph J. Reynolds removed nearly all of the local officials elected on June 25, 1866. After receiving the advice of local Unionists, especially J. B. Williamson, Reynolds replaced District Judge Matthew D. Ector with Williamson and

35. *Texas Republican*, September 14, 1867; Lt. Adam G. Malloy to Lt. Joel T. Kirkman, May 31, June 30, July 28, September 2, September 30, 1867, BRFAL, RG 105, NA.

36. *Texas Republican*, June 29, July 13, 1867; Randolph B. Campbell, "George W. Whitmore: East Texas Unionist," *East Texas Historical Journal*, XXVIII (Spring, 1990), 17–28.

37. *Texas Republican*, July 13, 1867.

County Judge Obadiah Hendrick with N. V. Board. Board, Williamson wrote, "is one of the unterrified union men of the county. . . . He has been much persecuted and desires a kind act from the Government he has never failed to support." Reynolds also removed two of the county commissioners, John Munden and L. P. Alford, but on the advice of Williamson, he allowed Sheriff S. R. Perry to remain in office. Perry could not take the test oath, but Williamson praised his work in finding jurors who could meet that requirement and thus in keeping the courts open.[38] The *Republican* called the removals "official tyranny" and described the appointees as men "devoid of merit or capacity" and "obnoxious personally and politically" to the white population. The *Flag* concluded that only the desire to feed at the "public crib" could explain the willingness of a man such as Board to take a military appointment.[39]

The registration of a black majority and removal of elected local officials generated fear and anger among some whites in 1867, and then, as the year drew to a close, an incident known as the Marshall Riot increased tension for both conservatives and radicals in Harrison County. A severe norther was blowing in Marshall on December 30 when Colbert C. Caldwell, a military appointee to the Texas Supreme Court, and several other radicals arrived to campaign for candidates in the upcoming constitutional convention elections. Caldwell wanted to hold his meeting in the main courtroom of the courthouse, but finding that he did not have the necessary written approval from County Judge Board, he agreed to use the basement hallways for the gathering. Caldwell spoke to the crowd of about three hundred for a few minutes, urging them to vote in February, and then one of the blacks accompanying the judge began singing "Rally Round the Flag, Boys." At that point, S. J. Richardson, the Marshall chief of police (and formerly a captain in the Confederate army), came into the hallway, fired a shot into the ceiling, and drove the freedmen out. Deputy Sheriff A. G. Adams came in to preserve order, but Caldwell believed that he was there to aid Richardson and took refuge at the federal military post in Marshall. Adams and Sheriff S. R. Perry, who had not been present at the courthouse,

38. Election Registers, 1867; J. B. Williamson to Gen. Charles Griffin, August 22, 1867, Governors' Papers: EMP. It is assumed that Williamson's advice to Griffin was passed on to Reynolds when he became commanding officer of Texas in September.
39. *Texas Republican*, November 23, 1867; *Harrison Flag*, November 23, 1867.

went to the army post to explain the incident. But they wound up arguing with Judge Caldwell in the Freedmen's Bureau office and becoming infuriated when he accused Adams of sympathizing with assassins. Adams promised to have "satisfaction" from the judge, who later reported that only an attaché of the Freedmen's Bureau armed with a shotgun saved him from grave danger. The post commander then arrested Sheriff Perry, Deputy Sheriff Adams, Chief of Police Richardson, and five others. To Caldwell's utter disgust, District Judge Williamson ordered the prisoners brought before his court on a writ of habeas corpus several days later and released them on bail.[40]

On January 11, 1868, Sheriff Perry and several of the others were rearrested, apparently on orders from General Reynolds and at the instigation of Judge Caldwell. Col. W. H. Wood of the U.S. Army then investigated and declared in early February that Chief of Police Richardson had caused the incident and that the others had only tried to keep peace. The report indicated that civil authorities in the county could handle the situation and that there had been no need for the military arrests. Wood recommended that the prisoners be turned over to civil authorities.[41]

Thus the Marshall Riot injured no one and created more excitement than was justified. On the other hand, the incident indicated the tense political atmosphere existing in the county as Congressional Reconstruction unfolded. Judge Caldwell, although certainly not an unbiased witness, provided some observations in January, 1868, that probably were not great exaggerations. He claimed to have been "expelled from the hotel because of my politics" and that lawyers "refused introduction to me in my presence, as they said, because I was a 'radical.'" "No man but a Johnson man will be tolerated here," the judge wrote. "Such an one would be lionized. He must *cuss Congress* and damn the *nigger.*" Blacks in the county, Caldwell believed, suffered so many wrongs and outrages that they might attempt to take matters into their own hands and thus give conservatives an excuse for violence. The judge did see a brighter side, however. "The last one of them [freedmen] will vote *if he can*"; so if federal authorities could prevent elec-

40. C. C. Caldwell to Maj. Longley (intended for Governor Pease), January 2, 1868, Governors' Papers: EMP; *Texas Republican*, January 4, 1868.
41. *Texas Republican*, February 22, 1868. The newspaper printed Colonel Wood's report in full.

tion "disturbances," radicals would control Harrison County's delegation to the constitutional convention.[42]

By early 1868 the Union League, an organization of Unionists and freedmen designed to work as an arm of the emerging Republican party, had formed a chapter in Harrison County. Its founder, C. E. Coleman, a Freedmen's Bureau teacher from Illinois, was described by the *Harrison Flag* as the "embodiment of putrefication and rottenness." In January the league selected four candidates—N. V. Board, C. E. Coleman, Mitchell Kendall, and Wiley Johnson—for the February 10–14 election of delegates to the constitutional convention. Board, the appointed county judge, was a scalawag; Coleman, a carpetbagger; and Kendall (who had served as a voter registrar) and Johnson were freedmen. The *Texas Republican* reported the meeting as a "ludicrously disgusting scene." Then, on January 27, radical leaders including Judge Caldwell and George W. Whitmore spoke to a gathering of about one thousand freedmen and fifty whites in Marshall, urging support for Congressional Reconstruction and black suffrage. The *Flag* described Caldwell as a "peddler of radical poison" and referred to Whitmore and the others as "filthy bubbles from the cesspool of radicalism" who "will soon burst and sink amid the contempt of the honest—to be gazed at and despised."[43]

White conservatives met on February 6, only four days before the election, and nominated Lemuel D. Evans, Thomas F. Purnell, J. M. Waskom, and J. M. Fain of Panola County. Waskom had been a slaveholding planter, but Evans and Purnell, the other two candidates from Harrison County were Conservative Unionists. Indeed, Purnell had served in the Union army and settled in Marshall after the war. These apparent concessions to political reality came far too late, however, to have any impact on the election. The four days of balloting went quietly with 2,417 of the county's 3,404 registered voters participating. Only 497 whites voted (56 percent of those qualified), whereas 1,920 blacks cast ballots (76 percent of those registered). The four radical candidates won overwhelmingly, receiving approximately 1,900 votes each to 500 for their opponents.[44]

In electing four radicals, including two of only nine black delegates chosen statewide, to the convention that wrote the "Radical" Constitution of

42. Caldwell to Longley, January 2, 1868, Governors' Papers: EMP.
43. *Harrison Flag,* February 1, 15, 1868; *Texas Republican,* January 25, February 1, 1868.
44. *Texas Republican,* February 8, 15, 1868, May 14, 1869; Election Returns, 1868.

1869, Harrison County's black majority demonstrated seemingly unchallengeable political power. R. W. Loughery of the *Republican*, however, refused to concede the apparent hopelessness of the conservative position and began to argue that whites should organize to oppose "Africanization." Their first attempt in May, 1868, drew such a small attendance that nothing could be accomplished, but a month later, after numerous editorials denouncing the "extraordinary" apathy of whites, another meeting was more successful. Resolutions condemned Congressional Reconstruction and black equality and called for the creation of a conservative club in each election precinct in the county. Direction would come from a central committee in Marshall that included Alexander Pope, one of the county's delegates to the secession convention, and S. J. Richardson, instigator of the Marshall Riot. Precinct committees were appointed in July, and the organizational process went ahead in August.[45]

White conservatives obviously had no intention of accepting black equality; nevertheless, they invited freedmen to join their precinct clubs and appealed to them with the argument that radicals cared only for blacks' votes whereas conservatives wanted racial cooperation in promoting prosperity. This economic argument had a negative side, too, as whites threatened blacks with a loss of work if they supported the radicals. The *Republican* advised against hiring or having any business relations with "radical loyal league negroes," and the conservative club in the fifth precinct adopted a resolution calling on all members to refuse employment to anyone who did not join their group. Economic coercion of this sort doubtless was impractical, but the idea apparently won widespread acceptance, at least in theory. For example, Joseph Bruckmuller, a German-born shoemaker turned shopkeeper, informed a friend in New Orleans that he would never give work to a white or black radical. Demagogues and their promises, Bruckmuller said, would not help the freedmen.[46]

Conservatives appeared to have some success with their economic appeals and threats. Thirty freedmen and forty-three whites signed the constitution of the club in precinct nine. A "Colored Conservative Club" of precinct five was created in Marshall, and Loughery reported that more than

45. *Texas Republican*, April 25, May 15, 29, June 5, July 17, August 7, 14, 21, 1868.
46. *Ibid.*, June 5, July 24, September 11, 1868; Joseph Bruckmuller to George Dinkel, September 7, 1868, in Peter Joseph Bruckmuller Papers, Eugene C. Barker Texas History Center, University of Texas, Austin.

150 blacks attended a meeting in early December, 1868, to hear speeches by black as well as white leaders. The editor exulted that freedmen were opening their eyes to the "enormities of radicalism" and expressed more pleasure later that month when the Freedmen's Bureau announced an end to all its activities except in education.[47]

In November, George Tucker, a black leader of the Union League in Marshall, published "An Address to the Colored Citizens of Eastern Texas," advising blacks to abandon their support for the league and the Republican party. Such activity, he said, brings so much opposition from whites (meaning, it seems, the loss of work) that it does more harm than good. All conservative efforts to win black support, however, proved largely futile. Even Tucker, at the same time that he advised blacks to drop support for the Union League, criticized Democrats for their "oppressive" threat not to hire blacks who opposed them politically. When the time came to go to the polls again in 1869, most Harrison County blacks would have little difficulty remembering that the radicals had brought them the right to vote and the promise of social advancement.[48]

Conservatives also might have used physical intimidation and violence to deal with the black majority. Such activities were common across the South and in some areas of Texas, but the presence of federal troops in Marshall prevented extensive, politically motivated violence in Harrison County. Instead, protection offered by the soldiers probably attracted freedmen from outlying areas. Capt. T. M. K. Smith wrote from Marshall soon after he took over the Freedmen's Bureau there in the spring of 1868: "Freedmen fleeing for their lives are continually coming to this place. . . . In almost every instance the offence charged against these freedmen was their attachment to . . . the U.S. Govt." The agent did not have enough men to do anything about the situation in surrounding counties, but he reported that "any outrage or injustice done to the freedmen in this county (Harrison) is promptly punished. Aggravated assaults though are of rare occurrence, owning no doubt to the presence of the troops in the immediate vicinity. If they were removed the same reign of terror would be instituted." Physical intimidation could not be a weapon against the black majority so long as troops remained in the county.[49]

47. *Texas Republican*, August 14, December 4, 25, 1868.
48. *Harrison Flag*, November 5, 1868.
49. Capt. T. M. K. Smith to Gen. J. J. Reynolds, June 24, 1868, BRFAL, RG 105, NA.

Local government remained stable through 1868 largely in the hands of military appointees, but the spring of 1869 brought upsetting changes. Congress required all civil officeholders to swear the test oath, and as a result Sheriff S. R. Perry, County Commissioner R. W. Blalock, and several other officials who had held office since June, 1866, were disqualified. In early May, General Reynolds appointed as sheriff Leonard C. DeLisle, a prewar resident of Marshall and former Confederate soldier who managed to take the oath. Henry Rawson, a native of England known for his unionism before the war, replaced Blalock. Rawson, who already held the position of postmaster, was on the way to becoming a leader among the county's Republicans. The *Texas Republican* complained that the test oath requirement had upset local government and denied the best men an opportunity to serve. Then, to make matters worse, within a month Sheriff DeLisle was murdered while attempting to arrest one Stephen Lott. DeLisle managed to wound Lott fatally also, and politics apparently had nothing to do with the incident. Nevertheless, the post commander at Marshall blamed Loughery's newspaper for inciting violence against loyal government officials. On June 1, Reynolds appointed H. J. Nichols, a young native of Vermont recently arrived in Marshall, to the sheriff's office.[50]

The county remained quiet during the second half of 1869 as preparations began for the election of November 30–December 3 to ratify the new constitution and elect state and local officers under its terms. Voter registration reopened for ten days in late November under the direction of Jacob Foster (the Pennsylvania native who had held the same position in 1867–1868), P. W. V. Board (son of County Judge N. V. Board), and John Loeber. The county's total electorate rose to 3,838, made up of 2,805 blacks (73 percent) and 1,033 whites.[51] Republicans, recognizing that victory depended only on getting the freedmen to the polls, organized thoroughly. One former slave described their approach as follows: "In the early days they held the election four days. They didn't vote in precincts but at the courthouse. The Democratic Party had no chance to 'timidate the darkies. The 'publican party had a 'Loyal League' for to protect the cullud folks. First the Negroes

50. Election Registers, 1869; Eighth Census, 1860, Schedule 1; *Texas Republican*, April 30, May 4, 1869; Jacob Wagner to Capt. B. F. Grafton, May 27, 1869, OCA, RG 393, NA.

51. Names of the registrars in 1869 are from Galveston *Daily News*, November 25, 1869, and identifying information is from the Eighth Census, 1860, Schedule 1, and Ninth Census, 1870, Schedule 1. Loeber could not be identified from any source. The number of voters is from the List of Registered Voters in Texas, 1869.

went to the league house to get 'structions and ballots and then marched to the courthouse, double file, to vote." [52]

As expected, Republicans swept the election in Harrison County, and their margins of victory were made even larger by the refusal of many conservative whites to vote. E. J. Davis, the Radical Republican candidate for governor, defeated the moderate Republican, A. J. Hamilton, 1,847 to 570, and George W. Whitmore won the contest for a seat in the U.S. House of Representatives by a similar margin. Given the hatred they had for Whitmore as the county's most notorious scalawag, conservatives doubtless found his victory especially galling. Henry Rawson continued his rise as a Republican by winning the state senate seat from Harrison County, and two freedmen, Mitchell Kendall and Henry Moore, gained seats in the lower house of the state legislature. Kendall, who had already served as voter registrar and delegate to the constitutional convention, was a forty-eight-year-old native of Georgia who worked as a blacksmith when not in public life. Moore, a sixty-year-old native of Alabama, could not read or write and listed state representative as his occupation in the census of 1870. According to his son, Moore had saved enough money to buy his freedom in Alabama and then lived with a "guardian" until emancipation. Just where or for how long Henry Moore lived as a free man before 1865 is not clear, but perhaps this background accounted for his position as a leader. [53]

Republicans also easily won control of county government. Five justices of the peace, elected precinct by precinct, took over the duties of the county court. Three of the five—Z. T. Perry in precinct one, John A. Price in precinct two, and James P. Lynch in precinct four—had no opposition, and the other two—Henry D. Smith in precinct three and A. S. Justus in precinct five—overwhelmed their opponents. Smith, who as the justice from the Marshall precinct would preside over the court, received 1,009 votes to a combined total of 300 for three opponents. In the race for sheriff, E. K. Taylor defeated A. G. Adams, the deputy who was involved in the Marshall Riot, by a vote of 1,829 to 614. Although five of the six new officials were natives of the South (Z. T. Perry could not be identified), none of them had held office previously in Harrison County. [54]

52. Rawick, ed., *American Slave*, Vol. V, Pt. 1, p. 123.

53. The 1869 election returns are in *Senate Miscellaneous Documents*, 41st Cong., 2nd Sess., No. 77, pp. 38–79. Jefferson *Radical*, December 11, 25, 1869, February 5, 1870; Rawick, ed., *American Slave*, Vol. V, Pt. 3, pp. 121–22; Ninth Census, 1870, Schedule 1.

54. *Senate Miscellaneous Documents*, 41st Cong., 2nd Sess., No. 77, pp. 38–79; Election Registers, 1846–1870; Eighth Census, 1860, Schedule 1; Ninth Census, 1870, Schedule 1.

The new county court began to govern in May, 1870, and the final key position in local government was filled in July when Governor E. J. Davis appointed J. B. Williamson to a six-year term on the district court. Williamson, a strong Unionist/Republican originally from Pennsylvania, was a familiar face on the bench, having served there since receiving a military appointment in 1867. Thus by the summer of 1870, white Republicans, largely on the basis of black votes, held every important office in local government. Conservative Democrats faced a seemingly impossible task in regaining their traditional dominance.[55]

Almost immediately upon winning control, Republicans began to waste their energies on intraparty squabbling. One faction led by Judge J. B. Williamson consisted primarily of white county officials, and the other led by state senator Henry Rawson depended largely on blacks and the Union League. The first dispute arose over Governor Davis' appointment of a mayor for Marshall. Williamson, Sheriff E. K. Taylor, and others supported Robert H. Martin, a longtime resident of the town, but Rawson wanted the position for himself. Taylor wrote Davis that "the Republicans of this county like Mr. Rawson; but are not willing for him to occupy all the positions in the county." He and Williamson both argued that the party would benefit from spreading appointments around. In the judge's words: "Our party prospects here grow better every day, and will continue to do so, if we will throw open the doors and admit all proper subjects, instead of closing them up for selfish ends." Davis made Martin mayor and drew a furious letter from Rawson attacking Williamson and insisting that the appointee was nothing but "a whiskeyhead and a Democrat."[56]

Factionalism grew more bitter when Sheriff Taylor died in October, 1870, and Davis had to appoint a replacement. The governor's first choice, James F. Miller, had the endorsement of Rawson and the Union League but could not qualify. The fight then became ugly as Rawson and the league turned to W. H. Poland, a native of Alabama who had lived in the county during the war, while the Williamson group supported H. J. Nichols, who had served as sheriff by military appointment in 1869 and 1870. Stilwell H. Russell, a young Texas-born lawyer destined to become one of the county's

55. Commissioners' Court Minutes; Election Registers, 1867–1870; Eighth Census, 1860, Schedule 1.

56. Robert H. Martin to E. J. Davis, August 30, 1870, E. K. Taylor to Davis, September 6, 1870, J. B. Williamson to Davis, September 6, 1870, Henry Rawson to Davis, September 14, 1870, Governors' Papers: EJD.

leading Republicans, praised Nichols to the governor as "a great acquisition to our Party" and claimed that Poland was well known for "cursing & abusing Republicans." Rawson, Mitchell Kendall (the black state representative), and others reminded Davis by telegram that the Union League, the "men who elected you," had unanimously endorsed Poland. C. E. Bolles, the district clerk and a Republican, told Secretary of State James P. Newcomb that neither man would do. Poland, he said, played a role in the Marshall Riot and Nichols was a good man except for one problem: "He is particularly bitter on colored men." Three-quarters of the blacks, Bolles wrote, find him unacceptable. Davis, facing a choice with a seemingly ironic twist between a former slaveholder (Poland) who had the support of blacks and a recently arrived native of the North who did not, settled on the former, making the appointment on November 7, 1870.[57]

Infighting among Republicans continued through the next two years. By September, 1871, the anti-Rawson faction, now led by S. H. Russell and several rising black leaders including David Abner and Walter Ripetoe, took over the local Union League. Russell became president; Ripetoe, vice-president; and Abner, treasurer. The League passed resolutions condemning Rawson for attempting to undermine District Judge Williamson and urging Governor Davis not to listen to him anymore. In May, 1872, the two factions again fought over whom Davis would appoint as mayor of Marshall.[58]

This factionalism took time and energy and, to the extent that it was public, made Harrison County Republicans look like squabbling office seekers, but thanks to the black majority, it in no way shook the party's hold on local government. "This county is squarely Republican," wrote one observer in October, 1872, and elections during the first two years after the restoration of civilian government bore out that statement. In a special election of representatives to the Forty-second Congress held October 3–6, 1871, Harrison County supported the incumbent Republican George W.

57. Election Registers, 1870; A. W. Rhem to E. J. Davis, October 8, 1870, Executive Record Books: EJD, I, 448; Stilwell H. Russell to E. J. Davis, October 29, 1870, N. V. Board to Davis, October 31, 1870, Henry Rawson, Mitchell Kendall, and L. J. Gallant to Davis, November 4, 1870, Governors' Papers: EJD; C. E. Bolles to James P. Newcomb, October 29, 1870, Newcomb Papers.

58. Minutes of a Meeting of the Union League of America in Marshall, September 2, 1871, Newcomb Papers; S. H. Russell to E. J. Davis, May 29, 1872, Henry Rawson to Davis, May 29, 1872, Governors' Papers: EJD.

Whitmore by a two-to-one margin (2,216 to 1,116) over his Democratic opponent, William S. Herndon, a Confederate veteran. (Herndon, however, won districtwide.) Republican margins were even more convincing in the general elections of November 1872. In national races, the county supported President Grant over his Liberal Republican challenger, Horace Greeley, by a vote of 2,374 to 775 and voted for Republican candidates for Congress by similar margins. These results, of course, went against the tide across Texas as Democratic conservatives, joined in some races by Republican moderates, gave victories to Greeley and the Democratic congressional candidates.[59]

In legislative and local elections, however, Republican strength brought more meaningful success. Henry Moore and Shack Roberts won the county's two seats in the state house of representatives, receiving 2,349 and 2,103 votes respectively compared to 661 for Robert L. Hightower and 784 for R. H. Cooper, their Democratic opponents. Moore, the incumbent elected first in 1869, and Roberts, a Methodist minister, would be two of only ten African Americans elected to the Thirteenth Legislature. Democrats did not bother to run candidates for sheriff and county treasurer, the two local offices that had to be filled, but those contests were as one-sided as the others. Stilwell H. Russell defeated W. H. Poland 2,273 to 884 in the race for sheriff, and William Umbdenstock, a German immigrant who had arrived in Marshall as a railroad hand during the 1850s, defeated H. J. Nichols for treasurer by a similar margin. Poland and Nichols had both held the sheriff's office, but the former had been a slaveholder and the latter was known for antiblack attitudes. Russell and Umbdenstock had no such disabilities and joined Judge Williamson as the county's leading white Republicans.[60]

Harrison County's efforts notwithstanding, the Thirteenth Legislature elected in 1872 was controlled by conservatives, and the next general election in December, 1873, unseated Governor Davis and brought total "redemption" to the state government. Voters in Harrison County gave Davis

59. A. W. Norris to James P. Newcomb, October 27, 1872, Newcomb Papers; Election Returns, 1871–1872; Kingston, Attlesey, and Crawford, *Political History of Texas*, 73, 75; Election Registers, 1871–1872. The unsuccessful Republican candidates for Congress were A. B. Norton and A. J. Evans, running at large, and R. K. Smith, running against Herndon for the seat from the First Congressional District.

60. Election Returns, 1872; Eighth Census, 1860, Schedule 1. Additional information on Umbdenstock is found in S. H. Russell to E. J. Davis, August 5, 1873, Governors' Papers: EJD.

2,313 votes to only 997 for Richard Coke, the "Redeemer" candidate, but the incumbent governor carried only twenty-six counties statewide. Similarly, the county sent a Republican senator, Webster Flanagan of neighboring Rusk County, and two black Republican representatives—Shack Roberts and Ed Brown (also from Rusk County)—to the state legislature where their party was in a hopelessly minority position. Democrats in Marshall, finally with something to celebrate, held a "jubilee" on December 11, 1873, in honor of their statewide victory. Two days later, however, Republicans, or as the Galveston *News* put it—"the colored people"—celebrated their continuing control of local government, which they had maintained with ease.[61]

The justices elected in December, 1873, each with more than 2,200 votes, constituted a more "radical" county court than did those chosen in 1869. L. J. Gallant, the justice in precinct two, was a native of Indiana who had come to Marshall as a Freedmen's Bureau teacher, and Edmund J. Brown, justice of precinct five, was black. The other three justices—M. T. Hoskins, J. K. Williams, and J. R. Ford—could not be located anywhere in Texas in the censuses of 1860, 1870, and 1880.[62] Thus, for a short time after the 1873 general election, Harrison County probably had the kind of government, one run by carpetbaggers and blacks, so infamous in the lore of Reconstruction in Texas.

The county court elected in 1873 proved highly unstable. First, James P. Lynch, one of the justices elected in 1869, challenged the right of his successor, J. R. Ford, to serve. Court minutes do not give the details, but Lynch, a Tennessee native resident in the county before 1860, replaced Ford during February, 1874. Next, in June, William S. Coleman, a Marshall lawyer, demanded that Justice Edmund J. Brown be removed from office on the grounds that a recent legislative act concerning the boundary between Harrison and Marion Counties made him a resident of the latter and that he was "mentally and morally unfit to fill any office whatsoever." Brown, according to the state election register, "abandoned his office" and left the county. A special election in September put H. L. Berry, a native of South

61. Kingston, Attlesey, and Crawford, *Political History of Texas,* 58–61; Campbell, *Southern Community in Crisis,* 310; Galveston *Daily News,* December 14, 1873.

62. Election Returns, 1873; Eighth Census, 1860, Schedule 1; Ninth Census, 1870, Schedule 1; Tenth Census, 1880, Schedule 1. Hoskins, Williams, and Ford could not be located with certainty even on the county's tax rolls for this period.

Carolina and former slaveholder, in Brown's place. L. J. Gallant, the carpet-bagger justice, died in August, 1874, necessitating yet another special election that was won by W. L. Hailey. Finally, the presiding justice, J. K. Williams, resigned in July, 1875, and was replaced by William Roy. Hailey and Roy, like three of the original justices on this court, could not be identified from any source and may also have been carpetbaggers.[63]

Factionalism and instability in the personnel nominated to run local government could not shake the majority support that Republicans enjoyed in Harrison County during the early 1870s. Even Robert W. Loughery, back in Marshall as editor of the *Tri-Weekly Herald* after brief stints with the Jefferson *Times* and Galveston *Times,* found the prospects for a Democratic victory hopeless. In May, 1875, he wrote, "We repeat: the political status of this county is settled for years to come; nothing we can do will change it." Loughery's view certainly seemed correct, but in fact Democratic control statewide created circumstances that assured Harrison County conservatives of political and legal support from Austin if they found any excuse to challenge Republican domination in Marshall. This was demonstrated in early 1874 when the state legislature voted to "address" District Judge John B. Williamson and remove him from the bench on several grounds, including the politically motivated charge that he was "not sufficiently learned in the law, and has not the mental capacity to become so learned." Governor Coke then appointed as judge Matthew D. Ector, the former Confederate general who had defeated Williamson for that position in 1866 and in turn had been removed in favor of Williamson in 1867. Local Democrats doubtless enjoyed this turn of fortune and the assurance that they could count on state government if any opportunity presented itself for taking control from the Republicans. Such an opportunity, however, appeared a remote possibility in 1875 and 1876.[64]

In the August, 1875, election, held at the instigation of Texas conservatives, to consider writing a new constitution to replace the Constitution of

63. Commissioners' Court Minutes; Election Registers, 1874–1875; Eighth Census, 1860, Schedules 1 and 2; Ninth Census, 1870, Schedule 1.

64. Marshall *Tri-Weekly Herald,* May 29, 1875; Election Registers, 1866–1867, 1874; *Journal of the House of Representatives of the State of Texas: Being the Session of the Fourteenth Legislature . . . January 13, 1874* (Austin, 1874), 100–103, 186, 208, 212; *Journal of the Senate of the State of Texas: Being the Session of the Fourteenth Legislature . . . January 13, 1874* (Austin, 1874), 189. General information on "addressing" judges under the terms of the Constitution of 1869 is found in Campbell, "Scalawag District Judges," 87.

1869, Harrison County voted 2,269 to 839 against a convention. Statewide, of course, the convention easily won popular approval, and seventy-five of the ninety delegates, elected three each from the state's thirty senatorial districts, were Democrats. Of the fifteen Republican delegates, three came from the senatorial district composed of Harrison and Rusk Counties. Sheriff S. H. Russell and David Abner, a leading black Republican from Marshall, and state senator Webster Flanagan of Rusk County each had more than 2,230 votes compared to fewer than 850 votes each for their Democratic opponents, two of whom—James Tucker and William S. Coleman—were from Harrison County. Democratic conservatives had campaigned with the argument that the "true interests" of blacks and whites were the same and that the "color line" should be ignored, but their pleas obviously were in vain.[65]

Russell and Abner were part of a hopelessly small minority at the convention, but they found the "Redeemers" willing to treat counties such as theirs as Republican enclaves in a Democratic state. In particular this meant that Harrison County would be designated as a separate house and senatorial district and left to its black majority. Loughery objected to this form of "Africanization" because it left his county "to the tender mercies of Radical vampyres [sic]." At least, he said, the convention could have imposed some sort of suffrage restriction to benefit white minorities. In spite of such complaints, however, Harrison County Democrats decided to support the new constitution largely on the grounds that it was better than the one drafted in 1869 and that Republicans opposed it. Shake off your apathy, Loughery told his readers, and vote. Harrison County will be redeemed some day.[66]

On February 15, 1876, when Texans ratified the new constitution and elected officials under its terms, Harrison County's Republicans found that in spite of their strength at the polls they were on the losing side in all district and statewide contests. They opposed the constitution by a vote of 2,713 to 1,036 and supported all of the unsuccessful Republican candidates for state offices by similar margins. In the governor's race, for example, William Chambers received 2,664 votes to 1,122 for Richard Coke. The local leader, William Umbdenstock, ran for state treasurer and carried the county 2,660 to 1,100 over A. J. Dorn, but he lost badly statewide. M. W. Wheeler

65. Marshall *Tri-Weekly Herald*, July 5, 22, August 5, 1875.
66. *Ibid.*, October 12, November 9, December 21, 1875, January 1, 1876.

defeated William S. Coleman, a Democrat from Marshall, 2,744 to 963 in the contest for a floater seat in the state house of representatives from a five-county district, but the latter went to Austin on the strength of white votes from the other counties. Finally, although J. B. Williamson carried Harrison County 2,710 to 1,060 over A. J. Booty of Panola County in the race for judge of the Second Judicial District, Booty won the election districtwide.[67]

By contrast, Republicans won all countywide races. Two black leaders, Walter Ripetoe and Shack Roberts, ran for the state senate and house of representatives respectively and overwhelmed their token opposition. J. B. Williamson, a candidate for county judge as well as district judge, had better luck in the local race and became presiding officer of the constitutionally restored commissioners' court. W. E. Singleton received 2,738 votes in the race for sheriff. Former sheriff Stilwell H. Russell claimed the position of tax collector, and S. H. Smothers, another black Republican, won the job of tax assessor. Three of the four county commissioners—Dr. W. C. Rain, J. E. Floyd, and A. E. Snow—were Republicans who won easily, but Democrat B. R. Bass defeated T. S. Buchanan by a vote of 304 to 287 in precinct one and became the first of his party to win an election in the county since 1866. Clearly, however, Bass owed his victory to the fact that commissioners were elected by precinct rather than on a countywide basis.[68]

The national election of 1876, which resulted in a disputed victory for Rutherford B. Hayes and "redemption" of the last southern states with Republican governments, followed a familiar pattern in Harrison County. Voters there cast sizable majorities for Republican candidates only to see their ballots lost in a flood of Democratic votes from other counties. For example, in the race for a seat in Congress from the First District, S. H. Russell carried his home county 2,966 to 1,277 over David B. Culberson, a Democrat from neighboring Marion County. Culberson, however, had a majority districtwide and went to Washington.[69]

Harrison County thus remained under Republican control in 1877 even after every southern state had been returned to government by white conservatives. Local Democrats, however, would not concede control indefi-

67. Election Returns, 1876; Marshall *Tri-Weekly Herald*, February 22, 1876; Kingston, Attlesey, and Crawford, *Political History of Texas*, 59.

68. Marshall *Tri-Weekly Herald*, February 22, 1876. Bass is identified as a Democrat *ibid.*, July 5, 1875. Identifications of blacks are from Ninth Census, 1870, Schedule 1.

69. Election Returns, 1876; Campbell, *Southern Community in Crisis*, 314–15.

nitely to the black majority and a relatively small group of white Republicans, and they would not allow the issues of Reconstruction to fade with the passage of time. Instead, insisting that radicals were guilty of misgovernment, conservatives organized, appealed to blacks, and managed a spectacular "redemption" of the county in 1878.

Conservatives in Harrison County concentrated their attack on the cost of government under the Republicans. Prior to 1871, county tax rates never rose above 32.5 cents on each $100 of property (plus a 50-cent poll tax on adult males), but they jumped to $1.50 on $100 (plus a $1 poll tax) in 1872 and $1.89 on $100 (plus a $1.50 poll tax) in 1875. At the same time, county indebtedness, which had been nonexistent in 1867, rose to more than forty thousand dollars. These increases in taxes and indebtedness came for a variety of reasons. First, from 1871 to 1873, county government attempted to support the free public education system established by the state legislature. This added $1 on $100 to the tax rate in 1872 before the state legislature largely scrapped the public education system in 1873. Second, beginning in 1874 tax rates reflected a subsidy given to the Texas and Pacific Railway in the form of $300,000 in bonds that required the payment of $21,000 in interest and the retirement of $6,000 in principal the first year. (The more than $40,000 in debt mentioned above obviously did not include the railroad subsidy.) This bond issue had been requested by a diverse group of citizens reflecting all political views and was approved in a special election, but then the charge arose that the company had misrepresented what it would do for Marshall and that it obtained votes through intimidation and fraud. Third, the county spent extensively on roads and bridges and built a new jail for $14,800 in 1875. Certainly some of these projects were worthwhile, and the county did not collect all of the taxes exactly as assessed—collection of the railroad subsidy tax, for example, was delayed until 1877 by legal actions. Nevertheless, conservatives had the tremendous advantage of being able to blame high taxes and public debt on the Republicans. To this, of course, they added the charge of misuse of public funds: a claim that could not be documented, but one that made good politics.[70]

Harrison County conservatives waited until just two months before the November 5, 1878, date of the first general elections scheduled under the Constitution of 1876 before they began to organize. In September a hand-

70. Real and Personal Property Tax Rolls, Harrison County, 1865–1873; Campbell, *Southern Community in Crisis,* 317–21, 323–28, 331; Commissioners' Court Minutes.

bill circulated in Marshall calling a public meeting "to nominate a Citizens' ticket of good and true men of both colors as candidates for the various county offices." Signers included former Unionists and Confederates, the county Democratic party chairman, businessmen, and at least one representative of the Texas and Pacific Railway. Before this "citizens'" group could meet, Republicans held their convention on September 25 and nominated a ticket headed by County Judge J. B. Williamson and including two blacks, John Hudson and S. H. Smothers, who ran respectively for the state house of representatives and county surveyor. The conservatives, however, refused to back down in spite of the Republicans' often-demonstrated control of the electorate and held a convention of the Citizens' party on October 12.[71]

Several well-known Democrats who had not participated in public life since the war decided to lend support to the new party. Edward Clark, the former lieutenant governor who held the governorship briefly following the resignation of Sam Houston in 1861, acted as chairman, and William T. Scott, the county's wealthiest planter and a three-term state senator during the antebellum years, accepted the meeting's nomination for the state house of representatives. George Lane, a former county judge elected first in 1860, ran for that position again. Solomon R. Perry, who had been elected sheriff as early as 1850 and also served in that capacity from 1865 to 1869, sought to return to what must have seemed "his" office. All four candidates for county commissioner were active Democrats, especially John D. Rudd, the county chairman, and Amory Starr, the son of James Harper Starr, a famed leader of the Republic of Texas. The Citizens' party made no nominations for four offices, including county surveyor, thus leaving one of the black candidates, S. H. Smothers, unopposed.[72]

During the campaign that followed this convention, the "Redeemers" presented themselves to the voters as a nonpartisan group seeking to restore fiscal responsibility and honesty to local government. They called themselves the Citizens' party rather than Democrats and termed their opponents "radicals," not Republicans. Their appeal to black voters, which was critical to any hope of success, followed several lines of argument already well developed by 1878. First, conservative spokesmen promised blacks that southern whites would protect all men's rights as least as effectively as

71. Marshall *Tri-Weekly Herald,* September 17, 26, 1878.
72. *Ibid.,* October 15, 1878; Marshall *Messenger,* October 18, 1878; Campbell, *Southern Community in Crisis,* 152, 34, 184, 338.

did the carpetbaggers and scalawags. As the Marshall *Messenger* put it in 1877: "The white people of the South are pledged to accord them [blacks] the political rights conferred upon them and will stand by these pledges faithfully." Resolutions adopted by the nominating convention of the Citizens' party sounded this same theme. A second argument emphasized how radical taxing and spending threatened the well-being of blacks as well as whites. "Bad" government injures everyone, the Citizens' party insisted; blacks and whites must unite to save themselves. Finally, the conservatives told blacks that white radical leaders had simply used their votes to take offices and the income from those positions for themselves. Jasper Black, an African American, published a letter in the *Tri-Weekly Herald* of October 17, making this point. Black wrote that after C. E. Coleman was elected to the constitutional convention of 1868–1869, he took the position and pay and went home to the North. In his own precinct, Black continued, where M. T. Hoskins was made justice of the peace, he took all the fines and fees possible and left. It was time, Black concluded, to stop voting blindly for radicals.[73]

Conservatives also assured blacks that the Citizens' party did not oppose the Republican party as such. They maintained that this was purely a local affair, and that they accepted blacks' support for Republicans at the state and national levels. To support this argument, both newspapers claimed that leading white Republicans in the county (primarily those connected with the railroad) supported the Citizens' party because they recognized that the "condition of things has been the result of bad government by their own party." Finally, Citizens' party spokesmen presented it as a move for general racial harmony. For example, Loughery of the *Herald* urged "peace and permanent reconciliation" and called for "a cordial and kind understanding between the two races that each will be willing to assist the other."[74]

The Citizens' party's campaign for black support came to a close on November 7, 1878, when Harrison County residents voted at ten polling places set by the commissioners' court back in April. The county had only six precincts, but precinct three, which completely surrounded Marshall, had a

73. Marshall *Messenger*, July 21, 1877, October 18, 1878; Marshall *Tri-Weekly Herald*, September 26, October 15, 17, 1878.
74. Marshall *Messenger*, October 18, 1878; Marshall *Tri-Weekly Herald*, October 29, 1878.

ballot box for each of the town's four wards as well as one for voters in that precinct who did not live in the town. The box for voters living in precinct three but outside Marshall was located at the office of Justice of the Peace William Roy. Roy's office, however, was within the corporate limits of Marshall, a fact that would prove critical to the outcome of the election.[75]

The election on November 5 apparently resulted in victories for radical candidates in all important contests, but their winning margins were much smaller than usual. Both conservative newspapers conceded that the Citizens' party had lost but expressed pleasure at the closeness of the vote. "As is well known," the Messenger wrote, "the radical majority of this county has long been from 1500 to 1700 [but] this tremendous majority has been reduced to a doubtful 100." Conservative success, the editor believed, would have a beneficial moral and political effect.[76]

A look at the returns indicates that the "Redeemers" had good reason to be encouraged. More voters (3,850) participated in 1878 than in any previous election during the decade, and yet the election was much closer than any since black enfranchisement. For example, where County Judge Williamson had 2,664 votes as opposed to 1,008 for several opponents in 1876, he defeated Lane by only 58 votes (1,954 to 1,896) in 1878. Other races showed similar results. For example, in the race for sheriff, A. A. Whisson defeated S. R. Perry by 2,008 to 1,833.[77]

The success of Citizens' party candidates can be explained either by their having gained the votes of a significant number of blacks (as many as five hundred) or by their having prevented many blacks from voting and stuffing ballot boxes to make up the difference. There is some evidence that blacks responded positively to the conservatives' appeals. African Americans joined the Citizens' party, wrote public letters of support, and made campaign speeches with its candidates. Years later, Simpson Campbell, a freedman who had belonged to W. L. Sloan, recalled the election as follows: "It was a democratic ticket and control by Southerners. They told us niggers if we'd vote that ticked we'd be rec'nized as white folks, but I didn't 'lieve a word of it. Old man Sloan told all his niggers that and they all voted that ticket but two—that was Charley Tang and Simp Campbell." Thus, in spite

75. Commissioners' Court Minutes; Marshall Tri-Weekly Herald, April 4, 1878.

76. Marshall Tri-Weekly Herald, November 7, 1878; Marshall Messenger, November 8, 1878; Election Returns, 1878.

77. Election Returns, 1876 and 1878.

of skepticism expressed by blacks such as Campbell, conservative arguments about common interests and fair treatment had the desired effect in some cases.[78]

Evidence of intimidation, either physical or economic, is very limited. R. P. Littlejohn, one of the Citizens' party leaders, claimed many years later that blacks were kept from the polls and a black election judge forced to resign, but radical leaders and black voters made no such charges at the time. There is a better possibility that fraud rather than intimidation played a role in the conservatives' success. Harrison County "Redeemers" eventually boasted of printing ballots of the same size and on the same color paper as that used by the Republicans and then switching the tickets so that the ignorant and unsuspecting blacks voted conservative. This legend, however, is based on stories by conservatives that differ on every detail, from the color of the ballots to the methods used to switch them for Republican tickets. Moreover, in the legal actions that followed the election (to be discussed below), radicals did not charge the conservatives with deceiving blacks with counterfeit ballots.[79]

Perhaps fraud made the election of 1878 close; it is impossible to say with certainty. But the conservatives did not win by cheating; instead, complete returns showed that they lost every contest. The Citizens' party's opportunity to turn defeat into victory came only when they discovered a few days after the election that the polling place for precinct three *outside* Marshall had been at William Roy's office *within* the town's corporate limits. This violated a state law requiring that each ballot box be located in the precinct in which those casting votes in that box lived. Technically, all the votes in Roy's box, as the precinct three box became known, had been cast by individuals voting in the wrong precinct. This proved critical because the box held more than one thousand votes, about one-quarter of all cast, and most were for Republican candidates. For example, in the county judge's race, Williamson received 758 votes in Roy's box and Lane had 266. Without these ballots the radicals would lose all the contested races to their conservative challengers.[80]

78. Campbell, *Southern Community in Crisis*, 344; Rawick, ed., *American Slave*, IV, Pt. 1, p. 192.
79. Campbell, *Southern Community in Crisis*, 345–46.
80. Marshall *Messenger*, November 8, 1878; Election Returns, 1878. W. S. Coleman to

Ten days after the election Citizens' party leaders obtained an injunction from District Judge A. J. Booty ordering County Judge Williamson not to count the ballots from precinct three. The order, of course, cited the improper location of the box. Williamson reacted by refusing to count any of the votes unless Roy's box was included, and conservatives assumed that he meant to issue certificates of election to the radical candidates on the basis of the original returns. The Citizens' party then got a second injunction that restrained Williamson from granting certificates of election and appointed three conservatives to count the returns "properly." Williamson had the original ballots, but the conservatives obtained what the *Herald* called "duplicates properly attested to by returning officers," then counted all except those in Roy's box, and declared the Citizens' party candidates elected.[81]

Late in the afternoon of November 18, conservative leaders, armed with the two injunctions against Williamson and their own version of the election results, occupied the key county government offices. George Lane was ill, so Amory Starr, acting as county judge, took control of Williamson's office and of the county seal and issued certificates of election to the conservative candidates. Jacob Wolff, the incumbent radical county clerk, refused at first to give up his office whereupon Joseph P. Alford, the clerk-elect, came in with "as many men as could conveniently enter the room" and ordered him out. Wolff attempted to refuse again but was told that his consent was not expected or necessary. He then vacated the office. S. R. Perry took over from Sheriff William E. Singleton under similar circumstances. The removals of radicals from other offices was completed the next day. Starr wrote a friend on the twentieth: "I held county commissioners court yesterday (Lane county judge being sick) and those officers who had not *turned over* to our men, I had posses sent out for and *turned* out. I'll have old Williamson in jail shortly if he don't return some papers he took out of the records. It's good fun but I've had no rest."[82]

Richard B. Hubbard, November 22, 1878, Governors' Papers: Richard B. Hubbard, Archives Division, Texas State Library, Austin (hereafter cited as Governors' Papers: RBH), says that there were 1,061 ballots in Roy's box.

81. Election Returns, 1878. This file for 1878 contains far more information, including affidavits by those involved, than is usually found in the election returns. Marshall *Tri-Weekly Herald*, November 16, 19, 1878.

82. Commissioners' Court Minutes; Jake Wolff to Maj. K. M. Walton, February 4, 1879, in Election Returns, 1878; Marshall *Tri-Weekly Herald*, November 19, 1878; Amory R. Starr

Conservatives celebrated their success to the extreme, holding public rallies in Marshall and smaller towns in the county. The *Messenger* ran a huge headline, "HARRISON COUNTY REDEEMED," and the *Herald* published a long satirical article entitled "The Salt River Expedition," making fun of the radicals sailing reluctantly away "up Salt River." County Judge Williamson, however, did not give in without a fight. On the afternoon of the eighteenth, he sent election returns to Austin showing that, with the votes in Roy's box counted, John Hudson had defeated William T. Scott in the state representative race. "I certify," he wrote, "that a few hours before these returns were made out, my office and seal were taken possession of by a mob and hence the seal is not attached." The next day, he began to issue certificates of election to the Republican candidates and on the twenty-first began to appeal to Governor Richard B. Hubbard, who had final authority in that only he could issue the commissions required to hold office. His second appeal to Hubbard accused the Citizens' party leaders of "political *hatred*" and concluded: "We are able in this county to do as they have done, take the law in our own hands, but will not."[83]

Of course, conservatives appealed to the governor as well. George Lane, for example, complained that "radical scoundrels" had "robbed the county and mismanaged its affairs." Therefore, he wrote, we "made a hard pull ... for the offices" and "have full hope our friends will give us truly all the aid we will be entitled in a due administration of the law." Hubbard, a conservative Democrat, reacted by refusing to issue any commissions to officers in Harrison County and asking Attorney General Hannibal H. Boone for a legal ruling on the situation. Boone issued an opinion on November 30, pointing out that only an incumbent county judge could issue certificates of election. This meant that the commissions issued by Starr were "without warrant of law" whereas those issued by Williamson were legal and that individuals holding them could be commissioned by the governor unless someone challenged their right to office on legal grounds. This opinion forced the Citizens' party candidates to file contest-of-election suits against their Republican opponents in December, 1878. In the meantime, the "Re-

to R. H. Irion, November 20, 1878, Henry Raguet Family Papers, Eugene C. Barker Texas History Center, University of Texas, Austin.

83. Marshall *Messenger,* November 22, 1878; Marshall *Tri-Weekly Herald,* November 19, 1878; returns filed by J. B. Williamson, November 18, 1878, in Election Returns, 1878; J. B. Williamson to Richard B. Hubbard, November 21, 22, 1878, Governors' Papers: RBH.

deemers," acting under a second opinion from the attorney general, remained in office pending the outcome of their suits and any legal action that might be taken against them by the Republican candidates.[84]

The conservatives' contest-of-election suits hinged on the argument that the ballot box for precinct three had been located illegally within the town of Marshall and therefore could not be counted. Counsel for the Republicans insisted that the polling place had been properly established by the commissioners' court and that the Republican majorities cast there were legal. The radicals also condemned the way their opponents had "violently and forcibly" taken control of county offices and pointed out that not counting the box from precinct three would disfranchise nearly one-third of those who had voted. Thus at the very least, they argued, a new election should be held to offer a voice to people who had lost their votes through no fault of their own.[85]

The suit brought by George Lane against J. B. Williamson came to trial in Judge A. J. Booty's court on December 31, 1878, and was decided on January 2, 1879. Not surprisingly in light of Booty's political views and the fact that he had enjoined Williamson from counting Roy's box, the decision gave Lane the office of county judge. Williamson asked for a new trial, was rejected by Judge Booty, and appealed to the Supreme Court of Texas. In the meantime, conservatives won another victory based on the improper location of Roy's box when the Committee on Privileges and Elections of the Texas House of Representatives decided that William T. Scott rather than the black Republican candidate, John Hudson, would take Harrison County's seat.[86]

The Texas Supreme Court handed down its ruling in *J. B. Williamson* v. *George Lane* on December 12, 1879, and confirmed conservative control of the offices that they had already held for more than a year. Chief Justice

84. George Lane to Richard B. Hubbard, November 22, 1878, Hubbard to Hannibal H. Boone, November 29, 1878, Governors' Papers: RBH; Opinion of Attorney General Boone, November 30, December 11, 1878, in Election Returns, 1878; Campbell, *Southern Community in Crisis*, 351–52.

85. This summary of the arguments in the contest-of-election suits is based on original case papers filed in District Court Civil Case Papers, Office of the District Clerk, Harrison County Courthouse, Marshall, Tex. The papers filed in *George Lane v. J. B. Williamson* are missing, probably because the case was appealed to the state supreme court, but those for the others, all of which are virtually identical, remain.

86. Marshall *Tri-Weekly Herald*, January 2, 4, 1879; Campbell, *Southern Community in Crisis*, 353–54.

George F. Moore's opinion hinged on the ruling that the contesting of an election was a political rather than civil matter and that the court heard only suits at law. This meant that the court had no jurisdiction in the case of Williamson's appeal and allowed Judge Booty's original decision in favor of Lane to stand.[87] Republicans also fought Citizens' party leaders in court by charging five of them with violating the federal Enforcement Act of 1870 that outlawed any infringement on the right to vote as protected in the Fifteenth Amendment. However, after a three-day trial in federal district court in Jefferson, a jury of eleven whites and one black found the defendants not guilty.[88]

"Redeemers" thus ended Reconstruction in Harrison County in one spectacular victory, probably with the aid of some fraud and intimidation, but primarily with the aid of a legal technicality and the power of their friends in the state courts and legislature. Democratic conservatives then maintained control of local government through the same organization and largely the same techniques and appeals that had won for them in 1878. During the 1880s, Republican candidates in federal elections generally received huge majorities, but the Citizens' party, pledging itself to inexpensive government, racial harmony, etc., controlled county government.[89]

Reconstruction threatened to bring genuinely radical social and political change to Harrison County. The county's overwhelming black majority made Republican government almost a certainty, and a sizable group of Whig Unionists offered experienced leadership at the outset. The white-southerner minority certainly felt threatened as they raged against scalawag and carpetbagger officeholders, "Negro rule," taxes, and corruption until an election technicality allowed conservative Democrats to regain control in 1878. When the era closed, however, other than accepting the absolute destruction of slavery, Harrison County had not undergone any radical changes of a permanent nature. County Judge George Lane symbolized

87. *J. B. Williamson v. George Lane,* 52 Texas 335.

88. Campbell, *Southern Community in Crisis,* 355–56. The defendants argued, with *United States v. Reese* (1876) as a precedent, that the only offense that could be charged under the Enforcement Act was denying the right to vote on the basis of race, color, or previous condition of servitude. Since they were accused of refusing to accept "colored back tickets," they had not committed any such offense.

89. Worth Robert Miller, "Harrison County Methods: Election Fraud in Late Nineteenth-Century Texas," *Locus: Regional and Local History of the Americas,* VII (1995), 111–28; Campbell, *Southern Community in Crisis,* 358–61.

this perfectly in 1878 by occupying exactly the same office that he had held in 1860.

More than likely, economic conditions in Harrison County during the 1860s and 1870s contributed to the bitterness of the struggle for political control. The local economy, in spite of greatly improved railroad connections, remained overwhelmingly rural and dependent on cotton and was slow to recover from wartime disruptions and the end of slavery. As late as 1879, cotton production stood at 17,619 bales, 3,821 fewer than in 1859. Total population increased from 15,001 in 1860 to 25,172 in 1880, but blacks who were relatively poor accounted for most of the growth (from 8,874 in 1860 to 17,196 twenty years later). Harrison did not get the economic boost provided many Texas counties by the tremendous influx of immigrants from older states and abroad during the years after 1865. Marshall, thanks to its success in attracting the Texas and Pacific Railway, grew to a population of 5,624 by 1880, but Dallas was nearly twice as large by that date, and even the much newer town of Waco in central Texas had more than 7,000 people. The total assessed value of taxable property, which stood at $1,819,648 in 1865, rose only to $2,414,958 by 1876, an increase of 33 percent but still a smaller amount than the total value of non-slave property back in 1860.[90]

Apparently, economic stagnation also affected the status of the county's economic elite after 1865. Of the richest 5 percent of taxpayers in the county immediately after the war, 33 percent of those individuals or members of their families remained at that level in 1880, 28 percent had fallen from the elite, and 35 percent could not be located anywhere in Texas. From the point of view of the elite class, this compared unfavorably with the situation in Dallas and McLennan Counties, where at least 50 percent of the wealthiest taxpayers in 1865 maintained that status in 1880. Almost certainly the lack of economic expansion in Harrison County stemmed much more from its great reliance on slavery before the war and its location in an

90. U.S. Bureau of the Census, *Agriculture of the United States in 1860,* 144–47; U.S. Bureau of the Census, *Report on Productions of Agriculture (1880),* 170–73; U.S. Bureau of the Census, *Population of the United States in 1860,* 484–86; U.S. Bureau of the Census, *Statistics of the Population of the United States (1880),* 344, 409; Real and Personal Property Tax Rolls, Harrison County, 1860, 1865, 1880. The rapid growth of the black population may be explained by the relative safety of Harrison County owing to the presence of troops and Freedmen's Bureau agents there for much of Reconstruction.

older region of Texas than from Reconstruction policies; nevertheless, the two coincided, and angry whites could easily claim the existence of a relationship.[91]

Blacks eagerly embraced all the opportunities of freedom. This was typical, of course, in all areas of Texas, but in Harrison County freedmen had overwhelming numbers on their side and the support of a local Freedmen's Bureau agent and protection of federal troops stationed at Marshall from 1865 until 1870. Blacks supported and attended schools, voted, held office, and exercised civic responsibilities such as jury service. Freedmen determined the winners of all elections in the county for ten years beginning in 1868, but—thanks to believing the promises of conservatives, plus some degree of fraud and intimidation—did not maintain the united front necessary to prevent the overthrow of Republican government in 1878. Even then, the first fifteen years after emancipation brought considerable social and economic progress. For example, more than three-quarters (78 percent) of a sample of 250 black households from the census of 1880 were headed by nuclear families. Only 38 percent of those families having children aged six to sixteen reported that at least one of those children attended school within the previous year, but this was not dismally deficient in a heavily rural county. White families did only a little better at sending their children to school. Most blacks, of course, reported their occupation as "farmer" (62.4 percent of all household heads in a sample of 250), and most of those (53 percent) were sharecroppers. However, 32 percent of the household heads who called themselves "farmers" rented for cash rather than on shares, and 15 percent actually owned land in amounts ranging from 15 to 240 acres. The great majority of individuals in all three classifications of farmers (sharecroppers, cash renters, and landowners) reported the ownership of horses, cows, and hogs. Freedmen constituted society's poorest class, but considering that most had emerged from slavery with virtually no property and that Harrison County had not prospered or grown during Reconstruction, the progress of many was notable.[92]

Overall, Harrison County drew little relief during Reconstruction from conditions that worked to ease tension in other places. For example, there

91. Real and Personal Property Tax Rolls, Harrison County, 1865 and 1880.
92. Demographic and economic information on the black population of Harrison County in 1880 was drawn from a sample of 250 African-American households from the Tenth Census, 1880, Schedules 1 and 2.

was no significant ethnic minority such as Germans to increase and temper the strength of white unionism. The county did have a larger than usual group of Whig Unionists, some of whom had considerable experience in politics and may have been able to build local support for the Republican party. Most of these older men, however, were soon replaced by newer white party leaders who tended to squabble among themselves and become targets for conservative invective. Finally, Harrison County did not enjoy notable expansion of its population or economy between 1865 and 1880 and therefore could not focus on, for example, making Marshall the greatest city in East Texas. In short, Harrison County, as one of the oldest and most southern localities in Texas, and one having little for its white population to concentrate on in public life except the issues of restoration to the Union, experienced Reconstruction in its most controversial form.

# 5

## JEFFERSON COUNTY

Antebellum Jefferson County did not typify the slaveholding, cotton-planting Old South. Located in the southeastern corner of Texas, a region of marshy grasslands crossed by belts of heavy forests, the county offered little opportunity for plantation agriculture. According to the census of 1860, 70 residents of Jefferson, representing 14 percent of all families, owned a total of 309 slaves; and the county's farmers reported the production of only eighty-four bales of cotton. John Stamps, the largest slaveholder with twenty-six bondsmen, was a railroad contractor rather than a planter. Instead of relying on the production of cotton, Jefferson County residents based their economic lives on small-scale agriculture, cattle herding, and, increasingly during the 1850s, on commerce. The milling of forest products such as lumber and shingles, an industry destined to become very important in the postwar years, also showed signs of its future by 1860. Beaumont, the county seat town located on the Neches River, and Sabine Pass, a smaller town situated just above the mouth of the Sabine River on the Gulf of Mexico, became steadily busier as the commercial outlets of southeast Texas, exporting cotton and forest products and importing a variety of manufactured items and plantation supplies. By 1860 the Texas and New Orleans Railroad gave Beaumont transportation links to Houston some eighty-three miles to the west and Orange, twenty-two miles to the east on the Louisiana border.[1]

1. Brief descriptions of Jefferson County, Beaumont, Sabine Pass, and the Texas and New

## Map 5

## Jefferson County

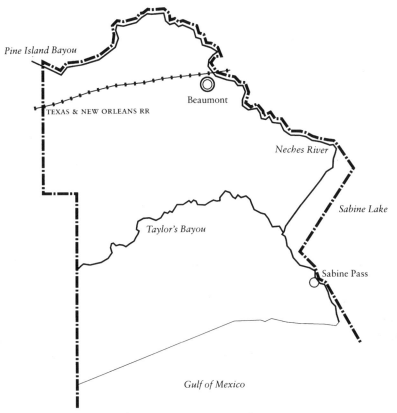

Pine Island Bayou

Beaumont

TEXAS & NEW ORLEANS RR

Neches River

Sabine Lake

Taylor's Bayou

Sabine Pass

Gulf of Mexico

Adapted, with permission, from the Jefferson County map in the *Texas Almanac* for 1996–1997.

Because of its location and development as a commercial center, Jefferson County had a notably diverse population. A majority of its 1,995 residents in 1860 were natives of the South, but, unlike the southern-born in most parts of Texas, many in Jefferson were families of French descent who had moved from southwestern Louisiana. The county also had a generous sprinkling of men, generally employed at nonagricultural occupations as merchants, boat pilots, and so on, or in skilled trades, who were native to the North or foreign nations. Finally, black slaves constituted 15.5 percent of the population.[2]

Although it did not have an economy or population typical of the Old South, Jefferson County responded to the presidential election of 1860 and the secession crisis that followed in much the same way as the plantation regions of Texas. Three-quarters (257) of the county's voters supported John C. Breckinridge, the Southern Democratic candidate, in 1860, and one-quarter (85) voted for John Bell of the Constitutional Union party. These proportions were closely comparable to the vote statewide. In the secession referendum a few months later, 94 percent of those participating voted for disunion. Support for secession appears much greater than it was statewide (76 percent), but in fact disunion received one vote fewer (256) than did Breckinridge in 1860. Apparently most of the county's Unionists (defined as the eighty-five who voted for Bell), either seeing the hopelessness of their situation or feeling intimidated by the strident secessionism of A. N. Vaughan's Beaumont *Banner,* stayed home. Only fifteen voters cast "no" ballots on February 23, 1861. However, some of Jefferson's well-known men, including Sheriff Andrew J. Tevis and George W. Tevis (sons of the founder of Beaumont), County Clerk George W. O'Brien, George F. Block, and William Lewis wanted to uphold the Union. After the firing on Fort Sumter, the county's Unionists either supported the Confederacy or avoided involvement in the conflict as completely as possible; nevertheless, they represented a core of potential leaders for the process of Reconstruction after the war.[3]

Orleans Railroad are found in Webb, Carroll, and Branda, eds., *Handbook of Texas,* I, 132, 909, II, 525, 751–52. Information on the population and slaveholding is from the Eighth Census, 1860, Schedules 1 and 2. See also Charles P. Zlatkovich, *Texas Railroads: A Record of Construction and Abandonment* (Austin, 1981), 90.

2. Eighth Census, 1860, Schedules 1 and 2.

3. Kingston, Attlesey, and Crawford, *Political History of Texas,* 73; Timmons, "Referendum in Texas on the Ordinance of Secession," 15, 18; Beaumont *Banner,* November 6, 20, 1860,

The actual fighting of the Civil War came closer to Jefferson than to most regions of Texas, but like the state as a whole, the county escaped the horrors of major battles and the rigors of military occupation. In September, 1862, three United States ships overcame the fortifications at Sabine Pass and landed a raiding party that burned the railroad depot just north of the town and destroyed the railroad bridge over Taylor's Bayou before withdrawing. One year later a major federal invasion force of twenty ships and five thousand men was turned back at Sabine Pass by Confederate artillery commanded by Lt. Dick Dowling. The United States did not attack southeast Texas for the remainder of the war.[4]

Reconstruction in Jefferson County began in July, 1865, when United States troops, the 37th Illinois Volunteers commanded by Maj. Ransom Kennicott, occupied Sabine Pass and Beaumont without any serious incident and began to parole ex-Confederates. The appointment of an interim county government by provisional governor A. J. Hamilton took several months longer, however, and gave some indication of the difficulties to follow.[5]

Jefferson's Unionists sought from the beginning to influence Governor Hamilton's appointments to offices in their county. James Armstrong, a veteran of the Texas revolution and member of the convention that wrote the first state constitution of Texas in 1845, went to Austin in August, 1865, to urge the appointment of union men. Armstrong had lived in Jefferson County during the 1840s, moved to Williamson County for the remainder of the antebellum years and the Civil War, and then returned to Beaumont. In 1867, the local Freedmen's Bureau agent would refer to him as "a man of unswerving Union principles and capable of filling any office." Armstrong was accompanied to Austin by Henry C. Pedigo, another leading southeast

February 19, 1861. Evidence on the unionism of these men is found in Andrew J. Tevis to Edmund J. Davis, November 8, 1870, Governors' Papers: EJD; Registration Book A [a list of loyalists compiled by Freedmen's Bureau agents in Texas in April, 1867], U.S. Department of War, Records of the United States Army Continental Commands, 1821–1920, Fifth Military District, District of Texas, Record Group 393, National Archives; W. T. Block, Jr., "Captain George W. O'Brien: A Torchbearer of Our Texas Civilization" (upublished paper); Block, "A History of the W. T. 'Will' Block, Sr., Family of Port Neches" (unpublished paper); and William Lewis to Andrew Jackson Hamilton, August 12, 1865, Records of the Adjutant General, Reconstruction Records, 1865–1873, Archives Division, Texas State Library, Austin.

4. Alwyn Barr, "Texas Coastal Defense, 1861–1865," *Southwestern Historical Quarterly,* LXV (1961), 12, 23–25; Ralph A. Wooster, "The Battle of Galveston," *Texas Gulf Historical and Biographical Record,* XXVIII (1992), 31.

5. Maj. F. W. Emery to Maj. Ransom Kennicott, July 11, 1865, *OR,* Vol. XLI, Pt. 2, p. 1072.

Texas Unionist from Tyler County. William Lewis, a Massachusetts-born lawyer and longtime resident of Beaumont, did not go to Austin but wrote to Hamilton, urging the appointment of "a union man died in the wool" as judge of the Fifteenth Judicial District, which included Jefferson County.[6]

The governor appointed Pedigo to the district judgeship on August 24, but did not name his choices for key positions in county government until October 12. Then, for reasons unknown, he simply appointed all the men who had won those offices in 1864 at the last elections held during the Civil War. John J. Herring resumed the office of chief justice; A. J. Tevis, that of sheriff; and Alexis Blanchet, Jr., James B. Langham, Samuel Remley, and Thomas Snow, the four county commissioners' positions. In creating county governments across the state, Hamilton often appointed a few officials to the posts that they had held during the war, but returning an entire local government to office was unusual. The choice of Sheriff A. J. Tevis is easily explained by his unimpeachable Unionist credentials, but there is no evidence that the other appointees had equally strong records. In any case, Hamilton's appointments should have been very reassuring to the majority of whites in Jefferson County. All six were southern-born, and four (Blanchet, Langham, Remley, and Tevis) had been slaveholders or were from slaveholding families. Moreover, they were the same officers elected while the county was still a part of the Confederacy.[7]

Developments in 1865 probably persuaded Jefferson County voters that Reconstruction would demand little in the way of political change, and the election, on January 8, 1866, of a delegate to the constitutional convention indicated that the majority did not intend to admit that secession had been a mistake. James Armstrong lost the election to Colonel Ashley W. Spaight, a resident of Liberty County who had commanded Spaight's battalion in the Confederate army. The vote was close in Jefferson County, fifty-six to forty-seven, but the defeat of a Unionist by a Confederate veteran, especially in Armstrong's home county, clearly demonstrated the

6. Information on Armstrong is from Webb, Carroll, and Branda, eds., *Handbook of Texas*, I, 69; Registration Book A, 70–71, RG 393, NA; and Eighth Census, 1860, Schedule 1. Information on Pedigo is from the Eighth Census, 1860, Schedule 1; and Campbell, "Scalawag District Judges," 80. Information on Lewis is from the Eighth Census, 1860, Schedule 1. The activities of the three men in August, 1865, are explained in Lewis to Andrew Jackson Hamilton, August 12, 1865, in Records of the Adjutant General, Reconstruction Records.

7. Election Registers, 1864–1865. Biographical and slaveholding data on these six men are from the Eighth Census, 1860, Schedules 1 and 2.

political atmosphere as Presidential Reconstruction developed. Once the commissioners' court and district court resumed normal business and the constitutional convention met in Austin early in 1866, Jefferson County's conservatives must have breathed a sigh of relief.[8]

Restoration of civil government was not, however, the only task of Reconstruction; there was also the matter of the former slaves and their place in society. White resistance to black freedom created the first serious problems in Jefferson County after 1865. Ironically, the end of slavery left blacks in some ways more vulnerable than before. "After freedom," a former Jefferson County slave named Valmo Thomas remembered, blacks "could be more or less abused by anybody. The old master he had to take care of them, but after they were free anybody could bother them. They didn't have no protection, you see." Captain Frank Holsinger, the first Freedmen's Bureau agent assigned to the county, bore out the truth of Thomas' assertion in one of his earliest reports from Beaumont. A white named Henry Bullock, he reported, had shot Jackson Northweather, a freedman, in Bullock's words, "just to see him kick." A lot of other whites, Holsinger said, were just as dangerous to local freedmen. By May, 1866, the situation was even more threatening, at least in the eyes of Lt. Charles C. Hardenbrook, the new bureau agent in Beaumont. He reported that, immediately upon the withdrawal of federal troops from the county, secessionists planned to burn the school for freedmen and murder him, his wife, A. J. Tevis (with whom he boarded), and the bureau schoolteacher. The agent asked to be relieved of his duties and replaced by the local Unionist, William Lewis.[9]

Citizens of Beaumont responded to Hardenbrook's fears by holding a public meeting chaired by George W. O'Brien. A resolutions committee that included County Judge John J. Herring and Unionist George W. Tevis

8. Record of Election Returns, 1860–1867, County Clerk's Office, Jefferson County Courthouse, Beaumont, Tex.; Webb, Carroll, and Branda, eds., *Handbook of Texas*, II, 648–49; Commissioners' Court Minutes, County Clerk's Office, Jefferson County Courthouse, Beaumont, Book C, 191; District Court Minutes Books, District Clerk's Office, Jefferson County Courthouse, Beaumont, Book D, 215. For the purposes of electing a delegate to the constitutional convention of 1866, Jefferson was in a district with Liberty, Chambers, and Orange Counties.

9. Rawick, ed., *American Slave: Supplement, Series 2*, IX, 3829; Frank Holsinger to William H. Sinclair, March 19, 1866, Charles C. Hardenbrook to Sinclair, May 7, 10, 1866, BRFAL, RG 105, NA. For a detailed account of the work of Holsinger and Hardenbrook in Beaumont, see Barry A. Crouch, "The Freedmen's Bureau in Beaumont," *Texas Gulf Historical and Biographical Record*, XXVIII (1992), 11–22.

drafted a statement pledging "support by all means, moral and physical" for Hardenbrook and all officials of the United States government. Thirty-three citizens signed the resolution and sent copies to the Houston *Telegraph* and the bureau agent. Hardenbrook, however, doubted the sincerity of most of the signees and remained suspicious for several months. On June 22, although he had received the support of four soldiers dispatched from Houston and reported that all was quiet in the county, he asked again to be relieved of his post.[10]

As is often the case in such disputes, it is impossible to determine who to believe. Hardenbrook probably exaggerated the threat to his safety, and some of the citizens doubtless overstated their willingness to support the bureau. However, the bureau agent's difficulties indicate that a good portion of the community would admit only that the war had been lost and the slaves freed. Acceptance of on-going federal intervention in any form, especially to aid the freedmen, was another matter. Men such as A. J. Tevis and William Lewis would cooperate with Union authorities and seek to help the freedmen, but the majority of whites in Jefferson County wanted only minimal political and social change.

On June 25, 1866, when voters across Texas went to the polls to approve the Constitution of 1866 and elect new state and local officials, Jefferson County voted overwhelmingly (143 to 3) for the Conservative Unionist James W. Throckmorton over Elisha M. Pease for governor. The state representative's seat from the district including Jefferson, Liberty, Chambers, and Orange Counties went to A. D. Kent of Beaumont over George W. O'Brien. Unfortunately, no local returns for this election are available, and we cannot know which candidate carried the county. O'Brien had served in the Confederate army, but so had Kent. O'Brien, however, had opposed secession and chaired the meeting promising support for agents of the federal government. Moreover, his stance on Reconstruction in June, 1866, although in disagreement with plans brewing in Washington for a congressional takeover, was not one of extreme opposition to the national government. He wrote a friend in Liberty on June 4:

> It is a very difficult matter for us of this country to locate ourselves at present securely upon any political platform having reference to our un-

10. Houston *Tri-Weekly Telegraph*, May 25, 1866; Hardenbrook to Sinclair, May 10, June 22, 1866, BRFAL, RG 105, NA.

certain future, but I shall endeavor to locate myself somewhere outside of the ranks of the radicals before we meet and then let you know where I stand. At present it seems that about all left us is to "hold fast to the willows" . . . and while endeavoring to stem the current of malice and oppression apparently about to engulf us, to trust in the final resurrection of *truth* and *justice*.

O'Brien, it seems, sought a moderate position between that of Radical Republicans in Congress and militant ex-Confederates in Texas. Perhaps that explained his loss of the election.[11]

Elections to key county offices on June 25 appear to have reflected concerns related to Reconstruction in only a limited way. Hamilton's appointee, John J. Herring, continued as county judge, defeating R. H. Leonard, a lawyer born in England, by a vote of ninety-two to sixty-eight. The incumbent sheriff, A. J. Tevis, was not a candidate and G. W. Payne easily defeated William Fletcher and Alex Collins for that office. Perhaps Tevis chose not to run because of unpopularity stemming from his support of the Freedmen's Bureau, but there is no evidence on the matter. Two of the incumbent county commissioners, Alexis Blanchet and James B. Langham, ran, but an entirely new court composed of Otis McGaffey, Morgan Odom, Samuel Lee, and J. D. Magby was elected. McGaffey, Odom, and Lee were antebellum residents of the county (Magby could not be identified), however, and there is no indication that the issues of Reconstruction had anything to do with this result.[12]

The new county court met for the first time in September, 1866, as did the district court under its recently elected judge, Samuel A. Willson, a former officer in Hood's Texas brigade. Lt. Hardenbrook remained in Beaumont, but his interest in the work of the Freedmen's Bureau had waned, and he would soon be reassigned. Most residents of Jefferson County probably considered Reconstruction at an end, but Congress soon would overcome President Johnson and begin the whole process again. Jefferson County would feel the impact of Congressional Reconstruction beginning in the spring of 1867 and continuing for more than two years.[13]

11. Kingston, Attlesey, and Crawford, *Political History of Texas,* 59; Election Registers, 1866; George W. O'Brien to William P. Duncan, June 4, 1866, Julia Duncan Welder Collection, Sam Houston Regional Library and Research Center, Liberty, Texas.

12. Record of Election Returns, 1860–1867; Eighth Census, 1860, Schedule 1.

13. Commissioners' Court Minutes, Book C, 195; District Court Minutes, Book D, 260;

The first development came with the so-called jury-order controversy that arose during the spring of 1867 when Gen. Charles C. Griffin, commander of the Department of Texas, issued an order requiring all jurors to take the test oath of 1862. At the May session in Beaumont, District Judge Willson accepted the claim of Deputy Sheriff Lastie Hillebrant that fewer than fifteen men in the county could meet the requirement and adjourned his court. No district court was held in the county that year, but regular business resumed in 1868 without the requirement of the test oath.[14]

The jury order affected only the courts and people who had business there, while Congress' new voter registration requirements in 1867 touched all men who had an interest in the county's political life. Registration of eligible voters in Jefferson County was handled by a board of registrars composed of William Lewis (the Massachusetts-born Unionist), Allen Pipkin (a freedman who had come to the county from South Carolina with his owner, J. F. Pipkin), and Thomas Alyen (an unidentified white). Mark Wiess, a local former Confederate soldier, served as the board's clerk. Voter registration began in the county on July 22, 1867, and closed on September 28. It is impossible to say exactly how many men the board refused to register, but clearly the number was significant. The total registration, 186, included 88 whites and 98 blacks (53 percent). Thus enough whites either refused to register or were denied registration that blacks, although only no more than 25 percent of the population, constituted a majority of the electorate in 1868. Clearly some whites attempted unsuccessfully to register because twenty-nine names, enough to create a white majority, were struck off after having been originally placed on the rolls.[15]

Ironically, some of the most loyal men in the county, such as A. J. Tevis, were disqualified by congressional requirements while former Confederates who had not held public office before the war registered if they wished. Tevis, who took an oath to uphold the Constitution when he was elected

---

Campbell, "District Judges of Texas in 1866–1867," 363; Crouch, "Freedmen's Bureau in Beaumont," 18.

14. A general discussion of the jury-order controversy is in Campbell, "District Judges of Texas in 1866–1867," 368–74. The impact in Jefferson County is in District Court Minutes, Book D, 308–18, 323–61.

15. Board of Registrars of Jefferson County to Gen. Charles C. Griffin, August 1867, OCA, RG 393, NA. William Lewis, Allen Pipkin, and J. F. Pipkin are found in the Ninth Census, 1870, Schedule 1. Weiss served in Spaight's batallion and the 21st Texas Infantry; see Index to the Compiled Service Records of Confederate Soldiers, RG 109, NA. List of Registered Voters in Texas, 1869.

sheriff in 1860, resigned in 1861 rather than support the Confederacy. However, after being elected sheriff again in 1864 (without his consent) and seeing that service in local government was preferable to being forced into the army, he qualified for the position. He held the office only eleven days before being removed by the district judge for disloyalty to the Confederacy, but, for that service, the registration board disqualified him. Years later Tevis angrily (and with less than perfect literacy) summarized the situation: "Rebel captains lieutenants and their companys have all registered and are voters but myself and other men who stood firm against the secession movement and for the union through the hole storm and suffered all manner of abuse that could be put upon us by barbarous traters could not register."[16]

Tevis gained at least some measure of satisfaction in February, 1868, by carrying Jefferson County's vote in the election of a delegate to the convention that was to write a new constitution for Texas. The vote was light—only thirty whites and fifty-two blacks participated—and he defeated James Armstrong by a margin of forty-eight to thirty. (Four voters did not support either major candidate.) Armstrong, whose unionism probably helped account for his loss to Col. A. W. Spaight in 1866, now apparently found himself too conservative for the county's newly enfranchised blacks. He did win the seat in the constitutional convention, however, thanks to support from other counties in the district, and wound up moving into the ranks of A. J. Hamilton's moderate Republicans and then returning to the Democratic party.[17]

Congressional Reconstruction also affected Jefferson County by bringing changes in the personnel of local government. Beginning in the late summer of 1867, military authorities began removing the state and local officials elected in June, 1866, as "impediments to Reconstruction" or simply for general disloyalty to the United States. When nearly all of the state's district judges were replaced in the fall of 1867, Samuel A. Willson of the Fifteenth Judicial District resigned rather than face removal. Henry C. Pedigo from Tyler County, who had occupied the Fifteenth district bench as Governor Hamilton's appointee in 1865–1866, replaced Willson. Jefferson County's officials, however, unlike many of those elected on June 25, 1866, in other counties across Texas, remained in office until the spring of 1869.

16. A. J. Tevis to E. J. Davis, November 8, 1870, Governors' Papers: EJD.
17. Election Returns, 1866; Webb, Carroll, and Branda, eds., *Handbook of Texas,* I, 69.

Local Unionists made few complaints, and military authorities, it seems, did not find the conduct of the government led by County Judge John J. Herring unacceptable. Then in April, 1869, Congress required all state and county officials to swear the test oath that they had never voluntarily supported the Confederacy, and all the key officers elected in June, 1866, were replaced by military appointees.[18]

The men appointed on May 19, 1869, brought to Jefferson County the nearest approximation to a "radical" government that it experienced during Reconstruction. John H. Archer, the new county judge, was a native of England who had served as a lieutenant in the 7th United States Colored Infantry during the war and become an agent of the Freedmen's Bureau after being mustered out of the army in 1866. Assigned to Beaumont in March 1867, he served there until the bureau ceased operations in Texas at the end of December, 1868. Archer found much less to object to in the treatment of local freedmen than had his predecessors, Holsinger and Hardenbrook, and generally filled his monthly reports with the statement: "Nothing new to report." Not surprisingly, he had less trouble than previous agents and after the Bureau closed remained in the county to raise cattle. Because of his foreign birth, Archer did not fit the standard definition of a carpetbagger, but he had lived in the North before 1861 and came closer to carpetbagger status than any other official in Jefferson County during Reconstruction.[19]

The first military appointee as sheriff, Valery A. Blanchet, could not qualify for the position, probably because he had voluntarily served in the Confederate army. He was replaced in July, 1869, by Randolph W. Tevis, son of George W. Tevis and nephew of A. J. Tevis. Although belonging to a Unionist family, the new sheriff was a native Texan and longtime resident of the county. Of the four new county commissioners, only William Ratcliffe from Tennessee was southern-born. George F. Block came from Prussia, W. J. Barton was from England, and S. K. Burch was a native of New York. However, all four lived in Jefferson County before 1865 and cannot be classed as carpetbaggers. These six military appointees ran Jefferson County's government for approximately one year (spring, 1869, to spring, 1870). From every indication, the business of the district court and commissioners' court proceeded without any serious difficulties during that time.

18. Campbell, "District Judges of Texas in 1866–1867," 375; Election Registers, 1867, 1869; *Congressional Globe*, 40th Cong., 3rd Sess., Pt. 3, Appendix, 327.
19. Ninth Census, 1870, Schedule 1; Richter, *Overreached on All Sides*, 257–58.

Undoubtedly many residents disapproved of government by appointed officials, but the individuals who actually served appear to have given reasonable satisfaction.[20]

Congressional Reconstruction came to an end in Texas following the election held November 30–December 3, 1869, in which voters approved the new constitution completed earlier that year and elected state and local officials under its terms. This election posed a key test of strength for the fledgling Republican party. Unless it could capitalize on the momentum provided by congressional policies and military appointments, and build a coalition of white Unionists and black freedmen to control the state government and localities such as Jefferson County from the outset, it faced a very difficult future.[21]

Voter registration opened again across the state for ten days in November, 1869. The registrars in Jefferson County—George W. Kidd (a white native of Tennessee), Lemuel P. Ogden (a white native of Texas), and Allen Pipkin (the freedman who had held the same position in 1867)—added 91 whites and 18 blacks to the rolls, bringing their total numbers to 182 and 116 respectively. Blacks were still overrepresented among the county's voters, constituting 39 percent of the total when they were only about 26 percent of the population, but they were no longer a majority. Obviously, to give the Republicans any hope of victory, a significant number of whites had to join the freedmen in voting for the new party.[22]

On December 3, 1869, after four days of voting at a central polling place in Beaumont, the more conservative candidates carried Jefferson County in every state-level contest. A. J. Hamilton received 108 votes to E. J. Davis' 23. Wells Thompson defeated James W. Flanagan 101 to 7 in the lieutenant governor's race. James Armstrong, now back in the Democratic party, carried the county 113 to 8 over George W. Whitmore of Smith County in a contest for the United States House of Representatives, but Whitmore won the election districtwide. E. B. Pickett of Liberty, a former major in the Confederate army, defeated his opponent for a seat in the state senate, J. W.

20. Eighth Census, 1860, Schedule 1; Ninth Census, 1870, Schedule 1; Index to Compiled Service Records of Confederate Soldiers, RG 109, NA.

21. Moneyhon, *Republicanism in Reconstruction Texas,* 104–28.

22. The registrars were named in General Orders, No. 179, issued by Gen. Joseph J. Reynolds on October 8, 1869, OCA, RG 393, NA. Names of those registered at this time are also in List of Registered Voters in Texas, 1869. The percentage of blacks in the population is calculated from the Ninth Census, 1870, Schedule 1.

Thomas, 114 to 8, and W. T. Simmons of Beaumont was overwhelmingly elected to the Texas House of Representatives, getting 164 votes with no meaningful opposition.[23]

In the local elections, two countywide races brought greater voter participation than did the contests for state office. Edward C. Ogden defeated E. P. Gray 108 to 76 in the race for sheriff, and Wilbur F. Gilbert became district clerk by the slim margin of 55 votes to 52 for Jeff Chaison and 42 for Thomas H. Langham. By contrast, the elections of five justices of the peace, who would constitute the county court under the new constitution, went largely uncontested. N. B. Bendy, the candidate for justice of precinct one and ex officio presiding justice of the court, had no opponent; nor did S. K. Burch in precinct three and James Magness in precinct five. George F. Block easily defeated H. C. Smith in precinct two. Only Alex Blanchet in precinct four had significant opposition in the person of William J. Barton, one of the military appointees to the commissioners' court. Blanchet won thirteen to ten.[24]

Most of these winners of county offices, like their counterparts in the state-level contests, were conservatives. Sheriff Ogden, District Clerk Gilbert, presiding Justice Bendy, and Justices Blanchet and Magness belonged (or would soon belong) to the Democratic party. On the other hand, George F. Block and S. K. Burch were Unionists who had held office as military appointees, and yet they won without opposition. Perhaps no one in their respective precincts wished to run for the offices. However, both men were Unionists rather than Republican activists and apparently had the respect of their neighbors regardless of past differences over secession. At least, the election of Block and Burch indicates that loyalists did not face total proscription in the local elections of December, 1869.[25]

Activist Republicans took no consolation in the victories of a few Unionists and insisted that conservatives had won the election illegally. Charles W. Winn, a young native of Arkansas and former U.S. Army officer who edited the Sabine Pass *Union*, claimed in April, 1870, that Sheriff Ogden and others had won through "fraud and intimidation." He urged Governor

23. Election returns for 1869 are found in *Senate Miscellaneous Documents*, 41st Cong., 2nd Sess., No. 77, pp. 38–79. Information on Whitmore and Pickett is from Webb, Carroll, and Branda, eds., *Handbook of Texas*, II, 901, 375.

24. *Senate Miscellaneous Documents*, 41st Cong., 2nd Sess., No. 77, pp. 38–79.

25. For identification of these men with the Democratic party, see Beaumont *News Beacon*, August 29, 1873.

Davis to replace Ogden with A. J. Tevis; a move that would constitute a "damaging blow at the very hearts of our rebel neighbors." Winn also said that since the formation of a Union League council at Sabine Pass he had found "a considerable white element in this county friendly to our Party and cause that from fear of personal violence have long disguised their real sentiments." With the appointment of Tevis and a little more encouragement from the Union League, Winn promised, Republicans would take permanent control of Jefferson County.[26]

The truth of Winn's charges about fraud and intimidation cannot be proven or disproven. Certainly the Republican vote should have been larger in 1869, and some whites no doubt attempted to keep blacks from voting. However, the election was held under military supervision, there were no official charges of stealing votes or threatening voters, and elsewhere in the state blacks and Unionists voted in large numbers. Threats and fraud may have prevented Jefferson County's Republicans from making the best showing possible in 1869, but, as Winn's efforts during the next few years would show, the votes necessary to carry the county were not there and could not be found.[27]

During the summer of 1870, Winn and Tevis created a chapter of the Union League at Beaumont, all the while complaining bitterly about the opposition of state representative W. T. Simmons, James Armstrong, J. B. Likens (an attorney who had been a major in the Confederate army), and B. F. McDonough (a merchant from Indiana who had no record of Confederate service in a Texas unit). These men, Winn insisted, represented the Ku Klux Klan at Beaumont and tried to keep Republicans from settling in the town and to prevent the proper education of freedmen. Winn appealed regularly to James P. Newcomb, the Republican secretary of state in Austin, and George T. Ruby, the head of the Union League for Texas, and before the year ended both he and Tevis sought aid from Governor E. J. Davis. Winn asked Davis to appoint him registrar of voters for the county and to place Tevis, Edward Fink (a New York–born minister who headed the Union League council at Sabine Pass), and Bosen Godfrey (a freedman) on the board of appeal that reviewed complaints against the registrar and supervised elections. Davis complied, thus giving key positions to Republicans.[28]

26. Charles W. Winn to George T. Ruby, April 24, 1870, Newcomb Papers.

27. Moneyhon, *Republicanism in Reconstruction Texas*, 123–25.

28. Winn to Ruby, June 1, 1870, Winn to James P. Newcomb, June 10, 1870, July 28, 1870,

The governor also aided his party's cause in Jefferson County by appointing William M. Chambers of Chambers County as judge of the new First Judicial District. Chambers, a former slaveholder, secessionist, and Confederate soldier, had become a strong Republican after the war. A. J. Tevis sought even more help from Davis in late 1870 by asking the governor to retain the restrictions on the suffrage that had existed from 1867 to 1869. "My opinion," Tevis wrote, "is that the enemy cant register under the reconstruction law untill they receive pardon from the Congress. Capt. C. Winn is of the same opinion and if this plan is carried out the republican party is sure to gain the coming elections. Let the registration be done over again in these eastern countys and we have got them." Governor Davis could not help in this case, however, because restrictions on the suffrage under the Congressional Reconstruction acts did not apply once Texas' new constitution went into effect in 1870.[29]

Throughout 1870, Jefferson County Republicans insisted that they represented at least half the vote of the county and would have great success in future elections. As the year ended, Thomas J. Russell, a recent convert to the party, wrote Governor Davis: "A good Republican Congressman will be elected here at the next election by an overwhelming majority. The greater part of the people wish to bury old dead issues so deep that there can be no resurrection for the issues nor for the supporters of them. An active campaign well carried on will do the work effectively. Such men as Armstrong, Likens, and McDonough will sink into oblivion."[30]

Such predictions amounted to wishful thinking, however, once the county's conservatives organized and publicized their cause. The *Neches Valley News* began publication in Beaumont during 1870, calling itself "The White Man's Organ for the First Judicial District." The editor, W. L. Smylie, urged all Democrats to subscribe and promised to provide free copies to all Democrats who could not afford a subscription. This paper was joined by W. F. McClanahan's Sabine Pass *Beacon,* an equally strong Democratic journal. An editorial in the *Beacon* of June 10, 1871, urged

Newcomb Papers; Edward Fink to E. J. Davis, July 14, 1870, Minutes of the Union Republican Association of Jefferson County, July 12, 28, 1870, Charles W. Winn to E. J. Davis, September 15, 1870, Governors' Papers: EJD; Election Registers, 1870; Ninth Census, 1870, Schedule 1; Index to Compiled Service Records of Confederate Soldiers, RG 109, NA.

29. Campbell, "Scalawag District Judges," 80, 84–85; Tevis to Davis, November 8, 1870, Governors' Papers: EJD; Ramsdell, *Reconstruction in Texas,* 254–55.

30. Thomas J. Russell to E. J. Davis, December 30, 1870, Governors' Papers: EJD.

Democrats to organize and described the fight against their Republican foes as "justice and right arrayed against treachery and villiany . . . loyalty and patriotism against corruption and plunder." Editor McClanahan, a twenty-seven-year-old Mississippian, made fun of a recent Republican meeting in Sabine Pass, saying that only six men attended. "We'll bet," he wrote, "that Jefferson County can boast the loudest talking and yet the most insignificant and sickly Radical concern that can be found elsewhere in Texas."[31]

The contest to elect a United States representative from the First District during the fall of 1871 proved that, although both Republicans and Democrats exaggerated their strength, the latter were much stronger. George W. Whitmore, the Republican incumbent, ran against William S. Herndon, a former Confederate officer and conservative Democrat. Whitmore, who was from Tyler, personally campaigned in Jefferson County, speaking jointly with Herndon at a barbecue sponsored by Democrats in Beaumont on September 5. All the efforts of the incumbent and his local supporters failed, however, as Herndon carried the county by a vote of 200 to 101 and won the seat in Congress. The Republican candidate ran far better (34 percent of the vote) than in 1869 (6 percent), but the defeat was still overwhelming.[32]

The presidential election of 1872 presented additional problems for Jefferson County Republicans because President U. S. Grant was opposed by reform-minded members of his party calling themselves Liberal Republicans. Horace Greeley, the Liberal Republican candidate, received the endorsement of the Democratic party as well. Jefferson County's Democrats, who had been represented by George W. O'Brien at the party's national convention, agreed with this strategy. Supporting the Liberal Republicans nationally and Democratic candidates in state elections, they enjoyed watching local Republicans fight over Grant and Greeley. A good many voters apparently reacted by staying home, but the election once more indicated the strength of conservatives in Jefferson County. Greeley defeated Grant by 127 to 64 (66 to 34 percent of the vote), and James Armstrong, running as a Democrat, won a seat in the state legislature. Soon after taking

31. *Neches Valley News* (Beaumont), January 7, 1871; Sabine Pass *Beacon,* June 10, 1871; Ninth Census, 1870, Schedule 1.

32. Galveston *Tri-Weekly News,* September 8, 1871; Moneyhon, *Republicanism in Reconstruction Texas,* 212; Campbell, "George W. Whitmore," 23–24.

his seat in Austin in 1873, Armstrong introduced a resolution calling for the impeachment of District Judge William M. Chambers. Conservatives in Jefferson County were delighted, but after the case dragged on for a year, the judge won acquittal on all charges.[33]

In the aftermath of the election of 1872, to compound the difficulties of local Republicans, some of their leaders became embroiled in factional disputes. Dr. R. S. Morgan, who had arrived in Sabine Pass early in 1872 and, with Charles W. Winn's support, been appointed medical officer at the port, informed Secretary of State J. P. Newcomb that Winn had endorsed Greeley. In response, Winn's wife claimed that Morgan had made speeches for Greeley. Her husband, she told Newcomb, had always been a loyal Republican, but Morgan, as soon as he had an appointment, had turned against the party. He was a vile scoundrel, she said, who had accused her of trying to kill her child and had attacked her with a hatchet in her own yard. Winn, with Tevis, represented activist Republicanism in the county, and this wild dispute with Morgan could hardly have helped the party.[34]

During 1873 the *Neches Valley News* and Sabine Pass *Beacon* combined to create the Beaumont *News-Beacon* under the editorship of W. F. McClanahan, giving the Democrats a unified voice in the county. The party held a county convention in August, 1873, to choose delegates to district and state meetings to be held preparatory to the state and local elections on December 2. McClanahan, O'Brien, and others were prominently involved. The convention did not, however, make nominations for local offices, and the only evidence available on campaign activities in Jefferson County during the fall of 1873 is a brief comment in the Galveston *Tri-Weekly News* in September that Democrats there were preparing for the election "with every assurance of success."[35]

The election marked another clear victory for conservatives in state-level races as the Democratic candidate for governor, Richard Coke, received 277 votes to 71 (20 percent) for E. J. Davis. Returns for local races are unavailable, but what is known about the political records of the winners suggests

33. *Neches Valley News*, July 27, October 26, 1872; Galveston *Daily News*, November 14, 1872; Beaumont *News Beacon*, May 10, 31, 1873; Campbell, "Scalawag District Judges," 87.

34. R. S. Morgan to James P. Newcomb, May 13, November 18, 1872, S. E. Winn to Newcomb, May 29, 1873, Newcomb Papers.

35. Beaumont *News-Beacon*, January 11, June 7, August 29, 1873; Galveston *Tri-Weekly News*, September 8, 1873.

that those contests were not highly partisan. Alex Blanchet continued as justice of precinct four, and John J. Herring became the presiding justice. Both men had been elected to county offices in 1864 and been appointed by A. J. Hamilton in 1865. James D. Bullock, the new sheriff, and Ralph West, justice of precinct five, both native to the South, had lived in the county before 1865. However, two new justices, Peter D. Stockholm and Samuel Harper, were northern-born, and Stockholm was known as a Unionist. Thus, as in 1869, no Republican activists won office, but extreme partisanship was not the rule either.[36]

The "Redeemer" constitutional convention of 1875 did not have a delegate from Jefferson County, but the three men elected from its senatorial district were all Democrats—E. B. Pickett of Liberty County, Lipscomb Norvell of Jasper County, and W. W. Whitehead of Tyler County. When Texas' voters went to the polls on February 15, 1876, to approve the new constitution and elect state and local officers, Jefferson County voted overwhelmingly for the constitution (264 to 94) and for Coke against William M. Chambers (291 to 102). Chambers received 26 percent of the total, compared with Davis' 20 percent in 1873, probably because he was from neighboring Chambers County. The race for district judge proved interesting in that Jefferson County voted overwhelmingly for J. M. Crosson against the Unionist/Republican Henry C. Pedigo (285 to 94), but the latter gained enough votes in other counties in the district to win the position.[37]

The results of county elections in 1876 suggest that the issues of Reconstruction, which were never critically divisive at that level, had largely passed. W. A. Cushman, a native of Massachusetts who appeared on the county's tax rolls first in 1865, became county judge (that office having been restored by the new constitution). By contrast, the sheriff was Thomas H. Langham, a Texas-born Democrat whose family had owned slaves. Simeon Broussard, the son of a slaveholding family from Louisiana and former Confederate, won a seat on the commissioners' court along with George F. Block (Unionist), Benjamin Granger (a carpenter from New York residing in the county by 1860), and C. C. Caswell (a merchant from Georgia who

36. Election Returns, 1873; Election Registers, 1873; Eighth Census, 1860, Schedule 1; Ninth Census, 1870, Schedule 1.

37. Galveston *Daily News,* August 7, 1875; Ninth Census, 1870, Schedule 1; Election Returns, 1876; Election Registers, 1876.

arrived after the war and worked with the Republican party during the early 1870s).[38]

Jefferson County thus emerged from Reconstruction never having had a "radical" government controlled by carpetbaggers and freedmen. Indeed, during the entire period from 1865 to 1876, officials appointed by the military rather than elected by the voters controlled the county for only one year (spring, 1869, to spring, 1870), and most of the appointees were long-time residents of the county. Beginning in 1869, with the first elections under the "radical" constitution, Jefferson County's voters usually elected conservatives to county offices. Several well-known Unionists also won positions, but activist Republicans, with the possible exception of C. C. Caswell in 1876, were not elected. Overall, extreme partisanship did not dominate the politics of local government.

The county enjoyed moderate economic expansion between 1865 and 1876, and local taxes remained relatively low. Tax rolls show an increase in the total assessed value of taxable property from $512,680 to $691,432 during the period, a gain of 35 percent. The county tax rate reached its Reconstruction-era peak in 1871 at 55 cents per $100 evaluation (plus a 50-cent poll tax on all adult males). This was a tremendous increase over antebellum and immediate postwar rates, which usually stood at 12.5 cents on $100, but it was far lower than rates in many other counties. For example, the 1871 rate in Colorado County was $1.125 per $100 and $1 per $100 in Dallas, McLennan, and Nueces Counties. Reasons for higher taxes in these other counties varied; nevertheless, Jefferson County suffered relatively little from increased tax rates. The local economic elite, defined as families that comprised the richest 5 percent of taxpayers in 1865, had considerable success in maintaining that position as late as 1880. Of the fourteen families that made up the elite immediately after the war, six (42 percent) remained in that class fifteen years later.[39]

Race relations in the county suffered from incidents of violence by whites against freedmen, especially in the years immediately after emancipation, but there were no riots or major outbreaks of racial violence. Unlike the case in some counties, the proportion of blacks in the population of Jeffer-

38. Election Registers, 1876; Eighth Census, 1860, Schedules 1 and 2; Ninth Census, 1870, Schedule 1.

39. Real and Personal Property Tax Rolls, Jefferson, Colorado, Dallas, McLennan, and Nueces Counties, 1860–1880.

son increased during Reconstruction, rising from 15.5 percent in 1860 (309), to 26.1 percent in 1870 (498), and 34.4 percent by 1880 (1,199). Almost certainly the influx of freedmen resulted from economic opportunity in Beaumont, especially in the lumber industry. Of the county's 202 black households in 1880, 72 percent were in town. A majority of the heads of those households worked in sawmills or as day laborers, or, in the case of women, as cooks and laundresses. Wage-paying occupations such as those apparently held attractions for men and women seeking to escape reliance on a cotton crop produced through tenant farming.[40]

Jefferson County's freedmen, in spite of prejudice and some incidents of violence, made significant political, social, and economic gains during Reconstruction. Blacks gained the right to vote in 1867. No freedmen were elected to office, but Allen Pipkin served on the board of registrars in 1867 and 1869, Bosen Godfrey on the county board of appeal in 1870–1872, and Woodson Pipkin on the same board in 1872–1874. In 1874–1875, the county court chose Jackson Flowers and Bill Martin to serve on the county's grand jury. The social lives of freedmen centered on nuclear families as more than three-fourths of all black households in 1880 were occupied by a man, his wife, and their children. Of those households having children aged six to sixteen, 59 percent reported at least one child attending school within the previous year. As noted above, most of the county's blacks lived in town and worked as laborers, sawmill hands, shinglemakers, cooks, and laundresses. There were also three teachers, three ministers, and six skilled craftsmen such as carpenters. Only fourteen black household heads reported working farm acreage in 1880, but nine of those owned small farms. (One rented for cash; four, for shares.) The landowners all had horses, cows, and hogs and grew corn and sweet potatoes, and even those who farmed land belonging to others owned livestock.[41]

Thus Reconstruction did not revolutionize Jefferson County, but it brought meaningful change. Local government never came under radical control or adopted policies likely to bring drastic change in any way. Republicans gained some appointed positions, but generally found their aspirations frustrated. Conservative Democrats generally remained as com-

40. U.S. Bureau of the Census, *Statistics of the Population of the United States (1880)*, 410; Tenth Census, 1880, Schedule 1.

41. Election Registers, 1867–1874; Commissioners' Court Minutes, Book C, 371, 406; Tenth Census, 1880, Schedules 1 and 2.

pletely in control as before the war and felt no strong need to proscribe Unonists. On the other hand, whites had to accept the freedom of blacks and, at least temporarily, extensive interference by the national government in local affairs. This alone doubtless seemed radical to most whites and called forth strong opposition to Reconstruction and its supporters, particularly in state-level elections. Blacks found little except freedom at first, but the congressional takeover in 1867 provided opportunities that they eagerly embraced. Rights such as the vote and jury service would eventually be taken away, but at least one generation of blacks enjoyed them. The experience remained an example and a promise for the future.

# 6

## MCLENNAN COUNTY

Although settled for less than twenty years, McLennan County in 1860 stood ready to enter the Cotton Kingdom of the Old South. The United States census of that year, the first taken in the county, reported that its rich prairie soils had produced 2,329 bales of cotton in 1859. Ten years later, in spite of the Civil War, the crop would amount to 8,829 bales (a 279 percent increase), and in 1879 production would reach 12,777 bales. Cotton planters faced difficulties with transportation because the Brazos River, which ran through the center of the county, could not be navigated that far north by steamboats; but the river offered at least a seasonal means of floating crops to market. Moreover, rail transportation in the form of the Waco and Northwestern Railroad would link the county's main town to the Houston and Texas Central Railroad at Bremond by 1872. Thus, for the people of McLennan County on the eve of the Civil War, cotton would soon be king.[1]

McLennan's population in 1860 reflected its rapid development as part

1. Brief descriptions of McLennan County and Waco are found in Webb, Carroll, and Branda, eds., *Handbook of Texas*, II, 121, 847. Cotton production statistics are from U.S. Bureau of the Census, *Agriculture of the United States in 1860*, 145; U.S. Bureau of the Census, *Statistics of the Wealth and Industry of the United States (1870)*, 256; U.S. Bureau of the Census, *Report on the Productions of Agriculture (1880)*, 243. Information on transportation is in Pamela Ashworth Puryear and Nath Winfield, Jr., *Sandbars and Sternwheelers: Steam Navigation on the Brazos* (College Station, Tex., 1976), 16; Zlatkovich, *Texas Railroads*, 74, 94; and *Handbook of Texas*, II, 848.

# Map 6

## McLennan County

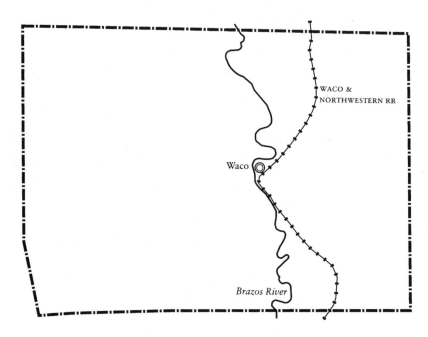

WACO &
NORTHWESTERN RR

Waco

Brazos River

Adapted, with permission, from the McLennan County map in the *Texas Almanac* for 1996–1997.

of the cotton-planting, slaveholding Old South. The county had 3,802 whites, 2,395 slaves, and 9 free blacks. There were 270 slaveholders, including twenty-seven who reported holdings of twenty or more bondsmen and six who owned at least fifty slaves. Slaveholders headed 41 percent of all households, and slaves were nearly 39 percent of the total population. By contrast, across Texas as a whole fewer than 30 percent of all households were headed by slaveowners, and bondsmen totaled only about 30 percent of the population. Antebellum McLennan County, although barely removed from the frontier, relied heavily on the South's peculiar institution, and the largely southern-born white population anticipated a bright future—so long as cotton prices remained strong and slavery undisturbed.[2]

During the election of 1860 and the secession crisis that followed, McLennan County's voters reacted as would be expected. They supported the Southern Democrat John C. Breckinridge over the Constitutional Unionist John Bell by a vote of 524 to 202 and favored secession by 586 to 191. These election results, however, regardless of the overwhelmingly prosouthern result, also indicate a relatively strong core of Unionist sentiment in the county. Nearly one-quarter of those who voted in McLennan on February 23, 1861, opposed secession, whereas some neighboring counties including Limestone (525–9) and Hill (376–63) cast far smaller proportions of Unionist votes. Moreover, unlike the case in many counties where Unionists apparently voted for Bell in 1860 but stayed home rather than vote against disunion in 1861, the antisecession total in the February 23 referendum in McLennan almost matched that for Bell in the election of 1860. Unionists in McLennan County appear to have had the numbers and strength to maintain the courage of their convictions.[3]

Located well into the interior of Texas, McLennan County escaped any threat of invasion during the Civil War and therefore avoided having to play host to defending Confederate armies as well. It was, however, heavily involved in the war effort. Camp Bosque, established in 1861 by Col. William H. Parsons, became a training center for Confederate soldiers. Waco served as a center for collecting cloth and clothing for the army, and the

2. U.S. Bureau of the Census, *Population of the United States in 1860*, 485; U.S. Bureau of the Census, *Agriculture of the United States in 1860*, 241; Eighth Census, 1860, Schedules 1 and 2; Campbell, *Empire for Slavery*, 2.

3. Kingston, Attlesey, and Crawford, *Political History of Texas*, 74; Timmons, "Referendum in Texas on the Ordinance of Secession," 15.

Waco Manufacturing Company, established in 1863, produced cotton and woolen fabrics for the same purpose. Nearly one thousand of McLennan County's men entered military service, and some emerged as outstanding leaders. Lawrence Sullivan "Sul" Ross rose to the rank of brigadier general and commanded Ross's Texas brigade from late 1863 into 1865. The Harrison brothers, James E. and Thomas, both attained the rank of brigadier general as did Hiram B. Granbury. William H. Parsons fought with Parsons' brigade in the Trans-Mississippi theater and became an acting brigadier general before the end of the war. Edward J. Gurley became colonel of the 30th Texas Cavalry, and Peter F. Ross, Sul Ross's brother, attained the rank of lieutenant colonel. Richard Coke, a lawyer who represented the county in the Texas secession convention, entered the army as a private and left as a captain. Many in McLennan County would look to men such as these for leadership after the war.[4]

When Texas surrendered in June, 1865, McLennan County, like most interior areas of the state, was not occupied immediately by federal troops. For months after the end of the war, a shortage of men and poor communications limited United States troops to Texas' borders and a few major towns. Confederate soldiers and officials returning to remote and relatively unpopulated areas such as McLennan County had to seek out federal authorities in San Antonio and Houston in order to be paroled. Thus, the Reconstruction process began in Waco during the summer of 1865 without any military presence or the immediate supervision of any representative of the United States government.[5]

McLennan's Unionists quickly sought to gain the ear of provisional governor Andrew J. Hamilton, who had arrived in Texas on July 21, 1865, with the job of restoring civilian government. In an effort to influence his appointments to positions in the interim county government, they provided Hamilton with the names of loyalists, and he responded on August 21 by filling all six key offices (county judge, sheriff, and four county commissioners) with men suggested locally. The six had strong Unionist credentials, but all were southern-born, four had been slaveholders, and two had previously held minor public offices.[6] Although they did not represent the majority po-

4. Winsor, *Texas in the Confederacy*, 10, 44–46, 58; Tony E. Duty, "The Home Front—McLennan County in the Civil War," *Texana*, XII (1974), 200; Webb, Carroll, and Branda, eds., *Handbook of Texas*, I, 370, 715, 779, 780, II, 342, 506–507, III, 365, 706.

5. Richter, *Army in Texas During Reconstruction*, 15–16, 27, 55, shows the locations and movements of occupation troops during 1865 and 1866.

6. B. F. Harris to John R. Billingsley, August 10, 1865, Robert Crudup and others to A. J.

litically, these new officeholders apparently differed little culturally and socially from most residents. Hamilton's choice for interim judge in the district that included McLennan County, Richard Coke, should have proven very comforting to prosouthern whites. Certainly it was dismaying to Unionists, who immediately protested to the governor that Coke was a rabid secessionist and warmonger who would never give justice or protection to loyalists. They urged the appointment of Andrew J. Evans, a Waco lawyer who had opposed disunion, but it was too late.[7]

Local government resumed seemingly routine operation in Waco during the fall of 1865. The commissioners' court under County Judge Robert Crudup chose grand jurors for a session of the district court, assigned road work responsibilities to residents, and provided for repairs to the courthouse. Judge Coke held a session of the district court during November with a grand jury that included a few noted Unionists. Calm appeared to be the order of the day. "I am pleased to report to you," a resident of Waco wrote Governor Hamilton, "that we are getting on finely under your wise and conservative administration. There seems to be a settled determination with the people to work in good faith for the restoration of the old order of govt. with the changes brought on by our own folly." This may have been true, but clearly McLennan's voters intended to have their traditional leaders restore the "old order." At the January 8, 1866, election of a convention to revise the Texas constitution in preparation for returning to the Union, they chose Edward J. Gurley, late colonel of the 30th Texas Cavalry, as their delegate.[8]

As McLennan's whites went about what amounted to a self-reconstruction in 1865, the county's blacks faced the adjustment from slavery to freedom. At first, a freedman named Aaron Ray remembered, they "naturally went wild. They shouted, danced, sang, and was more than happy. They just was drunk with the joy." Some left, never to return, "but most of the

Hamilton [fall, 1865?], Unsigned letter to A. J. Hamilton listing loyal and disloyal men in McLennan County [fall, 1865?], Governors' Papers: AJH. The names of Hamilton's appointees (all of whom were recommended as loyalists) and their previous officeholding experience are found in the Election Registers, 1850–1865. Demographic data and information on slaveholding are from the Eighth Census, 1860, Schedules 1 and 2.

7. Coke's nomination is in the Election Registers, 1865. The protest is Thomas Ford and others to A. J. Hamilton, August 26, 1865, Governors' Papers: AJH.

8. Commissioners' Court Minutes, County Clerk's Office, McLennan County Courthouse, Waco, Book 2, pp. 348–56; District Court Minutes, District Clerk's Office, McLennan County Courthouse, Waco, Book D, 266; S. M. Jenkins to A. J. Hamilton, October 18, 1865, Governors' Papers: AJH; Webb, Carroll, and Branda, eds., Handbook of Texas, III, 365.

oldest ones just calmed down about the next morning and then they began to ask 'where us going to stay, and how us going to eat?' There ain't no Yankee men come to give us nothing." A majority of the freedmen had no choice except to return to farm labor on places belonging to their former masters or other planters, working primarily for wages during the first year after freedom.[9]

McLennan County's blacks, in spite of their relatively large numbers, did not gain the assistance of the Freedmen's Bureau until January, 1866, and even then only incidentally. When Lt. Eugene Smith of the 10th United States Colored Infantry found so little to do at his original assignment as sub-assistant commissioner at Indianola that he requested a transfer to Texana or Matagorda, the bureau sent him to Waco. With the lieutenant came a detachment of forty cavalrymen, the first United States troops to be stationed in the county since the end of the war. Smith's earliest impressions foreshadowed an anything-but-smooth relationship between bureau agents and the county's white population. "In regard to the inhabitants [of Waco]," he wrote, "I cannot say much in their favor." Smith did find one thing in the county that pleased him—a model plantation run by the Dunklin brothers. Freedmen there worked on a task basis and were paid one-half of their wages in specie at the end of each month and the other half at the close of the year. The agent reported that the result of this arrangement was good work and fair treatment, and he urged the workers to save their money and practice the "Yankee way of doing business." In general, however, Smith disliked his assignment and quickly left when mustered out of the service in May, 1866. Other agents would soon follow, however, and their reactions to conditions in the county would be equally negative.[10]

On June 25, 1866, McLennan County's voters went to the polls to approve the revised constitution of 1866 and elect state and local officers according to its provisions. The results indicated a determination to return traditional leaders to office and concede nothing to the Unionists. The contest for county judge in which Wallace E. Oakes defeated Robert Crudup, 474 to 202, provided an excellent example. Crudup was the incumbent, his

9. Rawick, ed., *American Slave: Supplement, Series 2*, VIII, 3256–3257. The narratives of Steve Brown (III, 491) and Harrison Cole (III, 773) indicate that slaves continued to work for their masters or planters who lived nearby.

10. Richter, *Overreached on All Sides*, 46; Eugene Smith to William H. Sinclair, March 12, May 1, 1866, BRFAL, RG 105, NA.

well-known unionism having earned him an appointment from Governor Hamilton in 1865, but Oakes had been elected county judge in 1860 and then resigned the next year to enter the Confederate army. Two of the four new county commissioners also had won the same office in 1860. All six of the key county officials elected, none of whom were Hamilton's appointees, were southern-born, and five had held slaves before the war. In the vote for district judge, Thomas Harrison, former brigadier general in the Confederate army, overwhelmed the Unionist lawyer, A. J. Evans, 470 to 163. Col. Edward J. Gurley won McLennan's seat in the house of representatives in the Eleventh Legislature, and George E. Burney, who had served in the legislature during the 1850s and the war, was elected to the state senate. In statewide races, support for the more conservative candidates was even stronger. For example, James W. Throckmorton defeated E. M. Pease in the governor's race by 639 to 85 in McLennan County.[11]

The new commissioners' court assembled in July, 1866, and Judge Harrison held a session of the district court that fall. Both were uneventful, and no doubt the majority of McLennan County's whites assumed that their self-reconstruction had been successful. Agents of the Freedmen's Bureau, however, saw conditions in the county very differently during late 1866 and early 1867.[12]

Lt. Alfred F. Manning became the sub-assistant commissioner at Waco in July, 1866. He reported in September that no freedmen or Unionists had been murdered in that district since the war and that most citizens were peaceful and quiet. However, Manning also believed that freedmen could not get justice in civil courts and that the removal of federal troops would have grievous consequences. Unionists in the area told him stories about the horrible mistreatment of blacks, and after he was joined in Waco during December by bureau agent F. B. Sturgis, who contended that freedmen in that region were not much better off than slaves, Manning decided to act.[13] In January, 1867, he arrested J. C. McCrary of McLennan County, Dr. John

11. Election Returns, 1866; Election Registers, 1860–1866; Eighth Census, 1860, Schedules 1 and 2; Webb, Carroll, and Branda, eds., *Handbook of Texas,* I, 254, III, 365. W. Y. McFarland, a native of Tennessee and former slaveholder, also ran for district judge, receiving sixty-one votes.

12. Commissioners' Court Minutes, Book 2, p. 370; District Court Minutes, Book E, 97.

13. Richter, *Overreached on All Sides,* 169–70, 180–81. Sturgis was in Waco only temporarily while on his way to an assignment at Marlin. Alfred F. Manning to Joseph B. Kiddoo, September 29, 1866, F. B. Sturgis to H. A. Ellis, December 27, 1866, BRFAL, RG 105, NA.

Bell of Bosque County, and a Dr. Irving of Milam County for being the principal offenders in the 1865 castration of a young black man accused of raping McCrary's daughter. The arrests so infuriated local residents that Manning felt it necessary to call out a company of cavalry to protect the jail against the threat of mob violence. The agent justified his actions to bureau headquarters on the grounds that civil authorities had refused to act in the matter and that justice would never be done in a court presided over by men whose "own hands are reeking with the blood of innocents." To emphasize his point, he cited the recent case of an accused murderer whom the grand jury had refused to indict in spite of the eyewitness testimony of two freedmen. "Such are the courts and such is justice in Texas," he wrote.[14]

McCrary and Bell sought and obtained writs of habeas corpus from District Judge Harrison, but Manning, saying that he had acted as an officer of the U.S. Army, refused to obey without direction from his superiors at the bureau. Lawyers for McCrary and Bell then appealed to Governor J. W. Throckmorton, claiming that Manning's action "has given great dissatisfaction and is creating the impression that no man is safe in his rights if such things can be done." Throckmorton in turn wrote to Gen. Charles C. Griffin, commander of the District of Texas, insisting that the state's laws and courts would protect freedmen from harm by whites. The governor also informed Judge Harrison in Waco that he had promised justice in the handling of all complaints. In the meantime, Manning responded to requests by McCrary's and Bell's lawyers for a statement of charges by refusing to give any information on the grounds that he was accountable only to his superior officers. The matter was settled when General Griffin, after some hesitation, agreed to turn the arrested men over to civil authorities, and Manning received an order to that effect in early February. McCrary's daughter continued to testify to the alleged assault, and nothing came of the charges against the three men.[15]

Manning became so angry and disgusted that General Griffin reassigned

14. Alfred F. Manning to Joseph B. Kiddoo, January 20, 1867, BRFAL, RG 105, NA; Richter, *Overreached on All Sides*, 170.

15. Manning to Kiddoo, January 20, 1867, Manning to Flint and Chamberlain, February 4, 1867, Manning to Joel T. Kirkman, February 14, 1867, Charles B. Pearre to James W. Throckmorton, March 6, 1867, BRFAL, RG 105, NA; Richter, *Army in Texas During Reconstruction*, 90; James W. Throckmorton to Charles C. Griffin, January 31, 1867, Throckmorton to Thomas Harrison, January 31, 1867, Governors' Papers: JWT; A. J. Evans to Charles C. Griffin, June 8, 1867, OCA, RG 393, NA.

him in February, 1867. Bureau agents who succeeded him, however, presented equally negative views of the conditions for freedmen in McLennan County. Lt. Edwin Mauck served as sub-assistant commissioner in February, followed by Capt. A. W. Evans in March. Both officers commanded units of the 6th U.S. Cavalry then stationed at Waco and complained that they could give only limited attention to bureau duties. Evans asked for help, pointing out that local whites expressed the proper attitude in words but that their actions were "frequently very different." Troops were "indispensable," he thought, to protect freedmen and their schools. Captain Evans gave special praise to the bureau school that had been set up by David F. Davis, a New Hampshire–born graduate of Dartmouth College who had arrived in Waco late in 1866, destined to become McLennan County's most important carpetbagger during Reconstruction. The fourth bureau agent assigned to Waco in less than a year, Capt. James Jay Emerson of the 20th U.S. Infantry took command of the post and the sub-assistant commissioner's duties in April. Like Evans, he thought troops essential to the protection of freedmen and immediately began to ask for cavalry or horses to mount some of the infantrymen under his command.[16]

Unionist leaders in McLennan County apparently had an equally bleak view of local conditions by early 1867 and also called for help from the federal government. Nathan Patten, a New York–born loyalist who had lived in the county for many years, complained in April that people of his sort could not get justice from District Judge Thomas Harrison. The judge, Patten said, had been a member of a vigilance committee before the war that had come to his home to hang him for unionism. "What chance do they [Unionists] stand," he asked, "with rebel judges, rebel lawyers, sheriff, & jury? No show at all." He wanted an order delaying all court actions until loyal judges could hear them.[17]

Patten's complaint typified messages from Unionists across the state that contributed heavily to a decision by General Griffin to issue an order on

16. Richter, *Overreached on All Sides*, 162–63, 170; Edwin Mauck to Joel T. Kirkman, February 23, 1867, James J. Emerson to A. H. M. Taylor, April 16, 1867, in Records of the Subordinate Field Officers of the Bureau of Freedmen, Refugees, and Abandoned Lands, Sub-assistant Commissioner, Waco, Tex., U.S. Department of War, Record Group 105, National Archives (hereafter cited as BRFAL, Waco, Tex.); A. W. Evans to Joel T. Kirkman, April 5, 1867, James Jay Emerson to Joel T. Kirkman, May 31, 1867, BRFAL, RG 105, NA. Information on David F. Davis is in Davis to Edwin M. Wheelock, December 9, 1866 and Davis to Joseph Welch, November 3, 1868, BRFAL-Education, RG 105, NA.

17. Nathan Patten to G. A. Forsythe, April 13, 1867, OCA, RG 393, NA.

April 27, 1867, requiring all jurors to swear the test oath. Judge Harrison's reaction to this jury order, although unsatisfactory to Patten (nothing short of his resignation or removal would satisfy Patten), was unusual among the men who occupied district court benches. Whereas some judges closed their courts and others insisted on finding white loyalists who could swear the oath, Harrison, although failing to empanel a grand jury, put freedmen on McLennan County petit juries and tried a number of cases. One of the two trial juries empaneled on May 30, 1867, consisted of three whites and nine blacks. It included Shepherd Mullins and Stephen Cobb, who became the most politically active blacks in the county during the next few years.[18]

Judge Harrison's use of black jurors probably infuriated most whites. Even a local Unionist who claimed to be able to take the test oath said that he would not if it meant sitting on juries with blacks. On the other hand, because he had empaneled only petit juries and failed to find enough men for a grand jury, Harrison remained open to the charge that he and the commissioners' court (which provided lists of prospective jurors) had conspired to exclude Union men from the justice system. A. J. Evans, Nathan Patten, and others insisted in a June 8 letter that this was the case. The judge claimed that he had been motivated only by an "earnest desire and constant care to do justice to all men," but his failure to empanel a grand jury called that into question. At least, Harrison's determination to try pending cases allowed McLennan County freedmen to participate in the justice system well before that opportunity became generally available across the state.[19]

Through the summer and into the fall of 1867, the bureau agent, James J. Emerson, and other representatives of the government continued to paint a grim picture of local conditions. "Nothing but troops can prevent abuse of freedmen," Emerson wrote in July. At the end of August the agent reported that a white man named H. Evans had threatened to kill Ben Spait, a black, and had struck a freedwoman named Maria with a pistol. For the first offense Evans was put under a $1,500 peace bond; for the second, fined fifteen dollars. There is no justice for blacks or Union men, Emerson wrote, "owing to the class of men now sitting as Judges, Justices of the Peace, etc."

18. District Court Minutes, Book E, 107–109, 171–72. The jury-order controversy is detailed in Campbell, "District Judges of Texas in 1866–1867," 368–73.

19. J. B. Johnson to Charles C. Griffin, May 29, 1867, A. J. Evans and others to Charles C. Griffin, June 8, 1867, Thomas Harrison to James J. Emerson, August 13, 1867, OCA, RG 393, NA. Although he used blacks on petit juries, Harrison was apparently unwilling to allow them to serve on the grand jury.

Byrd W. Gray, an Alabama-born Unionist who carried out special inspections for General Griffin, reported from Waco in August that Judge Harrison and all the local officials should be removed. With the help of local Unionists, he put together a list of proposed replacements that included A. J. Evans as district judge and Robert Crudup as county judge. These men, Gray wrote in August, "have the moral firmness & courage to stem the swift current of opposition."[20]

These complaints and requests coincided with the takeover of Reconstruction by Congress during the spring and summer of 1867, giving federal agents and Unionists reason to believe that as the military directed the writing and implementation of a new state constitution conditions would indeed change. The registration of voters, black as well as white, under rules established by Congress began in Waco on July 10. Nathan Patten served as the supervisor of registrars for the district, and George B. Dutton, a thirty-eight-year-old native of New Hampshire who had arrived in Texas during the 1850s, headed the board of registrars for McLennan County. Registration ended on August 30 and then reopened for one week in September and another at the end of January, 1868. By that date, total registration came to 1,880 voters, 1,003 blacks and 877 whites. Blacks constituted 53 percent of the registered voters, although they were decreasing as a proportion of the county's population and would constitute only 34 percent of the total in 1870. The exact extent of white disfranchisement cannot be determined, but clearly a significant number either refused to register or were rejected when they tried. The black majority coupled with McLennan's approximately two hundred white loyalists assured a Unionist/Republican victory in the February, 1868, election of delegates to the constitutional convention.[21]

Congressional Reconstruction, while creating a black majority of the electorate, also gave Unionists interim control of the McLennan County government. Responding to complaints such as those made by B. W. Gray and McLennan's Unionists about the attitudes and conduct of the men

20. James J. Emerson to Joel T. Kirkman, July 1, 1867, Emerson to Kirkman, monthly report for August, 1867, B. W. Gray to Joel T. Kirkman, August 18, 19, 1867, BRFAL, RG 105, NA; Gray to Kirkman, August 19, 1867, Governors' Papers: EMP.

21. Report by Nathan Patten, Supervisor of Registrars, July 22, 1867, OCA, RG 393, NA; List of Registered Voters in Texas, 1869. Dutton is identified in the Eighth Census, 1860, Schedule 1. McLennan County in 1870 had 13,500 people—8,861 whites, 4,627 blacks, and 12 Indians. U.S. Bureau of the Census, *Statistics of the Population of the United States (1870)*, 64–67.

elected during Presidential Reconstruction, Gen. Joseph J. Reynolds issued orders on November 1 removing all six key local officials. Robert Crudup, A. J. Hamilton's provisional appointee as county judge in 1865 and unsuccessful candidate for that position in 1866, replaced Wallace E. Oakes, the man who had defeated him the previous year. N. A. McPhaul, a North Carolina–born Unionist, replaced John W. Hill as sheriff. The four new county commissioners represented a striking variety of backgrounds, especially for McLennan County in 1867. Lewis Moore's Unionist credentials had won him an appointment from A. J. Hamilton in 1865, but he was a native of Arkansas and former slaveholder. William Warwick, born in New Jersey, had lived in the county before the war as a small nonslaveholding farmer. The other two commissioners, Shepherd Mullins and Stephen Cobb, were among the very few blacks to hold that office anywhere in Texas. Mullins had come to Texas from Alabama as a slave and prospered quickly as a freedman. By 1867 he reported property including two lots in Waco and livestock valued at $1,174. Perhaps his economic status explains District Judge Harrison's willingness to have him serve on a jury that year. Stephen Cobb, a native of Missouri, was twenty-seven at the time of his appointment. He owned only eighty-eight dollars' worth of livestock in 1867, but his occupation as a minister may have given him the status necessary for service on the commissioners' court. The appointments of Mullins and Cobb were a recognition of black leadership virtually unknown in Texas at the time; however, both men had been recommended by Gray and local Unionists. There is no evidence of local white reaction, but Mullins and Cobb served without incident.[22]

General Reynolds completed the replacement of officials with key roles in local government on November 18 by giving District Judge Thomas Harrison's place on the bench to A. J. Evans. Evans, a South Carolina–born lawyer who settled in Waco in 1852, served in the Texas House of Representatives during the Seventh Legislature. He played an active role in the Constitutional Union party, but like many other Texas Unionists, served in the Confederate army once secession became a reality. After the war, his unionism reasserted itself, and he joined Nathan Patten as one of McLennan

22. These McLennan County removals and appointments are in Election Registers, 1867. Biographical information is from the Eighth Census, 1860, Schedule 1, and Ninth Census, 1870, Schedule 1. The taxpaying status of Mullins and Cobb is from Real and Personal Property Tax Rolls, McLennan County, 1867.

County's most vocal supporters of the national government. Evans had been the choice of local Unionists for district judge at the onset of Reconstruction in 1865, and finally in late 1867 he occupied the bench.[23]

Judge Evans held a district court session in Waco from November 25, 1867, to January 9, 1868, and dispensed justice apparently without incident. The commissioners' court, with Mullins and Cobb present, met in November and again in January. At the latter session, the court chose a panel of grand jurors for the spring, 1868, district court session that included two blacks, Jacob and George Moore.[24]

From February 10 through February 14, 1868, McLennan and two neighboring counties, Falls and Bell, elected three delegates to the constitutional convention. Nearly 98 percent (977) of McLennan's newly enfranchised blacks participated, voting unanimously for the convention and for A. J. Evans, Nathan Patten, and William E. Oakes as delegates. Whites cast 131 votes for the convention and provided nearly the same number of votes for the three Republican candidates. Evans and Patten were well known in McLennan as activist Unionists. Oakes, a resident of Falls County, had left home during the war and become a captain in the 2nd Texas Cavalry (U.S.A). He served on the Rio Grande and was mustered out in November, 1865. Only eighty-nine whites bothered to vote against the convention, and conservatives provided no serious opposition to Evans, Patten, and Oakes.[25]

Unionists maintained firm control of McLennan County during 1868 and 1869 as military rule of the state continued and the convention labored to write a new constitution. When William E. Oakes died on August 24, 1868, Shepherd Mullins took his place as a delegate, becoming one of only twelve blacks to serve in the convention. There were several changes in the key personnel of local government, but in all cases loyalists filled the positions. For example, Peter McClelland, a fifty-eight-year-old Virginia native who became a county commissioner in January, 1868, could swear the test

23. Election Registers, 1867; *Biographical Encyclopedia of Texas*, 42–43; *A Memorial and Biographical History of McLennan, Falls, Bell, and Coryell Counties, Texas* (Chicago, 1893), 118; Baggett, "Rise and Fall of the Texas Radicals," 15.

24. District Court Minutes, Book E, 178–341; Commissioners' Court Minutes, Book A, 98–99, 105; Ninth Census, 1870, Schedule 1.

25. Election Returns, 1868; Election Registers, 1868. Information on William E. Oakes (who must not be confused with Wallace E. Oakes, the county judge elected in 1860 and again in 1866) is from his obituary in the *Daily Austin Republican*, August 25, 1868.

oath. Revision of voter registration lists in October and November, 1869, in preparation for the referendum on the new constitution and election of officials was handled by McClelland, George A. O'Brien, and William Hay. O'Brien, a recently arrived native of Michigan, and Hay, a fifty-two-year-old black minister, also could swear the test oath.[26]

Control of local government, however, did not mean that everything went smoothly for Unionists and their black allies in McLennan County during 1868–1869. Instead, freedmen faced a level of violence virtually unparalleled in any other Texas locality, and both county officials and Freedmen's Bureau agents found themselves outmatched in attempting to respond. Waco had always been a difficult assignment at best for bureau sub-assistant commissioners, but conditions apparently worsened during the tenure of D. F. Stiles from December, 1867, to March, 1868. Most whites are hostile, Stiles reported in February, 1868, and "continually threatening to kill" blacks. Civil officers do what they can, he said, but they cannot get a local jury to convict those guilty of crimes against freedmen and Unionists.[27]

In March, Stiles was replaced by Charles Haughn, formerly an officer in the 51st United States Colored Infantry, who seems to have arrived ready to do combat with local whites. One of his earliest letters asked bureau officials if he could demand the payment of wages to freedmen for work performed since the issuance of the Emancipation Proclamation on January 1, 1863, or only for the time since actual freedom in 1865. Two weeks later he sought special authority to stop planters from driving tenants off their places without honoring their contracts. "When you think I'm getting too fast or too impertinent," he wrote, "please tell me." If Haughn feared that bureau officials might think him "too fast," there should have been no doubt as to the relationship that he would have with the white majority in McLennan County.[28]

26. *Daily Austin Republican,* August 25, 1868; Election Registers, 1868. The registrars are named in Joseph J. Reynolds, General Orders, No. 179, October 8, 1869, OCA, RG 393, NA. Identification of these men is from the Ninth Census, 1870, Schedule 1.

27. Richter, *Overreached on All Sides,* 272; D. F. Stiles to J. P. Richardson, February 3, 1868, BRFAL, RG 105, NA.

28. Richter, *Overreached on All Sides,* 272–73; Charles Haughn to J. P. Richardson, March 13, 27, 1868, BRFAL, RG 105, NA.

At the end of March, less than a month after Haughn's arrival, all federal troops were removed from Waco, and conditions rapidly worsened for the agent. He feared that more planters than ever would drive tenants off their land without compensation. "Already some planters are saying to them," he wrote on April 4, "you went & voted God damn you! Now lets see what the Yankees can do for you." At the beginning of May, he disclosed three cases of threats or attacks by whites on blacks and the murder of seven white men by "A Mob of Texans." The victims, he said, were from Illinois and were killed because of their unionism. "There is no protection by the civil authorities," Haughn reported in early June, "for anyone who believes in the Government of the United States." At the end of that month, he recounted five more cases of violence by whites against blacks, including one murder. "A freedman's life is in danger all the time," he wrote, and the civil authorities have to cater to "disloyal rabble." Virtually every communication during the spring of 1868 begged for troops.[29]

In late July, County Judge Robert Crudup confirmed Haughn's view of conditions in an appeal to District Judge Evans. "Judge Evans," he wrote in his unpunctuated style, "the U.S. Govt. set the negrs free & promised to protect them in there freedom are they doing it the negros are driven to the Democrats daily for protection what are we to do." Haughn continued to relate numerous cases of violence every month and apparently felt himself increasingly alone in attempting to deal with the problem. During September alone, he reported twenty-five threats or attacks by whites against blacks. In one case, four white men robbed a seven-year-old child of twenty-five cents and threatened to rape her. Haughn commented on the incident in one word: "Chivalry!!!" "I am obliged to fight the whole country," he informed headquarters, "Lawyers, Doctors, Philosophers & all. If I give an order to the sheriff, they must discuss the right and if there be any possibility of avoiding the order it will be avoided." Court continuances and hung juries also bedeviled his efforts to protect freedmen. Finally, in November, 1868, a company of infantry returned to Waco, but this brought no satisfaction to Haughn. His last communications before the bureau ceased

29. Charles Haughn to J. P. Richardson, April 4, 1868, Haughn to Charles A. Vernon, June 3, 1868, June 30, 1868, BRFAL, RG 105, NA. The attack by "A Mob of Texans" was reported in "Records of Criminal Offenses Committed in the State of Texas," XI–XIII, 133, BRFAL (pagination runs consecutively through the three volumes).

operation at the end of December insisted that the disposition of most local whites was "murderous" and that blacks stood no chance against violence and the lack of any protection for their rights.[30]

There is no clear-cut explanation for the prevalence of violence in Mc-Lennan County during Congressional Reconstruction. Haughn, given his obvious sympathy for the freedmen and equally obvious dislike for white Texans, may have exaggerated to some extent.[31] However, Judge Crudup confirmed his assessment, and there is striking evidence that McLennan remained notoriously violent even after Haughn moved to Nacogdoches, Texas, at the end of 1868. In January, 1869, Gen. Edward R. S. Canby, then commander of the Fifth Military District, posted two companies of infantry and one of cavalry in Waco and ordered a special tax in the county to raise funds for the "arrest, maintenance, and trial of criminals." Even then, according to a record kept by the army of violent incidents in each county during 1869 and 1870, McLennan was the most violent in Texas for the next two years. Perhaps this circumstance was explained by the rapid influx during the late 1860s of whites from other southern states. New arrivals had no personal acquaintance with freedmen already resident in the county and therefore had none of the ties or familiarity that in some cases led to sympathy and protection by whites for blacks.[32]

Regardless of the violence, McLennan's Republicans continued to control local government during the summer and fall of 1869 as the county prepared for the November 30–December 3 election to approve the new state

30. Robert Crudup to Judge A. J. Evans, July 28, 1868, Letters Received by the Office of the Adjutant General (Main Series), 1861–1870, Records of the Adjutant General's Office, 1780s–1917, Record Group 94, National Archives; "Records of Criminal Offenses," XI–XIII, 162–167, Charles Haughn to Charles A. Vernon, September 30, December 7, 31, 1868, BRFAL, RG 105, NA.

31. Haughn made every case of violence in which the assailant was unknown into an attack by whites on blacks. He reported, for example, on March 4, 1868, that Joe Pitts, a black, was killed near Waco by an unknown attacker. The race of the murderer was listed as white. "Records of Criminal Offenses," XI–XIII, 125, BRFAL, RG 105, NA.

32. General Orders, No. 4, by Gen. Edward R. S. Canby, January 16, 1869, Special Orders, No. 7, by General Canby, January 7, 1869, OCA, RG 393, NA; Richter, *Army in Texas During Reconstruction,* 152. The white population of McLennan increased 133 percent between 1860 and 1870 (from 3,802 to 8,873) while the black population increased 92 percent (from 2,404 to 4,627), with most of the whites arriving from older southern states. U.S. Bureau of the Census, *Population of the United States in 1860,* 485; U.S. Bureau of the Census, *Statistics of the Population of the United States (1870),* 64–66. Examples of whites during Reconstruction aiding blacks whom they had known before freedom are found throughout the slave narratives edited by George P. Rawick and cited elsewhere in this study.

constitution and choose officials under its terms. In preparation for the election, General Reynolds, who had resumed command of the military district, ordered that voter registration be reopened for one week in late October and ten days in late November. Whites, either new arrivals or those who had refused to register earlier, took advantage of this opportunity to such an extent that by election day total registration in McLennan County stood at 2,317, comprising 1,241 whites and 1,076 blacks. Thus by November 30, 1869, the black majority of February, 1868, was replaced by a 54 percent white majority.[33]

Clearly, to maintain control of the county, McLennan's Republicans needed another very high turnout of black voters plus the support of at least several hundred whites. This would not be easy to accomplish, especially since the split that had developed at the constitutional convention between moderate Republicans supporting A. J. Hamilton and Radicals supporting E. J. Davis came home to the local level during the summer of 1869. Nathan Patten wrote to J. P. Newcomb, editor of the San Antonio *Express* and a strong Davis supporter, that their prospects were bright in that area, provided that a good speaker could explain that the Republican party "is not a black mans party any more than a white." District Judge A. J. Evans, he complained, "has been at work industriously forming a *white party* at the same time calling himself a Republican." According to Patten, Evans, a friend of Hamilton's, had made a speech in Waco attacking Radical Republicans in general and himself and Shepherd Mullins in particular. Evans' audience, Patten said, "consisted of about 75 white disfranchised Rebs and 20 to 30 Freedmen." When the judge told the freedmen that Patten had opposed enfranchising them in the new constitution, the accused had stepped into the hall and called him an "*infamous liar.*" Thus the internal dissension that hampered Republican efforts to control Texas from the constitutional convention onward appeared very early in McLennan County.[34]

The election held November 30–December 3, 1869, drew nearly 1,500 voters to the polls and demonstrated notable strength for the Radical Republicans in McLennan County. In the race for governor, E. J. Davis defeated A. J. Hamilton 797 to 696 (53 to 47 percent), and J. W. Flanagan won the lieutenant governorship by an even wider margin, gaining 818 votes to 294 for his nearest competitor, A. H. Latimer. Judge A. J. Evans, who ran

33. List of Registered Voters in Texas, 1869.
34. Nathan Patten to James P. Newcomb, August 18, 1869, Newcomb Papers.

for the state senate as a moderate Republican, lost McLennan County to S. W. Ford, a friend of E. J. Davis, by a vote of 676 to 778, but he did well enough in the two other counties in the district, Falls and Limestone, to win the seat anyhow. Radical strength proved most impressive in the election of state representatives, three of whom were chosen at large from a district composed of McLennan, Falls, and Limestone Counties. Shepherd Mullins, whom the commander of federal troops at Waco called "a colored man of good standing and some what influential in the community," polled 772 votes in McLennan County, more than any other candidate. He and David Medlock, a resident of Limestone County who received 597 votes in McLennan, were two of only fourteen blacks elected to the Twelfth Legislature. Robert Crudup, the Unionist county judge, polled 637 votes in his home county and became the third state representative from the district.[35]

Republicans who tended to support the radical faction also won control of the most important offices in county government. Oscar H. Leland, a native of Vermont who had taught math at Baylor University since coming to Texas in 1856, became justice of the peace for precinct one and presiding officer of the county court. He had been drafted into the Confederate army, he explained to Governor Davis, but "at the close of the war I boldly avowed my political views and took my stand with the Radicals and against Andrew Johnson and his 'policy.'" He defeated three opponents with 386 votes from a total of 821 cast.[36] William H. Morris, who easily won the race for sheriff (1,426 to 22), was a native of Kentucky who had been General Reynolds' appointee to that office in September, 1868, and could swear the test oath. Of the other four men who served with Leland on the county court, only John Wood, who defeated Democrat T. L. McGee 55 to 34 in precinct three, had strong Unionist credentials. He had been named two years earlier by William Sinclair, an inspector for the Freedmen's Bureau, as one of the county's most notable loyalists. The partisan stance of S. M. Johnson (precinct five), a Virginian who arrived after the war, is not clear. S. B. Trice (precinct two) and John W. Hill (precinct four) probably tended

35. Election returns for 1869 are found in *Senate Miscellaneous Documents*, 41st Cong., 2nd Sess., No. 77, pp. 38–79. John B. Johnson to C. E. Morse, May 21, 1869, OCA, RG 393, NA; Alwyn Barr, "Black Legislators of Reconstruction Texas," *Civil War History*, XXXII (1986), 340–52.

36. *Senate Miscellaneous Documents*, 41st Cong., 2nd Sess., No. 77, pp. 38–79; Oscar H. Leland to Edmund J. Davis, May 28, 1870, Governors' Papers: EJD; *Memorial and Biographical History*, 776–77.

toward the Democrats in that Trice later sought nomination by that party and Hill had been removed from the office of sheriff by General Reynolds in 1867. In any case, relatively few voters participated in elections outside precinct one. Johnson, for example, defeated his opponent five to four, and Hill won fifty-six to forty-five.[37]

The strength of Radical Republicanism in countywide elections in 1869 is clearly demonstrated by the election of a well-known carpetbagger as district clerk. David F. Davis, the New Hampshire native who came to Waco as a Freedmen's Bureau teacher in 1866, won the office over two competitors with 666 votes from a total of 1,442. Davis had served as president of the Radical Republican state convention in 1868 and become a staunch supporter of Edmund J. Davis. His letters to the newly elected governor expressed a curious belief in a sort of mystical power behind the Radical cause. "All desire," he wrote Davis in January, 1870, "that you may not fall like Hamilton & all other men who have dared to forsake the *vital force* of the times. . . . Men are no more than feathers in the wind unless they truthfully represent it. It was the force which caused your constituency to swim rivers upon rafts . . . to vote for you." Three years in Waco had taught Davis that the majority of southern whites could not be moved by any power. But, he told the governor, if you "hold fast to the *vital force* . . . the colored vote & the living elements among the whites & the accessions from abroad will permanently bury the old ideas." In mid-January, when Robert Crudup resigned as county judge preparatory to taking his seat in the legislature, Davis sought and received appointment to the position. He then attempted to have other local officials replaced, practicing in the process a sort of multicultural politics well ahead of its time. "If I have room," he wrote Governor Davis, "I want a German, a Yankee, a true Southerner, & a colored man. The four elements which placed yourself in power." David F. Davis served less than half a year, but for that brief period McLennan County had a carpetbagger county judge.[38]

37. *Senate Miscellaneous Documents*, 41st Cong., 2nd Sess., No. 77, pp. 38–79; Election Registers, 1867–1869. Wood's name was included on a list of loyalists eligible for appointment to local office compiled by military authorities during the spring of 1867. This list is discussed in Robert Shook, "Toward a List of Reconstruction Loyalists," *Southwestern Historical Quarterly*, LXXVI (1973), 315–20. Trice's efforts to win nomination as a Democrat are shown in the Waco *Daily Examiner*, January 14, 1876.

38. *Senate Miscellaneous Documents*, 41st Cong., 2nd Sess., No. 77, pp. 38–79; Winkler, ed., *Platforms of Political Parties in Texas*, 115; David F. Davis to E. J. Davis, January 12, 15,

In early May, 1870, once Congress approved Texas' constitution and restored the state to the Union, McLennan County returned to government by elected officials. Local Republicans looked to the future with considerable optimism, but serious difficulties would continue to disrupt public life in the county and provide opportunities for the conservative opposition. One of these problems, intraparty factionalism, was of the Republicans' own making.

Under the new constitution and several laws passed by the Twelfth Legislature, Governor Davis had extensive powers of appointment. He filled all vacant positions in county government, appointed the mayors and aldermen of all newly chartered cities and towns, and chose the men to occupy the benches of the state's district courts. Many of McLennan County's Republicans wanted positions in government, and the resulting scramble heightened the factionalism that had already begun to develop before the election in 1869. For example, A. C. Fairman sought a district judgeship, saying "I believe that I am the only genuine Republican lawyer in Waco friend Evens [A. J. Evans] having forsaken us." Fairman was made a voter registrar rather than judge, but within several months Davis received demands from Shepherd Mullins and others for his removal. Fairman, they said, has become a Democrat and should be replaced by J. H. Townsend, a black graduate of Waterville College in Maine who moved to Waco in the late 1860s. The governor complied with their request.[39] Oscar H. Leland and John E. Stephenson both sought the position as superintendent of public instruction. Leland pointed out that he had been educated in New England and would bring that system to all Texans, black and white. Stephenson, who was from Alabama, wrote: "I never drink nor swear nor dissipate in any way."[40]

The struggle for control of the Waco city government in 1870 created especially bitter factionalism. At the request of D. F. Davis, Shepherd Mullins, Albert R. Parsons, and several freedmen, Governor Davis appointed Ben-

March 22, 1870, Governors' Papers: EJD. E. J. Davis was appointed governor on January 8, 1870, and he had the power to make interim appointments from that date until he took office under the new constitution in April.

39. Ramsdell, *Reconstruction in Texas*, 298–99; Campbell, "Scalawag District Judges," 76–78; A. C. Fairman to E. J. Davis, January 10, 1870, Shepherd Mullins and others to E. J. Davis, October 31, 1870, Governors' Papers: EJD; Election Registers, 1870.

40. Oscar H. Leland to E. J. Davis, May 28, 1870, John E. Stephenson to E. J. Davis, September 5, 1870, Governors' Papers: EJD.

jamin F. Harris, a devoted Unionist, mayor of Waco in the late summer of 1870. Almost immediately, Harris was charged with unlawfully taking city funds. His friends replied that supporters of A. J. Hamilton had cooked up the charges and that all genuine Republicans supported the mayor.[41]

Those who opposed Harris then focused on controlling the board of aldermen. John T. Flint, a New York–born lawyer who had lived in Bell County before the war, wrote Governor Davis: "The Parsons faction here is irresponsible, and if they go into power will offend the sense of justice of all decent men whether Republican or not." He recommended Peter Mc-Clelland, George B. Dutton, J. W. Wheeler, and several others. The governor, in what appears to have been an uncharacteristic attempt to appease moderate Republicans, promised to appoint enough of the men suggested by Flint to give the latter's group a majority on the board. Flint responded positively, although he could not resist saying again that appointing Harris as mayor was a blunder resulting from bad advice. Within a month, however, Davis received a letter from three black aldermen, William Blocker, Shadrack Willis, and Lewis Graves, complaining that Dutton, McClelland, and Wheeler were betraying the Republican cause in Waco. Intraparty squabbles of this sort did not necessarily ruin the Republican party in McLennan County, but certainly they did nothing to strengthen it either.[42]

Governor Davis' choice for judge of the Thirty-third District soon proved controversial also, adding to the difficulties facing Republicans. The Thirty-third District encompassed McLennan and Falls Counties when created by the legislature in July, 1870. An act of February 6, 1871, added Limestone County. John W. Oliver, the district's first judge, lived in Houston prior to his appointment on July 13, 1870. A thirty-five-year-old Mississippian, Oliver was also a Radical Republican whose political enthusiasm tended to overcome judicial balance. For example, even as he prepared to move to Waco, he discussed with J. P. Newcomb the establishment of a Republican newspaper at his new home. Local Radicals such as David F. Davis

41. "Republicans of Waco" to E. J. Davis, July 29, 1870, D. F. Davis to E. J. Davis, August 5, 1870, Albert R. Parsons to E. J. Davis, August 17, 1870, Governors' Papers: EJD. Albert R. Parsons was a native Alabaman and former Confederate soldier who became a Radical Republican. He later moved to Chicago and was one of the anarchists executed for the Haymarket bombings in 1886. Webb, Carroll, and Branda, eds., *Handbook of Texas*, III, 705–706.

42. John T. Flint to E. J. Davis, September 10, 1870, William Blocker, Shadrack Willis, and Lewis Graves to E. J. Davis, October 13, 1870, Governors' Papers: EJD; E. J. Davis to John T. Flint, September 17, 1870, John T. Flint to E. J. Davis, September 20, 1870, Executive Record Books: EJD.

were enthusiastic. "Every man is perfectly delighted with Judge Oliver," he wrote Governor Davis. "I hope length of time will never cause us to think any the less of him." Albert R. Parsons thought it a great help to have a judge who was in "active sympathy" with the Radicals and who would edit a paper to present their views. Oliver's active radicalism, however, soon led to serious confrontations with conservative Democrats and moderate Republicans in the Thirty-third District.[43]

According to his critics, Judge Oliver often refused to use jury panels selected by justice courts and had sheriffs choose men whose names he supplied. They also claimed that he removed officials such as county clerks on the basis of false charges. In October, 1871, he convinced Governor Davis to declare martial law in Limestone County on the grounds that Republicans there were not safe. By mid-November, 1871, conservative and moderate lawyers in the district were so angry that they petitioned the judge to resign. His actions, the petition read, had made him so "unpopular as a Judge and as a man, with the people of the District and with the members of the bar; that they no longer have in you the confidence necessary to be reposed in one in your position, and . . . the prospect of your future usefulness as Judge in this District is destroyed." McLennan County conservatives such as Thomas Harrison and Richard Coke were joined by moderates such as A. J. Evans and John T. Flint in signing the petition.[44]

Oliver ignored the demand for his resignation, so the lawyers took their charges to the Republican-controlled state legislature. In December, 1871, a committee of the house of representatives issued both majority and minority reports. The former dismissed the complaint as "conceived in political prejudice and born in that hatred which is engendered by defeat" and concluded, "in the hearts of the Republicans in the state at large Judge Oliver will ever be esteemed, and the party owes him a debt of gratitude it will not fail to pay." G. W. Patten, brother of Nathan Patten and a McLennan County Unionist, was one of the signatories. The minority report, however, contended that Oliver had made his office an "engine of oppression" and called for his impeachment as the only way to protect the liberties of citi-

43. Gammel, comp., *Laws of Texas*, VI, 195–97; Betty Ann McCartney McSwain, ed., *The Bench and Bar of Waco and McLennan County, 1849–1876* (Waco, Tex., n.d.), 254; Ninth Census, 1870, Schedule 1; J. W. Oliver to J. P. Newcomb, August 15, 1870, Albert R. Parsons to J. P. Newcomb, September 9, 1870, Newcomb Papers; J. W. Oliver to E. J. Davis, May 26, 1870, D. F. Davis to E. J. Davis, August 5, 1870, Governors' Papers: EJD.

44. Duty, "McLennan County in the Civil War," 224–25.

zens. A motion to table the matter failed, and the house voted 43 to 31 to impeach the judge. A five-man committee drafted eight articles of impeachment that went to the senate in early December. Then, fortunately for the judge, the legislature adjourned before anything could come of the charges.[45]

Undaunted by a demand for his resignation and the brush with impeachment, Oliver became involved during the spring of 1872 in a rancorous dispute with the county court of McLennan County. The judge made a practice of issuing drafts on the county treasury to pay the sheriff and court bailiffs for work beyond their usual responsibilities. Finally, on April 20, 1872, the court, with Republican Oscar H. Leland presiding, announced that it would not pay such drafts in the future. Oliver reacted by declaring Leland and the other two justices involved in the decision in contempt, fining them one hundred dollars each, and ordering them jailed until payment of the fines. The justices pled their case in a letter to the local bar headed "In the Dungeon on the Jail," and the Waco *Daily Advance* published a broadside headlined, "STOP THE MADMAN." "These things can go no further," the newspaper said. "Either they must stop of themselves, or a stop will be found for them." Local doctors then impaneled a lunacy commission and certified to Justice Leland that the judge was insane. Leland issued an order for Oliver's arrest, and a constable found the judge as he was leaving court and took him to the same jail in which the justices were being held. At that point compromise seemed in order to all parties. The judge released the justices in return for a dismissal of the lunacy complaint. Oliver remained on the bench until January, 1873, when he resigned, his controversial tenure almost certainly having done more harm than good to the Republican cause in McLennan County.[46]

Violence also continued to plague the county, even after the restoration of constitutional government in 1870. One of the most serious incidents, the so-called Waco Riot of August 6, 1870, involved a member of the new state

45. *Journal of the House of Representatives of the Twelfth Legislature. Adjourned Session—1871* (Austin, 1871), 743–44, 793–95, 802–803, 817, 819–21; *Journal of the Senate of the Twelfth Legislature. Adjourned Session—1871* (Austin, 1871), 519. G. W. Patten is identified in the Ninth Census, 1870, Schedule 1.

46. S. W. Ford to E. J. Davis, May 9, 1872, Governors' Papers: EJD; Waco *Advance* (broadside), May 7, 1872; Duty, "McLennan County in the Civil War," 226–32. Oliver was replaced by Joab H. Banton, Jr., a native of Texas. Election Registers, 1873; Eighth Census, 1860, Schedule 1.

police force created by the Davis administration. A group of young white men stole several watermelons from a black-owned store and then withdrew to Jim Johnson's saloon. In response, armed blacks, including a state policeman named William Mason, gathered at the store. Johnson convinced the men to return and pay for the watermelons, but as he and the others approached, the black men, not knowing what was intended, opened fire. Johnson was killed amidst gunfire from both sides, and Mason was arrested for murder. N. W. Battle, a local lawyer, successfully defended Mason, but the incident provided more ammunition for conservative opponents of Radical legislation. Waco's blacks generally have been peaceable, an Austin newspaper said, but one bad man "in the State Police changes the condition of affairs by his influence and example and a reign of terror is at once instituted."[47]

Republican factionalism, the controversial tenure of Judge John W. Oliver, violence involving the state police, and notably high taxes in 1871 combined to weaken seriously the Republican cause in McLennan County during the first two years of the Davis administration. A. R. Parsons wrote J. P. Newcomb in May, 1871, that "the people are rousing, the party has never had more vitality than now"—but the results of congressional elections that October would belie his optimistic words. Two years earlier, William T. Clark, the Republican candidate, had carried McLennan easily, receiving 853 votes to 579 for his opponent. But in the special election of representatives held October 3–6, 1871, he lost to the Democrat, D. C. Giddings, by a 1,520 to 1,162 vote. A year later, Congressman Giddings defeated A. J. Evans, 1,316 to 1,189, in spite of the fact that Evans lived in McLennan County. At the same time, in the election of state representatives from the Nineteenth District for the Thirteenth Legislature, the two top vote-getters in McLennan were James M. Anderson of Waco and Davis M. Prendergast of Limestone County, both of whom had been members of the secession convention. In contests for local offices, Lemuel Jones, a Democrat, won the position as justice of the peace for precinct three, replacing the Unionist, John Wood, who had died in July, and another Democrat, B. F. Richey, defeated the moderate Republican, George B. Dutton, for the office of county

<hr>

47. Patricia Ward Wallace, *Waco: Texas Crossroads* (Woodland Hills, Calif., 1983), 31; M. P. Hunnicutt to E. J. Davis, September 3, 5, 1870, N. W. Battle to "To Whom It May Concern," September 5, 1870, J. L. L. McCall to E. J. Davis, September 5, 1870, Executive Record Books: EJD.

treasurer. The county's white majority was asserting itself, and Republicans, having failed to build a sizable white constituency, faced a complete loss of control.[48]

As the state general elections of December 2, 1873, approached, McLennan County's Republicans had difficulty preparing to campaign effectively. J. W. Oliver and George A. O'Brien wrote J. P. Newcomb in late July complaining that state chairman James G. Tracy had not appointed anyone to fill the vacant position of county chairman and recommending George W. Patten for the job. "It is important," they wrote, "for Republicans to be up and doing." Democrats, no doubt encouraged tremendously by the nomination of Richard Coke for governor, held a county convention and ran candidates for all offices. The Waco *Examiner* ran a masthead endorsement of Coke, a longtime county resident, and bitterly attacked Republicans for renominating Governor E. J. Davis. "With characteristic stupidity," editor J. W. Downs wrote on August 29, "this detestable faction which has . . . almost ruined the state for the past four years, thus proclaim in advance their desired continuation of an era of folly and tyranny not paralleled in American annals." The editorial concluded, "The black flag is up— we take no prisoners."[49]

David F. Davis, who unsuccessfully sought reelection as district clerk, succinctly summarized the McLennan County election results in a letter to Governor Davis on December 10, 1873. "Party spirit ran high here during the election & swept everything before it which was not of the *hot Democratic sort*." Coke defeated Davis in the governor's race by a vote of 1,631 to 878, and his statewide victory touched off a great victory celebration in Waco. "Every house is brilliantly illuminated," the Galveston *Daily News* reported, "and every lady is upon the streets with happy and joyous faces." Locally, Democrats took full control of county offices. E. P. Massey, a Tennessean who had come to McLennan County after the war, became presiding justice of the county court. One of the county's most famous residents,

48. Albert R. Parsons to J. P. Newcomb, May 1, 1871, Newcomb Papers; *Senate Miscellaneous Documents*, 41st Cong., 2nd Sess., No. 77, pp. 38–79, has the vote in 1869. Returns on the congressional elections of 1871 and 1872 and the state legislative races are in Executive Record Books: E. J. Davis/Richard Coke. For the careers of Anderson and Prendergast, see Webb, Carroll, and Branda, eds., *Handbook of Texas*, I, 44, II, 407. Local returns for 1872 are in *Report of the Secretary of State of the State of Texas, 1872*, 71. O. H. Leland to E. J. Davis, July 20, 1872, Governors' Papers: EJD.

49. J. W. Oliver and George A. O'Brien to J. P. Newcomb, July 26, 1873, Newcomb Papers; Waco *Daily Examiner*, August 29, 1873.

Gen. Sul Ross, won the sheriff's office. Ross, the son of an antebellum slave-holder, had commanded a cavalry brigade during the war and was destined to become governor of Texas in 1887. In January the Waco *Daily Advance* announced that county government had been placed in the hands of men "who are undoubtedly the choices of the people," and congratulated "the people of McLennan County upon this event that places in office their chosen servants."[50]

David F. Davis, as might be expected, put the most positive face possible on the election results. "But I hope you are not discouraged," he wrote Governor Davis. "We both carried the city of Waco." In reality, however, the Republican majority of 1869 had been reduced to a 35 percent minority by December, 1873, meaning lasting "redemption" for McLennan County. The black population increased—from 4,627 in 1870 to 7,643 by 1880—but the white population grew much more rapidly—from 8,861 in 1870 to 19,726 in 1880. Blacks and the small core of Republican whites were lost in a sea of conservative whites, many of them recent arrivals from older southern states. In August, 1875, when McLennan as part of a seven-county district elected three delegates to a convention that would write a conservative constitution to replace the "radical" Constitution of 1869, Sul Ross, James R. Fleming, and George B. Erath received the most votes in the county. Fleming lived in Comanche County and, like Ross, had fought in the Confederate army, beginning his service under Gen. Nathan B. Forrest at age thirteen. The Comanche *Chief* praised his role in "redeeming his county and state from the misrule of the dominant party." Ross and Fleming ran as Democrats; Erath, a longtime Texan, Indian fighter, and original surveyor of Waco, campaigned as an independent.[51]

The election of February 15, 1876, to approve the new constitution and elect state officers provided the final blow to Republican aspirations in McLennan County. Democrats organized from the precinct level up and nominated a full slate of candidates in a county convention on January 12.

50. D. F. Davis to E. J. Davis, December 10, 1873, Governors' Papers: EJD; Kingston, Attlesey, and Crawford, *Political History of Texas*, 60; Galveston *Daily News*, December 6, 1873; Election Registers, 1873; Webb, Carroll, and Branda, eds., *Handbook of Texas*, II, 506–507; Waco *Daily Advance*, January 14, 1874.

51. D. F. Davis to E. J. Davis, December 10, 1873, Governors' Papers: EJD; U.S. Bureau of the Census, *Statistics of the Population of the United States (1880)*, 410; Waco *Weekly Patron and Examiner*, August 20, 1875; Galveston *Daily News*, August 7, 1875; Webb, Carroll, and Branda, eds., *Handbook of Texas*, I, 569, 610–11; Comanche *Chief*, March 9, 1876.

Former Republicans apparently were reduced to seeking cooperation with the Democrats or running without a party label. The *Daily Examiner* of January 14 reported that "we are much afraid that Brother Leland [Oscar H. Leland, presiding justice from 1869 to 1873], whose recovery from a long and severe attack of Radicalism appeared so promising, has relapsed" and would be an independent candidate for county judge. The next day Leland put a note in the paper announcing that he had indeed become a Democrat but was not a candidate. David F. Davis ran for the county judge's position as an "Independent."[52]

On election day, Democrats again demonstrated complete control of the county. They endorsed the new constitution and supported Coke for governor against the Republican, William M. Chambers, by a vote of 2,041 to 906. George B. Gerald, the colonel of a Mississippi regiment during the war and resident of Waco since 1869, easily defeated Davis for county judge. Sul Ross's brother, Peter F. Ross, won the sheriff's office. Three of the four new county commissioners, C. A. Westbrook, John Shackelford, and Henry J. Caufield, were longtime residents who had owned slaves before the war. The only anomaly in these results was the victory of Xenophon Boone Saunders, a Unionist in 1861 and Republican since 1867, in the race for district judge. Perhaps the fact that his opponent, Pennsylvania native J. P. Osterhout, had switched from secessionist Democrat to Republican in 1869 and accepted a district judgeship from E. J. Davis, accounted for Saunders' victory. In any case, this one success for a Republican, who had no Democratic opponent, did not alter conservative domination of the county.[53]

Inauguration of government under the Constitution of 1876 concluded an era of often spectacularly controversial change in McLennan County. Clearly, at the outset of the period in 1865 and 1866, the white majority intended to accept the end of slavery but to make no other alterations in their society. The 1866 election of Wallace E. Oakes as county judge, the same position that he had held in 1861, symbolized this intent. Congressional Reconstruction, however, brought changes that many conservatives could not have imagined even in 1865. Beginning in 1867, the enfranchisement of freedmen, coupled with the replacement of all important county office-

52. Waco *Daily Examiner*, January 1, 14, 15, February 17, 1876.
53. Waco *Daily Examiner*, February 17, 1876; Kingston, Attlesey, and Crawford, *Political History of Texas*, 60; Election Registers, 1876; Eighth Census, 1860, Schedules 1 and 2; *Memorial and Biographical History*, 880–81.

holders by military appointees, gave control of the county to Republicans. At one point, blacks, Shepherd Mullins and Stephen Cobb, occupied two of the four seats on the commissioners' court, and at another time a carpet-bagger, David F. Davis, served as county judge. Mullins was a delegate to the constitutional convention of 1868–1869 and a representative in the Twelfth Legislature. Blacks served as aldermen in Waco, held positions in law enforcement, and acted as grand and petit jurors. Local taxes, which had never been higher than 50 cents per $100 in property evaluation—and that in 1869 under an appointed government—jumped to $1 on $100 in 1871 when elected Republicans headed the justice court. The new state-mandated public schools were a major cause of the increase. Rates fell to 62.5 cents in 1872 and 30 cents in 1873 and would return to nearly $1 in 1875 and 1876 under conservative control. Nevertheless, Republican government and ruinous new levels of taxation became synonymous for many.[54]

With all these changes came a level of violence generally unmatched elsewhere in Texas.[55] Whites did not escape the impact of general lawlessness and racial tension. Charles Haughn, the Freedmen's Bureau agent, reported numerous cases of attacks by whites on whites, and the victim of the Waco Riot in August, 1870, was white. But freedmen suffered more acts of crime and terror, perhaps because the black population, although sizable, did not have the numbers or the degree of concentration necessary for self-protection. Perhaps, too, the fact that newly arrived whites had no personal familiarity with the county's freedmen led to a higher than usual level of violence. Some of the attacks on blacks may have been political, but most appear simply random and racial. Finally, regardless of its prevalence, violence did not prevent a significant increase from 1860 to 1880 in the number of blacks living in McLennan County (from 2,404 to 7,643) and did not play a major role in "redemption." The white population, however, grew so rap-

54. Real and Personal Property Tax Rolls, McLennan County, 1850–1876.
55. Barry A. Crouch, "A Spirit of Lawlessness: White Violence; Texas Blacks, 1865–1868," *Journal of Social History*, XVIII (1984), 217–32; and Gregg Cantrell, "Racial Violence and Reconstruction Politics in Texas, 1867–1868," *Southwestern Historical Quarterly*, XCIII (1990), 333–55, point to the widespread nature of violence in Texas but do not indicate that one place was more violent than another. This statement about McLennan County is based on examining the "Records of Criminal Offenses," XI–XIII, BRFAL, RG 105, NA, and evidence in Richter, *Army in Texas During Reconstruction*, 152.

idly that the proportion of blacks declined from 39 percent in 1860 to 28 percent by 1880.[56]

The changes brought by Reconstruction in McLennan County and the accompanying violence undoubtedly made the era seem revolutionary to many of those living through it. In a sense, they were correct. Politics and race relations, for example, would never be the same again. But in another sense, when the era ended, the white majority found their society and government remarkably the same as in 1865. No social revolution worked by Republican taxes had destroyed the upper class. Of the twenty-nine white families that constituted the wealthiest 5 percent of the county's taxpayers in 1865, fifteen (52 percent) remained in the wealthiest 5 percent in 1880. Only seven families (24 percent) had fallen from the taxpaying elite. Politically, the county by 1876 had returned to the control of men very much like those who had governed during the antebellum years. Indeed, a majority on the commissioners' court elected in 1876 had been slaveholding residents in 1860. Finally, although the county remained largely agricultural, its economy, aided by immigrants and the link with the Houston and Texas Railroad, expanded significantly during Reconstruction. Cotton production increased, and the total assessed value of taxable property rose from $1,450,090 in 1865 to $4,326,392 in 1876, an increase of 198 percent. During this period the value of town lots, most of which were in Waco, increased from $133,984 to $917,849.[57]

McLennan's freedmen worked enthusiastically for the changes that Reconstruction brought. At the first election in which they were allowed to participate, nearly 100 percent of those registered went to the polls. Black leaders held state and local offices, and freedmen regularly participated in the justice system. Economic progress did not match political gains during the era. A majority (56 percent) of black household heads in 1880 remained dependent on agriculture, most of them as tenant farmers or farm laborers, and another 11 percent were day laborers. However, 16 percent of those who reported farming as their occupation in 1880 owned farmland (an average of forty acres each), and 11 percent rented land for cash rather than working for shares. Those who owned land or rented for cash generally

56. U.S. Bureau of the Census, *Statistics of the Population of the United States in 1860*, 485; U.S. Bureau of the Census, *Statistics of the Population of the United States (1880)*, 410.

57. Real and Personal Property Tax Rolls, McLennan County, 1865, 1876, and 1880.

owned livestock, especially horses, and even among tenants the ownership of horses and hogs was common. Thus economic progress did occur; a more remarkable feat than is generally recognized, considering that blacks typically emerged from slavery propertyless with their labor as their only asset. Finally, freedmen stabilized their social lives and found opportunities for their children's advancement. In 1880, three-quarters of black households contained husband, wife, and children in a nuclear family. Nearly one-third of those with school-age children had at least one child attending school. As might be expected, living in Waco brought greater opportunities for schooling. There, 45 percent of the households with children aged six to sixteen had at least one in school. Town life, however, also seems to have weakened nuclear families. Only 59 percent of the households in Waco had nuclear families as compared with 84 percent in rural areas. Perhaps job opportunities for women in town—19 percent of the households there were headed by laundresses or cooks—created less need for men in the family.[58]

The people of McLennan County, especially the blacks, paid a higher price in terms of violence during Reconstruction than did those in many other counties across Texas. Any explanation is hypothetical at best, but somehow the mix of ex-Confederates, Unionists, federal officials, and freedmen in and around Waco became explosive, especially from 1867 through 1870. When it was over, conservative whites prevailed, primarily because they were in the majority. Blacks, however, had established a tradition of activism and participation that remained a legacy for generations. "Right after the freedom war," Charley Johnson, a former slave told a Works Progress Administration interviewer in 1937, "there were colored policemen and colored deputy sheriffs right here in Waco." Another McLennan County interviewee said, "I don't think it is right for any party to keep the colored folks out." Shepherd Mullins and Stephen Cobb would have agreed.[59]

58. Information on the black population of McLennan County in 1880 is based on a random sample of 250 households headed by African Americans. Tenth Census, 1880, Schedules 1 and 2.

59. Rawick, ed., *American Slave: Supplement, Series 2,* VI, 1979, III, 496.

# 7

## NUECES COUNTY

Nueces County, located immediately south of the Nueces River in the coastal bend region of Texas, remained thinly settled until after the Civil War. Fewer than a thousand people lived there in 1850, and ten years later the population stood at only 2,906, a majority of whom were of Mexican ancestry. Corpus Christi, settled during the 1830s and destined to become the region's major city, had only 175 residents in 1860. The county's economy depended on open-range grazing of cattle and sheep, although commerce through Corpus Christi showed promise and would increase rapidly after the war. Cotton production was virtually nonexistent, amounting to only thirty-nine bales in 1860, and accordingly slavery had a very limited presence. Nueces reported 216 slaves in the census of 1860, 7 percent of the total population. There were fifty-two slaveholders, representing 11 percent of the county's households, but most owned very few bondsmen.[1]

1. Brief descriptions of Nueces County and Corpus Christi are found in Webb, Carroll, and Branda, eds., *Handbook of Texas,* I, 415, II, 290–91. Information on the population, slaveholding, and cotton production in Nueces County in 1860 is from the Eighth Census, 1860, Schedules 1 and 2; U.S. Bureau of the Census, *Population of the United States in 1860,* 485, 487–89; U.S. Bureau of the Census, *Agriculture of the United States in 1860,* 145, 241. In 1860, foreign-born men and women made up 39 percent of the population of Nueces County. A great majority of them were natives of Mexico who had become citizens of the United States at the time of annexation. Their children born after 1845 were, of course, considered natives of Texas, but obviously they were of Mexican ancestry also, and, with their parents, made up a majority of the population.

Map 7

Nueces County

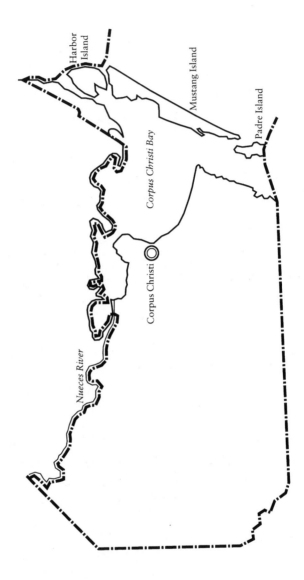

Harbor Island

Mustang Island

Corpus Christi Bay

Padre Island

Corpus Christi

Nueces River

Adapted, with permission, from the Nueces County map in the *Texas Almanac* for 1996–1997.

Given how little Nueces County had in common with the Old South, the stance of its voters during the election of 1860 and the secession crisis that followed seems surprising at first glance. John C. Breckinridge, the Southern Democratic candidate, carried Nueces by a vote of 125 to 44 for John Bell of the Constitutional Union party. Then, news that the Republican Abraham Lincoln had won the presidency led to a public meeting on December 4, 1860, in Corpus Christi. Those who attended endorsed immediate disunion and provided for the election of delegates to a state secession convention. Two strong secessionists, P. N. Luckett and Henry A. Maltby, received overwhelming support and went to Austin in January. In the February 23, 1861, referendum on the convention's decision to take Texas out of the Union, Nueces County favored secession by a vote of 142 to 42.[2]

Nueces thus appears typical of most Texas counties, supporting disunion by a three-to-one margin. There is some evidence, however, that the county's population did not have quite the degree of unity suggested by events in 1860 and 1861. First, in the gubernatorial election of August, 1859, Sam Houston, a strong Unionist, defeated the ultrasoutherner, Hardin R. Runnels, by a vote of 233 to 105. More than twice as many voters participated in this election as in the presidential election of 1860 or the secession referendum, and the result was victory for the candidate who always favored upholding the Union. Second, Nueces County Unionists lacked leadership during the crisis. Henry L. Kinney, the founder of Corpus Christi and a member of the Eighth Texas Legislature (1859–1861), opposed disunion, but in early 1861 he was planning to resign his seat and move to Matamoros, Mexico. Kinney had formed strong alliances with leading Mexicans in Nueces County and, had he not been planning to leave, may have influenced more Hispanics to vote against secession. Another local leader, Edmund J. Davis, who would become the most famous Unionist/Republican in Texas after the war, had lived in the county at times during the 1850s but in 1860 and 1861 was based in Brownsville serving as judge in a huge state judicial district covering all of South Texas. Perhaps as a resident of Corpus

2. Kingston, Attlesey, and Crawford, *Political History of Texas*, 74; Timmons, "Referendum in Texas on the Ordinance of Secession," 16; Eugenia Reynolds Briscoe, "A Narrative History of Corpus Christi, Texas, 1519–1875" (Ph.D. dissertation, University of Denver, 1972), 354–65. Luckett was a thirty-six-year-old native of Virginia and a doctor. Maltby, a twenty-nine-year-old originally from Ohio, edited the Corpus Christi newspaper. Eighth Census, 1860, Schedule 1.

Christi he could have encouraged those who opposed secession. Thus it appears that Nueces County secessionists seized the initiative and kept it during the momentous events of 1860–1861, whereas Unionists had little leadership and remained away from the polls.[3]

Nueces County had relatively few men to contribute to the Confederate army, and most who volunteered remained in the area to defend against Union attacks. United States naval vessels arrived off the coast early in 1862, threatening defensive positions on St. Joseph and Mustang Islands that protected approaches to Corpus Christi Bay and the town. In mid-August federal forces drove Confederate defenders from the islands and passes and moved in to attack. Gunboats shelled the town, but troops commanded by Maj. A. M. Hobby prevented a successful landing. Sailors from the U.S. Navy landed south of Corpus Christi but were soon driven away. Federal ships arrived again in November, 1863, and once more took the protecting coastal islands, allowing Union forces to attack the town successfully on Christmas Day. Occupation troops did not remain for the duration of the war, but moved in and out largely at will in 1864 and 1865.[4]

The Corpus Christi area of Nueces County thus saw a great deal more military action than was typical across the state. Civilians who wanted to leave had time to evacuate before Union attacks in 1862 and 1863; nevertheless, their town suffered more damage than most towns in Texas. Nueces also had significant internal divisions that would not disappear with the end of the war. For example, Edmund J. Davis, the Unionist district judge who regarded the county as home, left the state once fighting began. He became commander of the 1st Texas Cavalry in the United States Army and emerged from the war as a brigadier general. Cesario Falcon served as a captain in the 2nd Texas Cavalry (U.S.A.) in 1863 and 1864. John James Dix, Sr., a native of Massachusetts who had settled in Texas in 1834 and established a hotel in Corpus Christi in 1849, left the state because of his unionism. Late in 1864 a Nueces County grand jury indicted Dix and eight others for treason. Nothing came of the charges before the end of the war, but they were symptomatic of local political attitudes. Even though Nueces

3. Kingston, Attlesey, and Crawford, *Political History of Texas,* 56, 74; Webb, Carroll, and Branda, eds., *Handbook of Texas,* I, 469, 962; Briscoe, "Narrative History of Corpus Christi," 354–65; David Montejano, *Anglos and Mexicans in the Making of Texas, 1836–1986* (Austin, 1987), 39, 43.

4. Barr, "Texas Coastal Defense, 1861–1865," 6, 11–12, 27–28; Winsor, *Texas in the Confederacy,* 15, 87; Briscoe, "Narrative History of Corpus Christi," 367–68, 379–402, 433.

differed economically and demographically from most Texas counties, Reconstruction there promised to be a difficult matter.[5]

A brigade of black troops from the 25th U.S. Army Corps occupied Corpus Christi during July, 1865, and Union officers began to parole ex-Confederates. In September provisional governor Andrew Jackson Hamilton appointed county officials and a district judge. He made John J. Dix, just back from wartime exile, county judge, and Henry W. Berry, an Ohio–born hotel keeper who had been accused of cooperating with occupying federal forces in 1864, became sheriff. Two of the county commissioners, James Bryden and Matthew Cody, could swear the test oath of 1862 (the so-called Iron-Clad Oath) that they had never voluntarily aided the Confederacy, and the third, John McLane, was a personal friend of E. J. Davis. On the other hand, all five men had lived in the county before the war, and two, Cody and Berry, had held local office before. Unionists certainly approved of these men, whereas ardent secessionists, who probably objected, gave no indication of their feelings. By contrast, Hamilton's appointee as district judge, E. P. Upton, who should have been acceptable to local Unionists, soon drew their wrath for supposedly protecting former Confederate sympathizers.[6]

Judge Upton, a native of Maine (before it was separated from Massachusetts), came to Texas in 1858 and took up residence in Refugio County. He contended in 1867 that he had suffered "wrongs and indignities" for opposing secession, but Nueces County Unionists insisted that he had supported the rebellion. They were particularly infuriated when Upton refused to hold a scheduled session of his court in Corpus Christi in the fall of 1865. According to County Judge Dix and other Unionists, Upton dismissed the grand jury and closed the court in order to protect two former Rebels, Charles Lovenskjold and T. O'Callahan, from charges pending against them. The judge, they complained to Governor Hamilton, was in collusion with the criminals and should be removed from office. The truth of these charges is unknown. Lovenskjold, a native of Denmark and well-to-do lawyer, had lived in Texas for many years and would be an active Democrat

5. Briscoe, "Narrative History of Corpus Christi," 393–402, 433, 449–50; Marcus J. Wright, comp., *Texas in the War, 1861–1865*, ed. Harold B. Simpson (Hillsboro, Tex., 1965), 69, 162; Richter, *Overreached on All Sides*, 185.

6. Richter, *Army in Texas During Reconstruction*, 17; Election Registers, 1860–1865; Eighth Census, 1860, Schedule 1.

during Reconstruction. (O'Callahan could not be identified.) In any case, regardless of whether the two had committed criminal acts or the judge was in collusion with them, Hamilton removed Upton from the bench on January 1, 1866.[7]

The replacement appointee, Benjamin F. Neal, apparently was acceptable to Nueces County loyalists, although a glance at his record would raise serious doubts as to why. A native of Virginia, Neal came to Corpus Christi in 1846. He served in both the house and senate of the state legislature during the 1850s and commanded a Confederate artillery battalion during the war. Neal's battery fought in the defense of Corpus Christi in 1862 and 1863, and he emerged from the war with the rank of major. Also, in 1864 and 1865, while Texas remained a part of the Confederacy, he served as a district judge. Judge Neal thus had no Unionist credentials and must have been acceptable in Nueces primarily because he lived there. He held court in Corpus Christi during the late spring of 1866, empaneled a grand jury with many notable Unionists on it, and had an uneventful session. Nothing came of the celebrated case against Lovenskjold and O'Callahan.[8]

County Judge Dix and local Unionists also expressed concern in late 1865 about the treatment of blacks in Nueces County. Some freedmen, they said, are still treated as slaves, and others are denied pay for their work. Dix requested the appointment of a Freedmen's Bureau sub-assistant commissioner for the county, but headquarters took no action. No doubt a county with approximately three hundred blacks constituting 8 percent of the population did not stand at the top of the bureau's list of areas in need of a local agent.[9]

Unionists, in spite of their complaints about former Rebels and the treatment of freedmen, gained full control of Nueces County in 1866. In January they elected E. J. Davis, Texas' best-known loyalist, to the constitutional convention that would pave the way for an elected state government and

7. Huson, *District Judges of Refugio County,* 85; E. P. Upton to Charles C. Griffin, August 19, 1867, OCA, RG 393, NA; James Mahon and eleven other citizens of Nueces County to A. J. Hamilton, [October, 1865?], John Dix to Hamilton, December 13, 20, 31, 1865, Governors' Papers: AJH. Lovenskjold could be located in the census of 1860, but O'Callahan could not. Eighth Census, 1860, Schedule 1.

8. Huson, *District Judges of Refugio County,* 81–83; *Members of the Texas Legislature,* 5, 13, 17, 30; Election Registers, 1864–1866; District Court Minutes, District Clerk's Office, Nueces County Courthouse, Corpus Christi, Tex., Book C, 1–51.

9. Petition from John Dix and other Loyal Citizens of Nueces County, December 9, 1865, BRFAL, RG 105, NA.

representation in Washington. Once the convention completed its work, elections were held on June 25, 1866, to choose state and local officials under the terms of the new constitution. In the race for governor, J. W. Throckmorton, the more conservative candidate, defeated E. M. Pease, but only by a vote of 146 to 134 in Nueces, a much closer contest than those in most counties. And Unionists took the other key positions. Dix continued as county judge; Berry as sheriff; and Cody, Bryden, and McLane as county commissioners. The fourth seat on the commissioners' court was won by John Kellett, a native of Florida who became a Republican. Judge B. F. Neal remained on the Fourteenth District Court bench, easily defeating E. P. Upton, whom he had replaced at the beginning of the year in Nueces County. Once the commissioners' court met in August and the district court in December, the process of self-reconstruction must have seemed largely satisfactory to those who had opposed secession in the first place.[10]

John Dix remained concerned about mistreatment of the freedmen and wrote bureau headquarters again in September, 1866, seeking the appointment of an agent for the county. Even as county judge, Dix wrote, he could not guarantee the rights of blacks. The Freedmen's Bureau finally responded by making Dix himself the sub-assistant commissioner for Nueces County in April, 1867. By that time, however, Congress had taken over Reconstruction and ordered the entire process repeated, beginning with the election of a new constitutional convention in February, 1868. By enfranchising blacks and disfranchising anyone who had taken an oath to uphold the United States Constitution and then engaged in rebellion, Congressional Reconstruction promised even more strength for Nueces County Unionists and greater protection for the freedmen.[11]

A small force of federal soldiers (a noncommissioned officer and ten men) arrived at Corpus Christi on April 19, 1867. The army brigade that occupied the town immediately after the war had been removed within a year, and this small body of troops had the sole purpose of maintaining or-

10. Election Returns, 1866, have the results of state and district contests. No returns are available on the races for county offices in 1866. Names of the winners are from the Election Registers, 1866. Kellett is in the Eighth Census, 1860, Schedule 1. The Corpus Christi *Weekly Gazette*, December 20, 1873, identifies him as a Republican. For meetings of the commissioners' court and district court, see Commissioners' Court Minutes, County Clerk's Office, Nueces County Courthouse, Corpus Christi, Book C, 30–31; and District Court Minutes, Book C, 53.

11. John Dix to Joseph B. Kiddoo, September 25, 1866, BRFAL, RG 105, NA; Richter, *Overreached on All Sides*, 185.

der during Congressional Reconstruction. John Dix, now county judge and Freedmen's Bureau agent, reported that the soldiers, whom he quartered in the courthouse, had a good effect on "the would be refractory and turbulent" and gave the blacks a sense of security. Freedmen in the county, Dix wrote, worked hard and behaved well. In a similar vein, Col. Nelson Plato, a Union army veteran from New York who had settled in Nueces County after the war, informed Gen. Charles C. Griffin, commander of the District of Texas, that the Rebels had learned their lesson. They have, he wrote, "forsaken their *Paths of Sin* & once more look to *Uncle Sam* as their savior." [12]

Although pleased with the presence of troops, Judge Dix nevertheless found several things to be concerned about as Congressional Reconstruction began. First, he had become almost as unhappy with District Judge B. F. Neal as he had been with E. P. Upton in the fall of 1865. Emphasizing Neal's support of the Confederacy, Dix claimed that the judge made law enforcement a farce and called for his removal. E. J. Davis joined in the demand for a replacement, telling General Griffin that Neal was an "ignorant, prejudicial, and bitter fellow." Second, Dix worried about the registration of voters scheduled to begin during the summer. "I have some doubts about the working of the proposed plan of registration," he wrote. "The number of traitors that will be disfranchised by it, I fear will not be sufficient to secure a loyal convention." [13]

Developments during the spring of 1867 brought some reassurance to Dix regarding both of these matters. In response to numerous complaints from across the state concerning district court judges, General Griffin on April 27 issued the circular order requiring all jurors to swear the test oath that they had never voluntarily supported the Confederacy. This order came too late to affect the spring session of Judge Neal's court in Nueces County, which ended on April 19, but Dix welcomed it anyway. "Justice will be done to the freedpeople now more commonly," he wrote, "since a rebel is not permitted to sit upon a jury." [14] The prospects for voter registra-

12. John Dix to Joel Kirkman, April 23, 1867, BRFAL, RG 105, NA; Nelson Plato to Charles C. Griffin, April 23, 1867, OCA, RG 393, NA. Plato is in the Ninth Census, 1870, Schedule 1. He held the rank of major in the Union army in 1865. *OR*, Vol. XLVI, Pt. 2, p. 173.

13. Dix to Kirkman, April 23, 1867, BRFAL, RG 105, NA; Edmund J. Davis to Charles C. Griffin, April 23, 1867, OCA, RG 393, NA.

14. John Dix to Joel Kirkman, April 30, 1867, BRFAL, RG 105, NA; District Court Min-

tion that would deal stringently with former Confederates improved when E. J. Davis was made supervisor of the Fifth Registration District which included Nueces County. Dix compiled a list of blacks who would be eligible to vote and reported with satisfaction that many whites intended not to register. He reported also that Mexicans, because of their loyalty to the United States, would register and vote in support of Unionists.[15]

Dix thus enjoyed a position of considerable strength as Congressional Reconstruction began, but he and his officeholding allies still faced significant opposition. On June 5, 1867, more than forty Nueces County citizens petitioned General Griffin, seeking the removal of Dix as both county judge and bureau agent. The petitioners claimed that the judge and a few friends such as E. J. Davis, county commissioners James Bryden and John McLane, and county clerk Joseph Fitzsimmons, in spite of having less than perfect records themselves, pleaded special loyalty to the Union as a basis for controlling the local government and reaping financial benefits from it. Dix, the petitioners continued, issued arbitrary rulings based on things that happened during the war. Blacks in the county were not numerous and enjoyed "freedom and equal rights." Moreover, they said, courts would operate fairly for freedmen and others regardless of the test oath order for juries.[16]

As would be expected, General Griffin ignored this appeal, and Dix kept both his positions. Nevertheless, the petition pointed up the complexities and tensions of Reconstruction at the grass roots. No doubt most of those who had supported the Confederacy had the kind of prejudice against the Union and freedmen that Dix constantly pointed out. And Dix's concern for the former slaves was genuine. He used his offices to protect their interests, although whenever possible he encouraged former slaves to manage their own affairs because that "makes these men more self reliant and independent." He established a school in his Corpus Christi hotel, and Mrs. Dix labored there as an unpaid teacher. He was one of a small minority, north or south, who believed that the national government should give freedmen an economic foothold. "I trust," he wrote bureau headquarters in

---

utes, Book C, 150. The jury order is discussed in some detail in Campbell, "District Judges of Texas in 1866–1867," 368–73.

15. Circular No. 16 issued by Gen. Charles W. Griffin, May 16, 1867, Governors' Papers: JWT; John Dix to Joel Kirkman, May 2, 1867, BRFAL, RG 105, NA.

16. R. J. Denny and forty other citizens of Nueces County to Gen. Charles C. Griffin, June 5, 1867, BRFAL, RG 105, NA.

September, 1867, "that Congress will provide them homesteads at its next session." On the other hand, some of Dix's allies such as McLane and Bryden, who were accused of selling beef to the Confederate army, did not have spotless credentials as Unionists. Also, Dix himself expressed attitudes toward the white majority that were certain to bring trouble. For example, he argued in September, 1867, that all rebels should have been disfranchised at the time of surrender. "To expect to make loyal citizens of traitors," he wrote, "is simply impossible. It never has been done, and it it is folly to expect to do it now." Bitterness was frequently a two-way street during Reconstruction.[17]

Voter registration began in Nueces County on June 18, 1867, and continued until August 6. In late July and early August, a terrible outbreak of yellow fever disrupted registration as it did every other aspect of life in the region. From July 25 through August 17, 106 deaths occurred in Corpus Christi and, in the words of E. J. Davis, "thinned out our population." The registrars reopened the books for two weeks in late September and then for another four days at the end of January, 1868. James Downing, a native of England and former United States Army officer; Cesario Falcon, a Mexican who had become a citizen of the United States by virtue of the annexation of Texas and served in the Union army during the war; and Mitchell Thompson, a black drayman born in South Carolina, served as the first registrars. Downing transferred to Live Oak County in July and was replaced by George B. Worden, who in turn left Corpus Christi to escape the yellow fever and was replaced in September by John McLane, the Pennsylvania native who was also a county commissioner. Thus the registrars represented everyone in the county except southern-born whites.[18]

By the end of January, 1868, the Nueces County registration list included 261 names, 133 of European descent, 80 of Mexican descent, and 48 of African descent. Freedmen, who constituted 18 percent of all voters as opposed to about 8 percent of the county's population, were somewhat over-

17. John Dix to Joel Kirkman, November 30, September 2, 30, 1867, BRFAL, RG 105, NA; Frank Wagner, "John James Dix," in *The New Handbook of Texas*, ed. Ron Tyler (6 vols.; Austin, 1996), II, 657.

18. List of Registered Voters in Texas, 1869. An extra edition of the Corpus Christi *Advertiser* for August 14, 1867, reported the yellow fever deaths. Ninth Census, 1870, Schedule 1; E. J. Davis to Charles C. Griffin, July 25, 1867, E. J. Davis to N. Prine, September 14, 1867, OCA, RG 393, NA; E. J. Davis to Stephen Powers, August 18, 1867, James B. Wells Papers, Eugene C. Barker Texas History Center, University of Texas, Austin. George B. Worden could not be identified.

represented on the list, but Mexicans (at 31 percent of those registered) probably were underrepresented. E. J. Davis, supervisor of registrars in the district, certainly thought so. "I am satisfied," he wrote in early September, "that a large number of Mexicans who are entitled to register in this county have failed to do so. This class of our population was almost universally loyal during the late war, and their failure to take this opportunity to secure the right to vote is to be regretted. The explanation of this lies in the fact that the report was industriously circulated among them that the U.S. intended making war upon Mexico, and that this Registry was for the purpose of making soldiers of them." Davis promised to discover the exact source of the rumors, but he failed. In any case, African-American and Mexican-American voters constituted nearly a majority, and well over half of the European-ancestry group were native to the North or immigrants from abroad. This meant that Republicans in Nueces County did not have to overcome a southern-born white majority in 1868–1869. Instead they faced only a relatively small group of what John Dix called "rowdies and disaffected rebels" encouraged by a "trifling newspaper," the Corpus Christi *Advertiser*.[19]

As voter registration neared completion during late 1867, Congressional Reconstruction touched Nueces County in another way—the replacement of local officials by military order—although not nearly to the extent that occurred across the state. Unlike the many Texas counties that had elected former secessionists to lead local government in 1866, Nueces had continued in office Hamilton's Unionist appointees such as John Dix, and had few who could be removed as "impediments to Reconstruction." Only Sheriff Henry W. Berry—for reasons that are unclear, since he was a Hamilton appointee who had served without having complaints made against him— lost his office in early November. John McLane resigned from the commis-

19. List of Registered Voters in Texas, 1869. An examination of the lists shows that the names of thirty-two men of European ancestry, one Mexican, and two blacks were "struck" after having been registered. E. J. Davis to N. Prine, September 2, 9, 14, 1867, OCA, RG 393, NA. Natives of Mexico were 32 percent of the county's population in 1870, a close match with the 31 percent of those registered who were Mexican. However, the 32 percent did not include the children of Mexicans born in Texas after annexation and, therefore, understates the proportion of Mexican-Americans in the total population. Citizens of Mexican ancestry probably accounted for about half of the county's people and were therefore underrepresented (at 31 percent) in the registration. U.S. Bureau of the Census, *Statistics of the Population of the United States (1870)*, 372–73; John Dix to J. P. Richardson, November 30, 1867, BRFAL, RG 105, NA.

sioners' court and replaced Berry as sheriff. Also in November, 1867, Gen. Joseph J. Reynolds who had replaced General Griffin as commander of the District of Texas upon the latter's death from yellow fever in September, removed District Judge B. F. Neal. Undoubtedly the complaints lodged against the judge by Dix and Davis contributed to this removal. George R. Scott, a Unionist lawyer from Austin, took Neal's place on the bench. "I don't know him [Scott]," Davis wrote a friend in Brownsville, "but he is well spoken of."[20]

During the election held February 10–14, 1868, Nueces County voters overwhelmingly (119 to 1) approved the planned constitutional convention and chose E. J. Davis (114 to 5) as their delegate. Only seventy-six whites voted, but forty-four of the forty-eight registered blacks went to the polls. While the convention met in Austin from mid-1868 until early 1869, military Reconstruction continued, and Nueces County experienced considerable instability in the personnel of local government, especially on the district court bench and in the sheriff's office. George R. Scott, the district judge appointed in November, 1867, served only seven months before being replaced by Jerome B. Carpenter. Judge Carpenter, a Vermont native who had been admitted to the bar in Illinois before coming to Texas after the war, lasted only until February, 1869, before also being removed. His replacement, J. B. Hurd, served for the remaining year of military Reconstruction, although apparently without distinction. Virtually nothing is known of his tenure on the bench except one comment by E. J. Davis that the appointment of the "very weak and irresolute" judge was a "bad mistake." John McLane served as sheriff from November, 1867, until his removal in July, 1868. Military commanders appointed Elijah H. Wheeler and then Nicholas Dunn to replace McLane but each in turn refused to serve. Finally at the end of October, 1868, Peter Benson, a former member of the 14th New York Infantry who came to Corpus Christi after the war, took the position, but he served only six months before being replaced in April, 1869, by Dennis Kelly, a twenty-eight-year-old native of Ireland. John Dix provided stability by remaining county judge throughout this period, and the rapid turnover of district judges and sheriffs may not have greatly

20. Campbell, "Grass Roots Reconstruction," 99–101; Election Registers, 1867. George R. Scott is identified as a supporter of the Constitutional Union party in Baggett, "Rise and Fall of the Texas Radicals, 1867–1883," 15. Edmund J. Davis to Stephen Powers, November 24, 1867, Wells Papers.

harmed local government. Nevertheless, it is unlikely that the changes encouraged respect for or confidence in county officials.[21]

Public life appears to have been relatively quiet in Nueces County from 1868 to early 1870, but the region did not escape entirely the violence and controversy so common across the state during those years. John Dix, as agent for the Freedmen's Bureau, had the responsibility of reporting all criminal disturbances in the county. He reported few such cases during 1867 but in March, 1868, sent headquarters accounts of nineteen incidents, many of them murders. The list, which had been growing since 1865, included mostly acts of violence involving Europeans and Mexicans, but some cases involved attacks by whites against blacks. One D. W. Pickle, for example, fatally stabbed William Forbes in the back and then boasted, according to Dix, that he had acted simply because his victim was black. Dix did not report many more cases during the remaining months of his service as a bureau agent, but local whites consistently drew his disgust. "There is," he wrote in February, 1868, "and always has been . . . difficulty in controlling these people by civil law for the reason that they have never been educated to respect it." They neither "fear God nor regard man," he concluded.[22]

The spring, 1868, term of the district court in Nueces County brought an interesting challenge to military Reconstruction. Daniel Haverty, who faced a probable indictment for swindling, challenged the grand jury on constitutional grounds. First, he argued that County Judge John Dix who presided over the commissioners' court when it selected grand jurors, and Sheriff John McLane, who summoned the jurors to serve, were both employees of the United States (Dix as a Freedmen's Bureau agent and McLane as head of the board of registrars) and therefore ineligible to perform state judicial duties. Second, Haverty challenged three grand jurors because they were blacks and "not a citizen or qualified voter according to the Constitution and laws of the State of Texas." He also claimed that juror Guadalupe Cárdenas was not a citizen. District Judge George R. Scott overruled

21. Election Registers, 1868–1870; Ninth Census, 1870, Schedule 1. Judge Carpenter's bar membership in Illinois was noted in District Court Minutes, Book C, 166, when he applied for admission to the bar in Nueces County. E. J. Davis to James P. Newcomb, July 11, 1869, Newcomb Papers; Briscoe, "Narrative History of Corpus Christi," 483.

22. "Records of Criminal Offenses Committed in the State of Texas," XI–XIII, 39–40, 78, 95, 114, 127, 162, 168, BRFAL, RG 105, NA (pagination continues consecutively through the three volumes). John Dix to J. P. Richardson, March 10, 1868, February 29, 1868, BRFAL, RG 105, NA.

Haverty's objection to the role of Dix and McLane and declared that the challenge to the blacks was "not sufficient in law." Cárdenas, the judge declared, is a citizen. Haverty's action indicates one of the many kinds of disputes created locally by military Reconstruction, and it shows participation by blacks in the justice system in Nueces County several years before that practice became common across Texas.[23]

Voter registration reopened for two weeks in late November, 1869, in preparation for the referendum on the new state constitution and the election of officials under its terms. Bvt. Maj. E. G. Bush of the 10th United States Infantry, Guadalupe Cárdenas, and Matthew Cody, Sr. (a native of Ireland), served as registrars, vigilantly rejecting any man who had ever sworn an oath to support the Constitution of the United States and then supported the Confederacy. For example, the registrars refused to enroll Peter Dunn because he had been an alderman before the war and rejected John H. McMahan for having served as a deputy sheriff. By November 30, Nueces County had 280 voters of European origin (57 percent), 138 of Mexican origin (28 percent), and 76 of African origin (15 percent). Nearly three-quarters of the European-origin registrants came from the northern United States or foreign nations. Thus southern whites, the backbone of conservative opposition to Reconstruction, were in a decided minority.[24]

Statewide, the four-day election (November 30–December 3, 1869) was essentially a contest between Radical Republicans led by E. J. Davis and moderate Republicans led by A. J. Hamilton. Democrats, except for extreme conservatives, tended to support Hamilton. The results in Nueces County were, in the words of the Galveston News, "rather mixed." As would be expected, since it was his home county, E. J. Davis outpolled Hamilton in the governor's race 231 to 143. A radical carpetbagger named Albert J. Fountain who lived in El Paso carried Nueces County overwhelmingly in winning the seat for the Thirtieth District in the state senate. Two of the three men elected state representatives from that district—Ira H. Evans and Nelson Plato—were carpetbagger radicals from Corpus Christi who ran strongly in their home county. Evans, like Plato, had served in the Union army and settled in the area after the war. However, in the race for

23. District Court Minutes, Book C, 162–65.

24. List of Registered Voters in Texas, 1869; Reports by Board of Registrars, Nueces County, November 16–17, 18–22, 26, 1869, OCA, RG 393, NA; Ninth Census, 1870, Schedule 1.

United States representative, the moderate John L. Haynes narrowly defeated Edward Degener, a Bexar County radical, by a vote of 186 to 182 in Nueces County, but Degener won the election districtwide.[25]

Locally, Nueces County radicals won a key race when Dennis Kelly, who held the sheriff's office by military appointment, defeated Henry W. Berry, the moderate originally appointed to that position by Hamilton, by a vote of 158 to 149. Joseph Fitzsimmons, the loyalist candidate for district clerk, also won. The radicals, however, suffered a major defeat when Milas R. Polk, a North Carolina-born moderate whom Hamilton had made tax assessor/collector in 1865, defeated John Dix 144 to 123 for the position of presiding officer of the county court. Polk's victory, crowed Henry A. Maltby, former secessionist and editor in Corpus Christi and now publisher of the Brownsville *Daily Ranchero* in Cameron County, "put the venerable Capt. John Dix, Sr., overboard. That balances the other losses and more too." There are no contemporary explanations of Dix's defeat. Virtually all of the county's black voters, most of whom lived in Corpus Christi (the presiding justice's precinct), cast ballots, so it must be assumed that whites defeated Dix. Perhaps he had done too much for the freedmen, or maybe his obvious sense of New Englander superiority had offended some voters. (Even in Michigan, where he lived before moving to Texas, Dix had offended local citizens with his "haughty attitude.") Also, he was nearing sixty-five years of age and not in good health. Of the other four positions on the county court, all of which represented very sparsely populated precincts, only two were contested, and radicals (Samuel R. Miller and Norman G. Collins) won both. The two justices who had no opposition (Richard R. Schubert and John S. Greer) soon joined the Democrats.[26]

The mixed results of the election of 1869 in Nueces County showed that

25. Election returns for 1869 are found in *Senate Miscellaneous Documents*, 41st Cong., 2nd Sess., No. 77, pp. 38–79. Galveston *Daily News*, December 9, 1869; Ira H. Evans Vertical File, Eugene C. Barker Texas History Center, University of Texas, Austin; Webb, Carroll, and Branda, eds., *Handbook of Texas*, I, 482, 637–38, III, 381. The third state representative from the 30th District was George Spencer of Starr County, a native of Ireland. *Members of the Texas Legislature*, 62; Ninth Census, 1870, Schedule 1.

26. Local election returns are in *Senate Miscellaneous Documents*, 41st Cong., 2nd Sess., No. 77, pp. 38–79. Brownsville *Daily Ranchero*, December 11, 1869. Polk, although no radical, was a personal friend of E. J. Davis. See Polk to Davis, April 14, 1870, Governors' Papers: EJD. The comment on Dix's "haughty attitude" is from Dan R. Manning, trans., comp., and ed., "The Rancho Ramirena Journal of John James Dix," *Southwestern Historical Quarterly*, XCVIII (1994), 81. Schubert and Greer attended a meeting of Nueces County Democrats in 1873. Corpus Christi *Weekly Gazette*, August 23, 1873.

Republicans had the votes to maintain control, especially as they ended conflict between radicals and moderates and unified to oppose Democrats. However, unlike the situation in most Republican-dominated counties in East Texas, the party's strength lay with northern-born and immigrant voters and in the Mexican population rather than with freedmen. The census of 1870 showed that 32 percent of the people of Nueces County were natives of Mexico; an additional 10 percent, of other foreign nations. Combined with the northern-born, these groups constituted a majority in the county. The problem for Republicans lay in the fact that these groups of potential voters did not have the unifying interests shared by blacks and were less likely to vote as a bloc. Democrats could win support in particular races, especially district, state, and national contests involving no local residents. Also, Republican strength was concentrated in Corpus Christi, making it more difficult to control all precincts in the county. Under these circumstances, elections promised such mixed results for years to come unless Republicans satisfactorily handled issues such as maintaining law and order in the region from Corpus Christi to the Rio Grande, public education, and taxes. At least the party had more of a chance in Nueces County than it did in many areas of Texas dominated by white southerners determined to return to conservative rule.[27]

The county's new government proved more unstable during 1870 while Texas returned to its place in the Union than it had for most of Congressional Reconstruction. Milas R. Polk, just elected as presiding justice, was found in January, 1870, to be delinquent in his accounts with the county as tax assessor/collector, a position that he had held since 1865. County Judge John Dix, in his last official act as he neared death, removed Polk from office on January 16.[28] Because of the problems as tax collector, Polk could not qualify for his position on the county court either. A special election had to be held November 28–December 1, 1870, to fill the positions of presiding justice and those held by the two Republican justices elected in 1869 (Miller and Collins), both of whom also had failed to qualify. Republican candidates enjoyed a new advantage in this election because Governor Davis had

27. U.S. Bureau of the Census, *Statistics of the Population of the United States (1870)*, 372–73.

28. John J. Dix, Jr., to E. J. Davis, January 16, 1870, M. R. Polk to Davis, April 14, 1870, Governors' Papers: EJD. John J. Dix, Sr., died in January, 1870, and was replaced briefly by Matthew Cody, Sr. Election Registers, 1870.

ruled that the constitution required countywide rather than precinct-by-precinct voting in choosing justices. Justices had to reside in the precinct they represented; nevertheless, the large number of Republican voters in Corpus Christi could participate in the selection of the entire county court. Charles Weidenmuller, a native of Germany whose strong unionism caused him to move to Mexico during the Civil War, won the position of presiding justice. He defeated H. W. Berry, a moderate Republican turned Democrat, by twenty-five votes, 110 to 85. Collins outpolled F. C. Gravis, a Democrat born in Texas, by about the same margin, and Miller won without opposition. Membership of the county court remained unsettled, however, because Collins again failed to qualify, necessitating another special election in May, 1871. James O. Luby, a young clerk from Ireland, defeated Richard Miller by about twenty-five votes and finally gave the court a full complement of justices. Luby ran as a Republican but proved so acceptable to Democrats that he would receive their endorsement and run without opposition for reelection in 1873.[29]

In June, 1870, county government received another blow to its stability, at least temporarily, when Sheriff Dennis Kelly was murdered. Sheriff Kelly, while investigating a loud party at a Corpus Christi saloon, got into an argument with Tom Burke, who stabbed him fatally and ran for Mexico. Joseph Fitzsimmons, the radical district clerk, insisted that the murder was a political crime. Kelly, he wrote Governor Davis, was brave and efficient, "and I have no doubt was marked by the Ku Klux as a victim." No evidence existed to support this charge, however. John McLane, a leading Republican who had held the sheriff's office as a military appointee, replaced Kelly in July and had no further trouble. "Well," he wrote Davis in October, "our town is quiet beyond anything I have ever seen."[30]

The move toward stability in county government by late 1870 received another boost in November when the state district court held its first session

29. John McLane to E. J. Davis, October 23, December 2, 1870, in Governors' Papers: EJD; *Nueces Valley* (Corpus Christi), November 12, 26, December 3, 1870. Governor Davis' interpretation of the constitutional requirements on voting for justices of the peace is found in election proclamations that he issued during 1870. See, for example, the Austin *Daily State Journal*, November 4, 1870. For information on Luby, see Election Registers, 1871–1873; Ninth Census, 1870, Schedule 1; *Nueces Valley*, May 13, 1871; Corpus Christi *Weekly Gazette*, December 20, 1873.

30. John McLane to E. J. Davis, June 14, 1870, Joseph Fitzsimmons to E. J. Davis, June 14, 1870, Governors' Papers: EJD; John McLane to E. J. Davis, October 10, 1870, Executive Record Books: EJD.

with Judge Tilson C. Barden on the bench. Barden, a native of New York, had come to Texas as an officer in the 117th United States Colored Infantry in 1865 and mustered out as a captain in 1867 at Brownsville. After serving briefly as judge of the First District during the last year of Congressional Reconstruction, he was appointed by Governor Davis as judge of the Sixteenth District, a position that he would hold until 1876, when a new constitution made district judges elective once again. The spring, 1871, court session held by Judge Barden resulted in a grand jury report pointing to the problem of outlaws, primarily cattle thieves from Mexico, operating in and south of Nueces County and calling for all "party dissensions" to be "buried" in the interest of restoring law and order.[31]

Although Republicans and leading Democrats served on this grand jury and undoubtedly were sincere in calling for cooperation to end lawlessness, their nonpartisanship ended there. Indeed, the advent of the Davis administration in 1870 provided local party activists a focal point for their differences, and two partisan newspapers—the Democratic *Weekly Advertiser* and the Republican *Nueces Valley,* both of Corpus Christi—presented their arguments to the public. The latter supported Davis' program, which included a new state police force and public school system, and denied the Democrats' charges that the state government had too much power and was ruining the public with high taxes. The Democrats naturally sought to blame the Davis administration for the lawlessness between Corpus Christi and Brownsville.[32]

In the fall of 1871 the relative strength of the two parties in Nueces County received a test in the election of a United States representative for the Forty-first Congress. To the dismay of Republican activists, their incumbent congressman, Edward Degener, lost to the Democratic candidate, John Hancock, by a vote of 139 to 134. Although Hancock was a conservative Unionist who had left Texas during the war, local Republicans saw Degener's defeat as a sign of dangerous apathy on their part. "The county is Republican," the *Nueces Valley* commented on October 7, 1871, "and there is

31. Huson, *District Judges of Refugio County,* 94–97; District Court Minutes, Book C, 526–27. For information on the problem of Mexican cattle thieves raiding in the area north of Brownsville, see LeRoy P. Graf, "The Economic History of the Lower Rio Grande Valley, 1820–1875" (Ph.D. dissertation, Harvard University, 1942), 630, 642.

32. *Nueces Valley,* January 14, June 24, July 29, 1871; Corpus Christi *Weekly Advertiser,* April 8, 1870.

no reason why it should not go Republican at every election." Perhaps party leaders could have done more to gain support for Degener in Nueces, but theirs was not the only county to fail the incumbent. He lost the election to Hancock districtwide.[33]

The next spring, as Texas prepared to participate in its first presidential election since 1860, Nueces County Republicans worked hard to mobilize support for their candidates. In April a county convention passed resolutions endorsing the records of President Ulysses S. Grant and Governor Davis and chose John McLane and Dr. Thomas Kearney, the New York–born customs collector at Corpus Christi, as delegates to the Republican state convention in May. A "Republican and Grant Club" met regularly during the spring and summer before being replaced in August by a "Grant and Wilson Club" supporting the party's national ticket (U. S. Grant and Henry Wilson). All of the county's leading Republicans, such as Judge Tilson C. Barden, Nelson Plato, Charles Weidenmuller, and Joseph Fitzsimmons, participated in these activities. Plato, as editor of the *Nueces Valley,* constantly called for party unity and pointed to the Davis administration's works of civic improvement such as the public school system. The party also benefited from the involvement of Gen. Lewis G. Brown, the New York–born former commander of the 25th U.S. Army Corps on the Rio Grande, who had settled in Corpus Christi after the war. A businessman at first, Brown helped establish the *Nueces Valley* in 1870 and by 1872 was serving as chairman of the Republican executive committee for the Thirtieth Senatorial District. He refused to accept nomination for any office himself but obviously contributed to the party's cause.[34]

Nueces County Democrats followed the lead of the national party in 1872 by endorsing Horace Greeley, candidate of the new Liberal Republican party that sought to unite all voters opposed to Grant and the corruption of his administration. The *Nueces Valley* made fun of the Democrats' "Greeley Club," but the *Weekly Advertiser* was even uglier about the Grant Republicans. "We want none of their lip!" William H. Maltby wrote, "Teach them that they have been tolerated, because there is no help for it,

---

33. *Nueces Valley,* October 7, November 4, 1871; Webb, Carroll, and Branda, eds., *Handbook of Texas,* I, 482, 763–64.

34. *Nueces Valley,* July 29, 1871, April 13, 20, 27, May 11, July 13, August 17, 24, September 21, 1872; Ninth Census, 1870, Schedule 1.

and not countenanced nor respected as men who had the right to meddle with the political affairs of Texas. Stand back, oh, ye carpetbaggers, scalawaggers, and government stink pots!"[35]

Only a few county government offices had to be filled in 1872, the most important being those of sheriff and treasurer. Republicans held a county convention in October and renominated John McLane for sheriff and Prokose Hoffman, a liquor dealer born in Bohemia, for treasurer. Two of the ten delegates to this meeting from precinct one (Corpus Christi), Mitchell Thompson and George Wilson, were black, indicating that Republicans backed their pleas for "colored" votes with a willingness to allow black participation. None of the ten, however, had Hispanic surnames. The Democrats chose William L. Rogers, a stockraiser from Louisiana, to oppose McLane and Felix Noessel, an immigrant from Germany, as the candidate for treasurer.[36]

The results of the November, 1872, Nueces County election were again inconsistent. The Liberal Republican Greeley defeated Grant by a vote of 373 to 272, and John Hancock, the Unionist Democrat, won another term in Congress by nearly the same margin over his Republican opponent. However, Republican candidates generally ran stronger than Democrats in the election of representatives for the Thirteenth Texas Legislature. For example, James Downing, the former Union army officer, received 417 votes, whereas Henry A. Gilpin of Corpus Christi, his nearest Democratic opponent, had only 279. (Gilpin, a sixty-two-year-old stockraiser originally from Rhode Island, and the other two Democratic candidates—Stephen Powers of Brownsville and J. F. Tom of Pleasanton—won districtwide and went to Austin to serve in the state legislature.) More important, Republicans won the key local contests by convincing margins. McLane defeated Rogers for sheriff 428 to 204 and Hoffman took the treasurer's office by a 347 to 277 vote. The party still controlled the county, but as before, it could not deliver a bloc vote for all Republican candidates.[37]

35. *Nueces Valley,* September 28, 1872; Corpus Christi *Weekly Advertiser,* July 6, 1872, quoted in Briscoe, "Narrative History of Corpus Christi," 527.

36. *Nueces Valley,* October 12, 19, November 9, 1872; Ninth Census, 1870, Schedule 1.

37. *Nueces Valley,* November 9, 1872. The political loyalties of Stephen Powers, like those of many politicians in the area stretching from Corpus Christi to Brownsville to El Paso, were quite flexible during Reconstruction. He attended the Democratic national convention in 1868 and won election to the state house of representatives as a Democrat in 1872, but was cooperating with the Republicans by 1876. See Edmund J. Davis to Stephen Powers, August 23, 1868, March 14, 1876, in Wells Papers.

The fall of 1873 brought the first general election since 1869. Statewide, conservative Democrats stood poised to end radical rule in Texas by electing Richard Coke to replace E. J. Davis in the governor's office. Nueces County Democrats, perhaps emboldened by this prospect, finally matched the Republicans in local organizational efforts. A convention in August sent seven delegates, including county court members Richard Schubert and John S. Greer, to the Democratic state convention in Austin. Another local meeting created a county executive committee and chose candidates for local office. Using a new Democratic newspaper, the Corpus Christi *Weekly Gazette,* the party hammered away at the Davis administration for high taxes and corruption. Democrats, according to the *Gazette,* are longtime residents of Texas, whereas Republicans are newcomers who have flocked to the state like buzzards to a carcass. This charge was not entirely fair, of course, although men such as Nelson Plato, who once more led his party's campaign, were indeed carpetbaggers.[38]

Governor Davis, although he lost badly statewide as conservatives took control of Texas, carried Nueces County by a vote of 313 to 199 over Coke, perhaps because he lived in South Texas and had many personal friends in Corpus Christi. Democrats, however, swept the state legislative races. An Irish-born resident of Corpus Christi, P. F. Murphy, led all candidates for the house of representatives in Nueces County. He was joined in the house by Louis Cardis, an Italian immigrant who lived in El Paso, and Santos Benavides of Webb County. William H. Russell of Brownsville, having changed political allegiance since being appointed a district judge by Governor Davis in 1870, defeated Thomas Kearney of Corpus Christi for the state senate seat. (Unfortunately, local returns on the Russell-Kearney race are not available, so the relative strength of the two candidates in Nueces County is not known.) Contests for local office, like those for state-level positions, did not go exclusively in favor of either party. Republicans showed their strength by electing Daniel M. Hastings, a native of Boston, as presiding officer of the county court and Joseph Fitzsimmons as district clerk. But Democratic candidates took the remaining four positions on the county court. Two of the races were uncontested, but in the other two, Democrats won by sizable margins. W. A. Ball, a young Tennessean, defeated John Kellett (who had served as county commissioner from 1866 to 1869) by a vote

38. Corpus Christi *Weekly Gazette,* January 4, August 23, 30, October 11, 1873.

of 364 to 134, and Richard Schubert defeated Rafael Salinas 374 to 128. Perhaps even more surprising, Charles Weidenmuller, who had held numerous positions including presiding justice and mayor of Corpus Christi, lost the race for county treasurer to Felix Noessel, the unsuccessful Democratic candidate in 1872. The *Gazette* hailed the end of Davis' administration, saying he "can now retire from public life without a sigh for his loss," but it had few comments on the results for local government.[39]

Thus statewide "redemption" in 1873 left Nueces County with a mixed local government, a situation that did not change during the remaining three years of the Reconstruction era. Indeed, once the Davis administration ended, local politics apparently became somewhat less partisan and less focused on the issues of Reconstruction. Republicans and Democrats still battled at the polls, but they tended to make more of national and state elections than local contests and to concentrate more on the performance of county and regional officials than on their partisan qualifications. For example, in July, 1874, the Democratic *Weekly Gazette* praised District Judge Tilson C. Barden, a carpetbagger appointed by Davis, for being "impartial and upright" and a terror to criminals. When two seats on the county court had to be filled at a special election that same month, Reuben Holbein, who had served as county clerk before and during the Civil War, won without opposition in the fourth precinct, and Charles L. Lege, a German immigrant, defeated Rafael Salinas in the fifth precinct. The *Gazette* had nothing to say about the partisan affiliations of any of the candidates.[40]

In November, 1874, the Nueces County electorate voted Democratic in two national and state races, supporting Gustave Schleicher of San Antonio over Jeremiah Galvan of Brownsville in a contest for the United States House of Representatives and giving John M. Moore (a former Confederate soldier) a victory over James Downing (a former Union soldier) in electing a state representative. The editor of the *Gazette* enjoyed these results, but a few weeks later made a point of praising the work of the carpetbagger,

39. *Ibid.*, December 20, 1873, January 31, 1874; Galveston *Daily News,* December 14, 17, 1873; Webb, Carroll, and Branda, eds., *Handbook of Texas,* I, 295. Russell's defection to the Democrats drew the wrath of Governor Davis. "There is no more despicable character in the politics of this State than the man William H. Russell," he wrote in 1874, "and he is the last man I would in any way abet in his private or public schemes." Davis to Stephen Powers and Nestor Maxan, October 27, 1874, in Wells Papers.

40. Corpus Christi *Weekly Gazette,* July 4, 11, 1874. These elections were held because Richard Schubert had resigned and John S. Greer had not qualified. Election Registers, 1873–1874.

Nelson Plato, as collector of customs at Corpus Christi. The newspaper said it agreed with the many local citizens who believed that individual Republicans such as Colonel Plato have done a good job.[41]

In 1875, Texas conservatives called for the election of a convention to write a new fundamental law to replace the Constitution of 1869. The voters of Nueces County, as residents of a thinly populated senatorial district that reached from Corpus Christi to El Paso, faced very confusing choices in electing three delegates to this convention. William H. Russell, the Republican judge turned Democratic state senator, arranged a district convention that nominated himself, Charles Howard of El Paso, and R. Benavides of Webb County as a Democratic ticket. Other South Texas politicians, however, who for one reason or another disliked Russell and his allies, nominated an "Independent Democrat" ticket consisting of John S. "Rip" Ford of Cameron County, J. B. Murphy of Nueces County, and Louis Cardis of El Paso. Republicans, rather than nominating yet another slate, supported Benavides from one and Murphy and Cardis from the other. Districtwide the seats in the convention went to the three "Independent Democrats"—Ford, Cardis, and Murphy. Nueces County voters gave strong support to Ford, a former secessionist and Confederate colonel with solid credentials as a conservative, but also voted heavily for Murphy, Governor Davis' former law partner and one of the candidates favored by Republicans. Thus the selection of delegates did not mean that conservatives had firm control of the county—a fact that was borne out when the convention completed its work and elections were held on February 15, 1876, to approve the new constitution and elect state and local officers.[42]

Richard Coke, the conservative Democratic incumbent, overwhelmed

41. Corpus Christi *Weekly Gazette*, September 19, October 24, November 7, 28, 1874. The election of a state representative became necessary when P. F. Murphy resigned. *Members of the State Legislature*, 81.

42. Corpus Christi *Weekly Gazette*, June 26, August 7, 14, 1875; Webb, Carroll, and Branda, eds., *Handbook of Texas*, I, 617–18. William H. Russell, a native Texan, lived in Cameron County in 1880. Davis made him judge of the Fifteenth Judicial District in 1870. Tenth Census, 1880, Schedule 1; Election Registers, 1870. Coke made Charles Howard a district judge in 1874. Election Registers, 1874. Most of the information necessary to explain this confusing intramural contest among Democrats is in two letters from John L. Haynes to J. P. Newcomb, June 10 and August 9, 1875, Newcomb Papers. Information on the election and the Thirtieth District's representation in the convention is also found in the Galveston *Daily News*, August 7, September 4, 1875. The *News* incorrectly named Santos Benavides rather than J. B. Murphy as a delegate, but the Austin *Daily Democratic Statesman*, September 8, 1875, correctly names Murphy.

his Republican challenger, William M. Chambers, by a vote of 1,007 to 181 in the race for governor, and Democrats won important regional races as well. For example, William L. Rogers defeated John S. McCampbell in the contest for state representative, 675 to 471. In the race for county judge, however, Joseph Fitzsimmons received 635 votes and defeated two challengers, J. R. Spann (451 votes) and Peyton Smythe (113 votes). Fitzsimmons, the leading Republican activist in the county, served as chairman of the party's local executive committee in 1876. His campaign advertisements, printed in both English and Spanish in the *Gazette,* reminded voters that he had held the county clerk's position for ten years. The sheriff's office also went to a Republican as Thomas Beynon, a native of Wales, defeated Henry W. Berry, the moderate Unionist who had held the position from 1865 to 1867, by the slender margin of 592 to 587. Berry challenged the result, but the *Gazette* acceded: "We feel satisfied that the new Sheriff is acceptable, not only to those who voted for him, but to those who voted against him as well." Voters also elected four county commissioners, that office having been restored by the new constitution, but the contests exhibited little or no partisanship. The *Gazette* commented favorably on all candidates, and only one of the winners, Frank C. Gravis, a Democrat, can be identified according to party. The other three commissioners—Joseph W. Dunn, Andrew R. Valls, and John Vining—were natives of the South, but that apparently had no political implications.[43]

After 1876, as further evidence that the issues of Reconstruction carried little weight in local elections, the voters of Nueces County voted consistently Democratic in presidential and gubernatorial contests and yet supported well-known Republicans locally. In 1880, for example, Winfield S. Hancock received 890 votes to 169 for James A. Garfield in the presidential race, and Oran M. Roberts defeated E. J. Davis, 847 to 208, in the contest for governor. However, Joseph Fitzsimmons won the county judge's office, and Thomas Beynon continued as sheriff.[44]

Thus Reconstruction in Nueces County did not end with a definitive "redemption" by conservative Democrats as was true statewide and in many

43. Corpus Christi *Daily Gazette,* January 5, 7, 29, February 1, 12, 16, 22, 25, 1876. The newspaper did not give the results of the contests for county commissioner. Winners are in the Election Registers, 1876. Basic biographical information on candidates is from the Ninth Census, 1870, Schedule 1, and Tenth Census, 1880, Schedule 1.

44. Kingston, Attlesey, and Crawford, *Political History of Texas,* 60, 74; Election Registers, 1876.

individual counties, especially in East Texas. Instead, where local government was concerned, the political conflict of that era faded with the passing
years. This gradual easing of the struggle between "radicals" and "Redeemers" was no doubt made possible by the relatively small number of blacks
in the county and the sizable proportion of Mexicans, European immigrants, and natives of the North. Nueces County's population nearly
doubled in the ten years after 1870, and by 1880, 43 percent of all residents
were foreign born. (Most of those not born in the United States, 36 percent
of the total population, were natives of Mexico.) White conservatives simply could not appeal to a majority of voters on the basis of issues such as
"Negro rule" or loyalty to the South. Moreover, concern over lawlessness
in the region from Corpus Christi to Brownsville unified most citizens regardless of partisan views.[45]

As Reconstruction drew to a close, Nueces County's blacks could point
to considerable political and social progress. Freedmen voted and served on
juries. They held no major offices in local government, but some participated actively in the Republican party. In 1880, the great majority (84 percent) of black families lived in Corpus Christi, where the men worked primarily as draymen and laborers and the women as laundresses and cooks.
Undoubtedly most were poor, but apparently this did not prevent considerable social stability. For example, nuclear families constituted nearly two-
thirds of the 115 black households in the county, and 74 percent of the families with children aged six to sixteen had at least one of those children
attend school for part of the previous year. Reconstruction by no means
guaranteed the freedmen of Nueces County a future of opportunity and
equality before the law, but at least it allowed one generation to achieve
more than might have been expected of people just emerging from slavery.[46]

The Mexican population of Nueces County, having not been enslaved,
had less to gain during Reconstruction than did the freedmen. For example,
they could vote and serve on juries during the antebellum years and contin-

45. The population was 3,975 in 1870 and 7,673 in 1880. U.S. Bureau of the Census, *Statistics of Population of the United States (1870)*, 64–65; U.S. Bureau of the Census, *Statistics of
the Population of the United States (1880)*, 410, 443. A good example of the concern over lawlessness regardless of partisan affiliation is found in an account of a public meeting published
in the Corpus Christi *Weekly Gazette*, December 20, 1873.

46. Information on the black population of Nueces County in 1880 is based on census data
reported for all 115 households in the county headed by African Americans. Tenth Census,
1880, Schedule 1.

ued to exercise those rights after the war. The years from 1865 to 1880, however, in spite of the fact that Mexican voters contributed to Unionist/ Republican success at the polls, did not bring any notable increase in political power to Hispanic citizens. Cesario Falcon and Guadalupe Cárdenas served on the local board of registrars from 1867 to 1869, but no one of Mexican ancestry held a major county office during the years from 1865 to 1880. Moreover, there does not appear to have been any special effort to organize or appeal to the Mexican voters of Nueces County as a bloc. In Brownsville, John L. Haynes tried to influence Hispanics to vote for Edward Degener in the 1871 congressional election by reminding them that the Democratic candidate, John Hancock, had been affiliated during the 1850s with the antiforeign, anti-Catholic Know-Nothing party. Also, politicians in some heavily Mexican counties apparently used the Catholic Church in a partisan fashion. For example, after the presidential election of 1872, S. B. Newcomb of El Paso complained to his brother: "If the election in this county holds water we may as well give up the business. The old Priest fairly drove these poor ignorant Mexicans to vote like sheep. He hurled all the anathemas of the church against all who would dare vote the Republican ticket. He went from house to house threatening even the women. No species of intimidation could be half as effective as this with these people." Others may have used similar methods to appeal to Hispanics in Nueces County, but there is no evidence to that effect. Instead, they appear to have been left alone to vote and generally not included otherwise in political decision making.[47]

Reconstruction brought relatively minor changes, even temporarily, to the lives of Nueces County's Anglo and immigrant population. The county had no antebellum slaveholding elite who could attempt to retain or regain power, and blacks were not numerous enough to threaten white domination in any way. Tax increases proved disturbing—especially when state and local property taxes that never exceeded 80 cents per $100 in evaluation from 1860 to 1870 soared to $1.50 on $100 in 1871. However, Nueces County residents seem to have accepted these taxes with a minumum of complaint, even though rates remained above $1.00 on $100 for the next five years. Perhaps rapid growth helped ease the shock of higher taxes. The

47. Brownsville *Ranchero and Republican,* September 19, 1871, copy in the John L. Haynes Papers, Eugene C. Barker Texas History Center, University of Texas, Austin; S. B. Newcomb to J. P. Newcomb, November 12, 1872, Newcomb Papers.

county's total population increased from 3,975 in 1870 to 7,673 residents in 1880, of whom 3,257 lived in Corpus Christi. Moreover, during the years from 1865 to 1876, the total assessed value of taxable property in the county rose from $1,177,496 to $3,533,155, an increase of 200 percent.[48]

In short, Nueces County experienced less bitter controversy and racial violence during Reconstruction than did most settled areas of Texas. Located on the periphery of the cotton South with a population largely composed of Mexicans and immigrants, the county had relatively little difficulty with emotional issues such as "Negro rule" or government by carpet-baggers. Blacks were less than 10 percent of the population, and carpet-baggers, although more numerous than in most Texas localities, did not dominate local affairs. Even if they had, recent arrivals from abroad or the northern states would have cared very little. Somewhat curiously, Reconstruction polemics, such as charges that "Radical" government gave rise to high taxes and corruption, seem to have affected the county's voters in state and national elections, but not on the local level. From the 1870s onward, they favored Democrats in most contests for the state legislature, the governor's office, Congress, and the presidency. At home, however, where individual officeholders were better known and political issues less abstract, Unionists and Republicans continued to win office, and Republican appointees won the approval of their fellow citizens. These disparate allegiances reflected a county that did not experience Reconstruction with the same intensity as did a good many others in Texas; one that certainly did not see radical change between 1865 and 1876; and a district that enjoyed notable growth and prosperity rather than the oppression and hardships so often associated with the era.

48. Nueces County's economic elite, defined as the richest 5 percent of taxpayers in 1865, consisted largely of stockraisers. Of the seventeen families in this class at the beginning of Reconstruction, only two (12 percent) remained in that group in 1880, whereas eight (47 percent) had fallen from the elite and seven (41 percent) were no longer in the county. Thus the economic elite in Nueces County suffered greater losses during Reconstruction than did the same class in other counties examined in this study. The reasons, however, could not have been related to the readjustments required by the death of slavery and apparently had little to do with Reconstruction. (Incidentally, only three of the richest seventeen families in 1865 were headed by Hispanics, so the losses among the economic elite do not appear to have been explained by members of that ethnic group losing their property to Anglos.) Real and Personal Property Tax Rolls, Nueces County, 1860–1876; U.S. Bureau of the Census, *Statistics of Population of the United States (1870)*, 64–65; U.S. Bureau of the Census, *Statistics of the Population of the United States (1880)*, 347, 410.

# CONCLUSION

The most obvious generalization that emerges from a study of grass-roots Reconstruction in Texas is an equally obvious warning: Be very careful in generalizing about events and developments from 1865 to 1880 in so large and varied a state. Although men in Washington and Austin created a common framework of constitutional provisions, legislative requirements, and military directives, Texans experienced Reconstruction very differently from county to county. The era simply did not unfold the same way or have the same impact in counties as varied demographically and economically as Colorado, Dallas, Harrison, Jefferson, McLennan, and Nueces. Nevertheless, a considerable number of general observations may be made concerning grass-roots Reconstruction in Texas, some fairly broad and others much more qualified but still useful. These conclusions fall into two categories—those applicable to particular phases of Reconstruction as it developed from 1865 to 1880 and those general enough to apply to the entire era.

At the outset of Reconstruction in Texas, President Andrew Johnson and provisional governor A. J. Hamilton expected Unionists who had opposed secession in 1861 to play a major role. Most Unionists wanted to live up to that expectation, but the strength and nature of unionism varied considerably from county to county. For example, in Colorado County 36 percent of those voting in February, 1861, opposed secession, most of the opposition coming from Germans who dominated certain precincts and doubtless encouraged each other. By contrast, only about 5 percent of those who went to the polls in Harrison and Jefferson Counties voted against secession. Both counties had virulently prosecession newspapers and no concentrations of ethnic groups opposed to disunion. Under those circumstances, it seems apparent that most of those who disagreed with secession, such as the old-line Whigs of Harrison County, did not have the courage to vote. Dallas, McLennan, and Nueces Counties matched the statewide proportion of Unionist votes with about 24 percent, but Dallas had many natives of the Upper South and Midwest, whereas Nueces' population included significant numbers of Mexicans, natives of the Northeast, and immigrants from abroad. In McLennan County, where the population was predominantly southern-born, unionism appears to have been largely a matter of individual experience and persuasion. In short, each county had Unionists, but they did not have the similiarity in background or conviction that could have helped unify them in support of a single approach to Reconstruction.

Provisional governor Hamilton, when he chose interim county officials in 1865, often did not do as much as possible to encourage local Unionists or warn secessionists that losing the war could mean changes in political leadership. Having to make hundreds of appointments in a short time while deluged with advice and appeals from interested parties, Hamilton faced a difficult task. He generally succeeded in picking men with a reputation for some degree of unionism, but only a few of them, such as John J. Dix of Nueces County and N. V. Board of Harrison County, had absolutely refused to support the Confederacy. Most were southern-born, and many had owned slaves. In two counties—Dallas and Jefferson—a majority of the appointees were men who had been elected to county offices in 1864 before the close of the war. Moreover, a few of Hamilton's choices, such as District Judge Richard Coke in McLennan County and County Judge William H. Hord in Dallas County, were noted secessionists. Thus, Unionists often wound up confused or angry, and disunionists did not receive enough of a warning that losing the war could lead to demands for change far greater than just ending slavery.

The January 8, 1866, election of delegates to the constitutional convention under Presidential Reconstruction indicated for the first time the differing views that voters in the various counties had about secession and the changes Reconstruction should bring. Nueces County chose a candidate, Edmund J. Davis, known for committed opposition to secession and the

Confederacy. Colorado and Dallas Counties elected delegates who, although they had supported the South during the war, were not known as ardent proponents of disunion. By contrast, the delegates chosen to represent Harrison, Jefferson, and McLennan Counties had strongly supported the Confederacy, three of the four as officers in the Confederate army. Thus, at the outset of Reconstruction, several counties indicated a willingness to accept Unionist or moderate leadership while others insisted on supporting secessionists and ex-Confederates.

In the election on June 25, 1866, to approve the new constitution and elect officials under its terms, voters in all six counties gave majority support to James W. Throckmorton, the Conservative Unionist candidate for governor. The results of district and local races, however, again demonstrated notable differences among the counties in willingness to admit that defeat required changes in attitude and leadership. Harrison and McLennan Counties remained unrepentant, electing secessionists and former Confederate officers to most key positions—and in the process defeating incumbents appointed by Governor Hamilton. In the race for county judge of McLennan County, for example, voters elected Wallace E. Oakes, who had held that office in 1861, over Hamilton's appointee, Robert Crudup. Dallas County seemed to forsake the moderation exhibited earlier in the year and elected ex-Confederate officers as district judge and county judge, also defeating Hamilton appointees. By contrast, Nueces County kept in office virtually all the Unionists appointed by Hamilton, including the wartime exile John J. Dix as county judge. Similarly, Colorado County, thanks to its German voters, returned to office its appointed county judge and did not turn local government over to former Confederates. Jefferson County voters retained the county judge appointed by Hamilton but defeated two of his county commissioners. In that county, however, the impact of Reconstruction on local government had been minimal because Hamilton had left in office all of the men elected in 1864.

Congressional Reconstruction obviously required all counties to follow the same procedures from 1867 through 1870 in writing a new constitution and restoring state and local government under its terms. This meant, for example, that each had a three-man board of registrars composed of a freedman and two Unionists, to enroll white and black voters who met the new standards of eligibility. In one significant way, however, the experience of the six counties differed during Congressional Reconstruction. The three that had elected secessionists and former Confederates to lead local government in 1866 (Dallas, Harrison, and McLennan) saw those officials removed in November, 1867, and replaced by military appointees. On the other hand, the three that had put Unionists or moderates in control locally in 1866 (Colorado, Jefferson, and Nueces) had no general removal of officials until the test-oath requirement went into effect in the spring of 1869. Thus the degree of federal intervention in county government between 1867 and 1870 varied considerably, depending on the attitude of local citizens.

Voter registration began during the summer of 1867 in all six counties and continued intermittently until the end of January, 1868. In each county, owing to the disfranchisement of whites or their refusal to register, blacks constituted a disproportionately large (relative to their numbers in the total population) part of the electorate. Then, during the February 10–14, 1868, election of delegates to the constitutional convention, sizable majorities of freedmen in each county voted while many whites did not participate. This was true even in counties such as Nueces and Colorado that had relatively large numbers of Unionist and moderate white voters. As a result, Colorado and Harrison chose three of the nine black delegates originally elected to the constitutional convention of 1868–1869, and radical Republicans represented five of the six counties. Only Jefferson County had a moderate delegate, and he owed his seat to voters in the other counties in the district rather than those in his own.

The first major test of Republicans' ability to control county government in Texas once Congressional Reconstruction ended came in the election held November 30–December 3, 1869, to approve the Constitution of 1869 and elect officials according to its provisions. In this case, as in all others except the election of delegates to the convention in 1868, the results varied notably among the counties. Four of the six (Colorado, Harrison, Mc-Lennan, Nueces) elected Republicans to most local offices. Even then, however, there was considerable variation from county to county in the electorate responsible for Republican success. Colorado County Republicans won thanks to German and black voters; Harrison Republicans, to the overwhelming black majority; McLennan Republicans, to a combination of blacks and Unionist whites; and Nueces Republicans, to Unionist Anglos and Mexicans. In the other two counties (Dallas and Jefferson), conservative white majorities asserted themselves to give control of local government to Democrats. But there, too, circumstances varied. The election in

Dallas County involved conventional Republican versus conservative contests and showed extensive partisan voting. Jefferson County differed in that several of the men elected to the county court were noted Unionists who had held office as military appointees. Activist Republicans, however, did not win there.

Thus four of the six counties had largely Republican governments when civilian government returned to Texas in 1870 and from the point of view of white conservatives had to be "redeemed." In three of the four (Colorado, Harrison, and McLennan) factionalism plagued the Republicans, rising in part from the moderate-radical split in the party statewide before 1870 and in part from a simple desire for public office, but these internal divisions apparently did not ruin their chances at the polls. Democrats regained dominance in McLennan County at the first opportunity presented after 1870—the general election of December 2, 1873. This victory came in the same election in which Richard Coke of Waco won the governorship, giving conservatives control of the legislative and executive branches of the government, and probably resulted from great local enthusiasm plus the influx into McLennan of white voters from the older southern states. Colorado, Harrison, and Nueces continued largely under Republican control even after statewide "redemption." Indeed, radicals showed more strength in Colorado and Harrison in 1873 than in 1869. Nueces County's voters tended to produce mixed results, suggesting that the issues of Reconstruction had less strength there, probably owing to the presence of many European and Mexican immigrants, than in counties populated primarily by southern-born whites and blacks.

In August, 1875, when Texans elected a constitutional convention to remove the last vestige of radical government statewide, Colorado and Harrison Counties remained "unredeemed." Colorado County's support for Republican delegates was in vain, thanks to conservative voters in the other county (Lavaca) in its senatorial district. Harrison, however, helped elect three of the convention's fifteen Republicans, including one of only six black delegates. Nueces County voters had to choose between two slates of Democratic candidates for the convention, but as later elections would show, this did not signal the rejection of virtually all Republicans as occurred in Dallas and McLennan. Voters in those two counties and Jefferson sent conservative Democrats to the convention.

The election of February 15, 1876, in which voters approved the Constitution of 1876 and chose yet another set of new officials, ended the era of Reconstruction in Texas. Local conditions, however, still varied significantly from county to county. The people of Jefferson and Nueces Counties, although the former had never experienced Republican control and the latter had never been "redeemed" by a thorough conservative victory, seemed ready to move beyond Reconstruction issues in local government. They voted Democratic in statewide races but elected Republicans as well as Democrats to key positions locally. Apparently personal qualities and the handling of grass-roots issues made the difference. By contrast, voters in Dallas and McLennan Counties engaged in a typical "Radical versus Redeemer" conflict. Local newspapers reminded voters of the records of candidates during the Civil War and Reconstruction, and Democrats won virtually every contested office. Indeed, the Republican party was already on the verge of extinction in Dallas and McLennan as it had no district and local candidates in the former and its former leaders ran as "independents" in the latter. Reconstruction issues were also very much alive in Colorado and Harrison Counties, but there Republicans still had the upper hand, winning the race for county judge in both and electing blacks to important positions as well. Conservatives in these two counties complained bitterly that their political brethren statewide had abandoned them to "Africanization."

Within a few years, the experiences of Colorado and Harrison Counties, which had been similar since 1869, diverged. Conservatives regained control of Harrison in November, 1878, thanks to a mistake by Republican leaders in locating a vitally important ballot box outside its precinct. Taking advantage of this technicality and the assistance of Democrats at the district and state level, Harrison County "Redeemers" took over local government and dominated from that time forward. More than likely, pressure tactics against black voters and ballot-box fraud also played a role in conservative successes in 1878 and the elections of the next few years, but this cannot be proven. Colorado County, on the other hand, remained under Republican control well beyond the era of Reconstruction, electing blacks to local offices through the 1880s and not electing a Democratic county judge until 1890.

The foregoing chronological summary demonstrates just how difficult it is to generalize about grass-roots Reconstruction. Conditions were rarely if ever exactly the same in all six Texas counties at any particular time during the years from 1865 to 1876 and, in some cases, beyond. However, an examination of how certain of those local conditions shaped Reconstruction at the county level permits some useful general conclusions about the entire process.

First, federal authority, which was present in the form of troops and Freedmen's Bureau agents in all six counties for varying periods of time between 1865 and 1870, had a major impact on local developments. Bureau agents, backed by even a few troops, offered freedmen a degree of protection from physical harm and defense of their economic interests that generally would have been lacking otherwise. Undoubtedly blacks would have benefited had the federal presence continued after 1870, but even in a short time it helped open the way for one generation of freedmen to make notable progress and convince one generation of whites that basic rights had to be respected. Federal authority also encouraged white Republicans and enhanced their opportunities to gain and keep political power at the local level. In short, the presence of federal authority made grass roots Reconstruction possible.

Second, the involvement of scalawags—loyal whites born in the South—was a key to Republican party strength at the local level. Contrary to the mythical view still widely held in Texas, carpetbaggers—northern-born whites who came to Texas after the war—did not dominate grass-roots Reconstruction governments. Each county studied, except Dallas, had at least one important carpetbagger officeholder, but such men never had the numbers to control a single county. Similarly, claims that blacks controlled Reconstruction governments at the grass-roots level are equally incorrect. Each county had a black on the military-appointed board of registrars from 1867 to 1869, and African Americans held important offices in Colorado, Harrison, and McLennan Counties at various times after 1867. However, blacks never controlled any county's government. Rather than carpetbaggers or blacks, scalawags constituted the great majority of Unionists and Republicans who were politically active and held office at the local level between 1865 and 1876. Conservative "Redeemers," the great majority of whom were southern-born whites, struggled for control, for the most part, against men much like themselves when it came to race, birthplace, and antebellum residence.

Most of the scalawags had lived in Texas before the Civil War, and county residents knew them personally. If the individual in question was known for courage and integrity, as was often the case, he was accorded a certain degree of respect in spite of his political stance. By contrast, carpet-baggers, as recent arrivals, and blacks, whom most whites regarded as inferior, provided focal points for personal as well as political opposition. Scalawags made mistakes and argued among themselves, but they generally provided leadership for the success, however limited, of Republican government at the grass roots.

Third, the rate of population growth and economic expansion appears to have helped determine local reactions to Reconstruction. Although all six counties enjoyed an increase in population and the value of taxable property, Dallas, McLennan, and Nueces grew far more rapidly between 1865 and 1876 than did Colorado, Harrison, and Jefferson.[1] The three rapidly expanding counties, especially Dallas and McLennan, were in newly settled areas of Texas and each had a town on its way to becoming a major city. (Dallas would have more than 10,000 residents by 1880; Waco, more than 7,000. Corpus Christi had only 3,257 people in 1880 but still stood as the major coastal city from Galveston to the Rio Grande.) Two of the counties with less growth, Colorado and Harrison, had older agricultural economies that were beginning to grow stagnant, and their major towns would never become large cities. (Columbus had fewer than 2,000 residents in 1880; Marshall, more than 5,000 but would not reach 10,000 until after 1900.) In two of the most rapidly growing counties, Dallas and Nueces, leaders tended to emphasize expanding economic opportunities and limit to some extent the bitterness of grass-roots partisan politics. In contrast the two counties having the slowest growth rates, Colorado and Harrison, experienced high levels of Reconstruction-era bitterness. McLennan County, however, with its tremendous growth rate and extreme violence, did not fit this pattern.

Neither Reconstruction policies nor varying rates of population growth and economic expansion displaced the economic elite in these six counties. In all six, approximately two-thirds to three-quarters of the richest 5 per-

1. The discussion of the impact of Reconstruction on the economies and the economic elites of these six counties is based on developments from mid-1865 until 1880. Thus it does not emphasize the impact of the Civil War and the tremendous economic losses in slave property that came in 1865 just as Reconstruction began. Instead, it seeks to begin at that point and examine the effect of the era that followed. An effort to separate the impact of the war from the impact of Reconstruction may be seen as attempting to divide the inseparable, but in light of the "Redeemers" standard charge that the latter ruined the South, it is worth making.

cent of taxpaying families in 1865 remained in the county in 1880. This geographic persistence rate compared favorably with that of well-to-do families in other states during the years following the Civil War. For example, a study of two counties in the plantation region of west Tennessee found a persistence rate of 51 percent from 1870 to 1880 for heads of white farm households who owned land. The comparable statistics for landowners in middle Tennessee and the mountainous eastern region of the state were 60 percent and 66 percent respectively. In Trempealeau County, Wisconsin, the persistence rate from 1870 to 1880 for all gainfully employed males owning real property valued at $5,000 or more was 50 percent. Among native whites who belonged to the proprietorial class in Atlanta, Georgia, between 1870 and 1880, persistence rates stood at 64 percent. These statistics are not perfectly comparable with those presented for the six Texas counties in this study. In the first place, somewhat different population groups are examined. Moreover, the investigations of counties or cities in Tennessee, Wisconsin, and Georgia depended on the experience of heads of households only, whereas the statistics for Texas counties included wives and sons as well as heads of households. This would reduce the effect of deaths on the Texas persistence rates and increase it in comparison with the others. Nevertheless, the Texas rates were generally as high or higher over a period of fifteen years and indicate a relatively strong degree of geographical continuity for the economic elite during Reconstruction.[2]

For the most part, the economic elite also maintained their affluent status during Reconstruction. In five of the six counties, at least half of the taxpaying elite families that were geographically persistent from 1865 to 1880 remained in that class at the end of the fifteen-year period. Statistics for comparisons of social persistence in other counties during this era are virtually nonexistent because most studies cover the period either from 1860 to 1870 or from 1860 to 1880 and therefore reflect the impact of the Civil War as well as Reconstruction, but it is worth noting that persistence in the economic elite in these five counties was greater than *geographic* persistence among the gainfully employed in Trempealeau County, Wisconsin, from 1870 to 1880.[3] Only in Nueces County, where the economic elite in

2. Robert Tracy McKenzie, *One South or Many? Plantation Belt and Upcountry in Civil War–Era Tennessee* (Cambridge, Eng., 1994), 102–104; Merle Curti, *The Making of an American Community: A Case Study of Democracy in a Frontier County* (Stanford, Calif., 1959), 67–68; Richard J. Hopkins, "Occupational and Geographic Mobility in Atlanta, 1870–1896," *Journal of Southern History*, XXXIV (1968), 200–213.

3. Curti, *Making of an American Community*, 68. Examples of studies that cover the Civil

1865 depended on livestock rather than land and cotton, was Reconstruction marked by more than 50 percent displacement of the richest taxpayers. And it is doubtful that developments related to the adjustment of blacks to freedom and restoring civil government in Texas had much to do with changing fortunes in ranching.

Fourth, the proportion of foreign-born residents in each county definitely affected the impact of Reconstruction. Germans in Colorado and Mexicans in Nueces did not vote as blocs, but their support proved important to Republican successes that continued even after the era ended statewide. These ethnic groups generally had opposed secession and a war to defend slavery and after 1865 tended to be less susceptible to arguments about "Negro rule" and congressional tyranny.

Finally, the proportion of blacks in each county appears to have played the most important role in determining the course of Reconstruction. Counties with relatively small proportions of blacks had the least controversy locally. Although Jefferson County went Democratic in 1869 and Nueces County continued to elect at least some Republicans through the 1870s, political spokesmen used characteristic Reconstruction-era rhetoric primarily when discussing issues and elections at the state and national levels. They did not commonly extend that sort of bitterness to individuals involved in local politics. Dallas County's leaders also tended to minimize political rancor locally during most of Reconstruction, but this probably resulted from a fortuitous (for most whites, at least) combination of demographics and economic conditions. Dallas County, with a white population that came primarily from the South and with relatively few blacks, could easily vote in a conservative local government at the first opportunity. Moreover, its leaders and spokesmen did not want to let political controversy interfere with what they foresaw as opportunities for tremendous economic growth during the postwar years.

Counties with relatively large percentages of freedmen usually suffered great bitterness in local politics after 1865. This was true even of Colorado County, which had a significant German-born population as well as many blacks. Conservative Democrats there never ceased angry attacks on local Republican leaders in spite of the fact that many of those officials could not

War as well as Reconstruction are Jonathan M. Wiener, "Planter Persistence and Social Change, Alabama, 1850–1870," *Journal of Interdisciplinary History,* VII (1976), 235–60, and A. Jane Townes, "The Effect of Emancipation on Large Landholdings, Nelson and Goochland Counties, Virginia," *Journal of Southern History,* XLV (1979), 403–12.

have won without support from white voters in the German community. McLennan County had constant controversy and an extreme degree of violence, at least in part because it had a large enough black population to constitute a threat to white control. Conservatives apparently did not feel secure enough to relax about local politics and concentrate on their expanding economy. Harrison County, because it had a black majority to provide support for the Republicans, endured a classic confrontation between "Radicals" and "Redeemers" that left a legacy of partisan extremism for generations to come.

For the blacks themselves, regardless of their relative numbers and in the face of pervasive racial prejudice and frequent violence, Reconstruction contained much that was positive. Nothing freedmen could do would have destroyed most conservative whites' belief in their inherent inferiority, and the apparently random nature of assaults and murders meant that blacks could rarely consider themselves safe from attack. Nevertheless, as soon as they were given an opportunity by federal intervention, freedmen eagerly sought to demonstrate that they were capable of exercising the responsibilities of citizenship. A large proportion of adult males registered and voted, those chosen served on juries, and some held appointive and elective offices. Blacks, it seems from the reports of Freedmen's Bureau agents and military officers, rarely if ever met violence with violence. But those who lived in Harrison and Colorado Counties seem to have enjoyed some strength from their numbers. For example, the so-called Eagle Lake Riot of 1873 in Colorado County suggested that blacks did not always submit quietly to violence or even rumors of violence.

While exercising basic political and civil rights for the first time, freedmen in the six counties also worked with at least some success to improve their economic status and stabilize basic social institutions. In Jefferson County, a coastal area that had not developed a cotton-based economy, most blacks lived in Beaumont, where the men worked in the lumber industry or as laborers and the women as cooks and laundresses. They were poor, but the increase in blacks as a proportion of the population after 1865 suggests that town life and wage labor had an attraction for them. Nueces County freedmen had a similar experience—working in Corpus Christi as laborers, draymen, cooks, and laundresses—although they did not grow notably faster than whites as a percentage of the population. In three of the four largely agricultural counties (Colorado, Harrison, and McLennan), most blacks were sharecroppers or farm laborers, but approximately 20 percent of those who gave their occupation as farmer owned land in 1880. Only in Dallas County did blacks not enjoy this success, which, although modest, was notable under the circumstances. In all six counties, families composed of a man, his wife, and their children were a basic institution in the lives of freedmen in 1880. Moreover, one-third or more of the families having children aged six to sixteen had at least one of those children attend school within the previous year. Blacks who lived in town were somewhat less likely to have male-headed families but were more likely to have children in school. Somewhat ironically, town life tended to break down the family at the same time that it brought greater educational opportunities.

In conclusion, Reconstruction set neighbor against neighbor in all the counties of Texas, but its impact varied greatly from one county to another. Overall, the story played out in a largely democratic (by the standards of that day) and non-revolutionary manner. Many conservative whites argued that Congressional Reconstruction from 1867 to 1870 brought dictatorial oppression and radical change as the military took over, officials elected in 1866 were removed, former officeholders who had supported the Confederacy were disfranchised, and blacks were enfranchised. Federal intervention did indeed make a significant difference in local government for a short time. But it did not prevent economic growth or bring basic alterations in the distribution of wealth, and black suffrage was the only important political change that continued, at least for a while, after 1870. Once the Constitution of 1869 was put into operation Democrats and Republicans contested democratically for control of county government, and for at least the next decade results seem to have reflected the popular will. Freedmen exercised essential rights of citizenship and, given their starting point, generally made considerable economic and social progress. The national government's help, beginning with the Freedmen's Bureau in 1865 and continuing in a variety of ways until 1870, was a key to these gains, but it ended long before blacks could maintain equality before the law on their own. Change that radical would not come for nearly another century (and some would question whether it has come yet).

Reconstruction at the grass roots in Texas, although it varied greatly from one locality to another, hurt whites far less than is often claimed and benefited at least one generation of blacks a good deal more than is often recognized. Ever since, however, a majority of white Texans have regarded the era as one of the darkest pages in their state's history and generally held to the attitudes of the "Redeemers" who opposed an activist government that taxed and spent, regardless of the purpose. Witness the fact that the Constitution of 1876, adopted with the deliberate intent of rolling back "radical" changes brought by Congressional Reconstruction, remains in 1997 (albeit with many amendments) the state's fundamental law. The legacy of Reconstruction as experienced at the grass roots in Texas lives on.

# BIBLIOGRAPHY

## PRIMARY SOURCES

### MANUSCRIPTS

Colorado County Courthouse, Columbus, Texas
    District Court Civil Minutes.
    Election Record, 1854–1866.
    Election Returns, 1866–1876.
    Police Court Minutes, 1862–1876.
Dallas County Commissioners' Court Office, Dallas, Texas
    Commissioners' Court Minutes, 1860–1876.
Dallas Historical Society Archives, Dallas, Texas
    Rawlins, A. B. Papers.
Dallas Public Library, Dallas, Texas
    District Court Minutes (Dallas County).
Harrison County Courthouse, Marshall, Texas
    Commissioners' Court Minutes.
    District Court Civil Case Papers.
    District Court Civil Minutes.
Jefferson County Courthouse, Beaumont, Texas
    Commissioners' Court Minutes.
    District Court Minutes Books.
    Record of Election Returns, 1860–1867.
McLennan County Courthouse, Waco, Texas
    Commissioners' Court Minutes.
    District Court Minutes.

National Archives, Washington, D.C.
  Seventh Census of the United States, 1850. Schedule 1
    (Free Inhabitants), and Schedule 2 (Slave Inhabitants).
  Eighth Census of the United States, 1860. Schedule 1
    (Free Inhabitants), and Schedule 2 (Slave Inhabitants).
  Ninth Census of the United States, 1870. Schedule 1 (Inhabitants).
  Tenth Census of the United States, 1880. Schedule 1 (Population), and Schedule
    2 (Productions of Agriculture).
  Records of the Adjutant General's Office, 1780s–1917, Record Group 94.
    Letters Received by the Office of the Adjutant General (Main Series), 1861–
      1870.
  Records of the Department of War, Record Group 105.
    Records of the Assistant Commissioner for the State of Texas, United States
      Bureau of Refugees, Freedmen, and Abandoned Lands, 1865–1869.
    Records of the Subordinate Field Officers of the Bureau of Freedmen, Refu-
      gees, and Abandoned Lands, Sub-assistant Commissioner, Columbus,
      Texas, and Waco, Texas.
    Records of the Superintendent of Education for the State of Texas, Bureau of
      Refugees, Freedmen, and Abandoned Lands, 1865–1869.
  Records of the Department of War, Record Group 109.
    Index to the Compiled Service Records of Confederate Soldiers Who Served
      in Organizations from the State of Texas.
  Records of the Department of War, Record Group 393.
    Records of the Office of Civil Affairs for the Department of Texas and the
      Fifth Military District, 1865–1870.
    Registration Book A [a list of loyalists compiled by Freedmen's Bureau agents
      in Texas in April, 1867], Fifth Military District, District of Texas.
Nueces County Courthouse, Corpus Christi, Texas
  Commissioners' Court Minutes.
  District Court Minutes.
Sam Houston Regional Library and Research Center, Liberty, Texas
  Welder, Julia Duncan. Collection.
Texas State Library, Austin, Texas
  Election Registers, 1846–1890. Records of the Secretary of State.
  Election Returns, 1860–1880.
  Executive Record Books: Edmund J. Davis, Richard Coke.
  Governors' Papers: Edmund J. Davis, Andrew Jackson Hamilton, Richard B.
    Hubbard, Elisha M. Pease, and James W. Throckmorton.
  List of Registered Voters in Texas, 1869.
  Records of the Adjutant General, Reconstruction Records, 1865–1873.
  Records of the Comptroller of Public Accounts, Ad Valorem Tax Division,
    County Real and Personal Property Tax Rolls, 1860–1880.

University of Texas, Austin, Eugene C. Barker Texas History Center
  Brown, John Henry. Papers.
  Bruckmuller, Peter Joseph. Papers.
  Evans, Ira H. Vertical File.
  Haynes, John L. Papers.
  Leyendecker Family Papers.
  Newcomb, James P. Papers.
  Raguet, Henry. Family Papers.
  Throckmorton, James W. Papers.
  Wells, James B. Papers
  Wright, Josepha. Papers.

## TEXAS NEWSPAPERS

Austin *Daily Democratic Statesman,* September 8, 1875.
Austin *Daily State Journal,* November 4, 1870.
Austin *Tri-Weekly State Gazette,* April 28, 1869.
Beaumont *Banner,* 1860–1861.
Beaumont *News Beacon,* 1873.
Brownsville *Daily Ranchero,* December 11, 1869.
*Colorado Citizen* (Columbus), 1859–1875.
Columbus *Weekly Times,* 1868–1869.
Comanche *Chief,* March 9, 1876.
Corpus Christi *Advertiser,* August 14, 1867.
Corpus Christi *Daily Gazette,* 1876.
Corpus Christi *Weekly Advertiser,* 1870–1872.
Corpus Christi *Weekly Gazette,* 1873–1874.
*Daily Austin Republican,* August 25, 1868.
Dallas *Herald,* 1860–1876.
Galveston *Daily News,* 1865–1875.
Galveston *Tri-Weekly News,* 1871–1873.
Hallettsville *Herald and Planter,* October 23, 1873.
*Harrison Flag* (Marshall), 1860–1868.
Houston *Telegraph and Texas Register,* May 2, June 2, 1837.
Houston *Tri-Weekly Telegraph,* May 25, 1866.
Jefferson *Radical,* 1869–1870.
Marshall *Messenger,* 1877–1878.
Marshall *Tri-Weekly Herald,* 1875–1878.
*Neches Valley News* (Beaumont), 1871–1872.
*Nueces Valley* (Corpus Christi), 1870–1872.
Sabine Pass *Beacon,* June 10, 1871.
*Texas Republican* (Marshall), 1849–1869.
Waco *Daily Advance,* 1872–1874.

Waco *Daily Examiner,* 1873–1876.
Waco *Weekly Patron and Examiner,* August 30, 1875.


PUBLISHED DOCUMENTS

*Congressional Globe . . . and Appendix.* Washington, D.C., 1869.
Deaton, Charles, comp. *Texas Postal History Handbook.* Austin, 1980.
Gammel, H. P. N., comp. *The Laws of Texas, 1822–1897.* 10 volumes. Austin, 1898–1902.
*Inventory of the County Archives of Texas, No. 94: Guadalupe County.* San Antonio, 1939.
*Journal of the House of Representatives, Twelfth Legislature.* Austin, 1870.
*Journal of the House of Representatives of the Twelfth Legislature. Adjourned Session—1871.* Austin, 1871.
*Journal of the House of Representatives of the State of Texas: Being the Session of the Fourteenth Legislature . . . January 13, 1874.* Austin, 1874.
*Journal of the Senate of the Twelfth Legislature. Adjourned Session—1871.* Austin, 1871.
*Journal of the Senate of the State of Texas: Being the Session of the Fourteenth Legislature . . . January 13, 1874.* Austin, 1874.
*Members of the Texas Legislature, 1846–1980.* Austin, 1980.
*Report of the Joint Committee on Reconstruction at the First Session Thirty-Ninth Congress.* Washington, D.C., 1866.
*Report of the Secretary of State of the State of Texas, for the Year 1872.* Austin, 1873.
*Reports of Cases Argued and Decided in the Supreme Court of the State of Texas.* 65 vols. St. Louis, 1848–1886.
*Senate Miscellaneous Documents,* 41st Cong., 2nd Sess., No. 77 (Serial 1408).
United States Bureau of the Census. *Agriculture of the United States in 1860; Compiled from the Original Returns of the Eighth Census.* Washington, D.C., 1864.
———. *Population of the United States in 1860; Compiled from the Original Returns of the Eighth Census.* Washington, D.C., 1864.
———. *The Statistics of the Population of the United States; Compiled from the Original Returns of the Ninth Census (June 1, 1870).* Washington, D.C., 1872.
———. *The Statistics of Wealth and Industry of the United States . . . from the Original Returns of the Ninth Census (1870).* Washington, D.C., 1872.
———. *Statistics of the Population of the United States at the Tenth Census (June 1, 1880).* Washington, D.C., 1883.
———. *Report on the Productions of Agriculture as Returned at the Tenth Census, 1880.* Washington, D.C., 1883.
*United States Statutes at Large.*
*The War of the Rebellion: A Compilation of the Official Records of the Union and Confederate Armies.* 130 vols. Washington, D.C., 1880–1901.

Winkler, Ernest William, ed. *Platforms of Political Parties in Texas.* Austin, 1916.

## PUBLISHED MEMOIRS, TRAVELERS' ACCOUNTS, AND CONTEMPORARY WORKS

De Wees, William B. *Letters from an Early Settler of Texas.* 1852; rpr. Waco, Tex., 1968.

Manning, Dan R., trans., comp., and ed. "The Rancho Ramirena Journal of John James Dix." *Southwestern Historical Quarterly,* XCVIII (1994), 81–98.

Rawick, George P., ed. *The American Slave: A Composite Autobiography.* Series 1, 7 vols.; Series 2, 12 vols.; *Supplement, Series 1,* 12 vols.; *Supplement, Series 2,* 10 vols. Westport, Conn., 1972, 1977, 1979.

Stein, Bill, ed. "The Slave Narratives of Colorado County." *Nesbitt Memorial Library Journal: A Journal of Colorado County History,* III (January, 1993), 3–32.

## SECONDARY SOURCES

### BOOKS

Ashcraft, Allen C. *Texas in the Civil War: A Résumé History.* Austin, 1962.

*Biographical Encyclopedia of Texas.* New York, 1880.

Buenger, Walter L. *Secession and the Union in Texas.* Austin, 1984.

Campbell, Randolph B. *An Empire for Slavery: The Peculiar Institution in Texas, 1821–1865.* Baton Rouge, 1989.

————. *A Southern Community in Crisis: Harrison County, Texas, 1850–1880.* Austin, 1983.

Campbell, Randolph B., and Richard G. Lowe. *Wealth and Power in Antebellum Texas.* College Station, Tex., 1977.

Cantrell, Gregg. *Kenneth and John B. Rayner and the Limits of Southern Dissent.* Urbana, Ill., 1993.

Cobb, Berry A. *A History of Dallas Lawyers, 1840 to 1890.* Dallas, 1934.

Cochran, John H. *Dallas County: A Record of Its Pioneers and Progress, Being a Supplement to John Henry Brown's History of Dallas County (1877).* Dallas, 1928.

Colorado County Historical Commission. *Colorado County Chronicles: From the Beginning to 1923.* 2 vols. Austin, 1986.

Curti, Merle. *The Making of an American Community: A Case Study of Democracy in a Frontier County.* Stanford, 1959.

Foner, Eric. *Reconstruction: America's Unfinished Revolution, 1863–1877.* New York, 1988.

Huson, Hobart. *District Judges of Refugio County.* Refugio, Tex., 1941.

Jordan, Terry G. *German Seed in Texas Soil: Immigrant Farmers in Nineteenth-Century Texas.* Austin, 1966.

Kingston, Mike, Sam Attlesey, and Mary G. Crawford. *The Texas Almanac's Political History of Texas.* Austin, 1992.

Lowe, Richard G., and Randolph B. Campbell. *Planters and Plain Folk: Agriculture in Antebellum Texas.* Dallas, 1987.

McKenzie, Robert Tracy. *One South or Many? Plantation Belt and Upcountry in Civil War–Era Tennessee.* Cambridge, Eng., 1994.

McSwain, Betty Ann McCartney, ed. *The Bench and Bar of Waco and McLennan County, 1849–1876.* Waco, Tex., n.d.

*A Memorial and Biographical History of McLennan, Falls, Bell, and Coryell Counties, Texas.* Chicago, 1893.

Moneyhon, Carl H. *Republicanism in Reconstruction Texas.* Austin, 1980.

Montejano, David. *Anglos and Mexicans in the Making of Texas, 1836–1986.* Austin, 1987.

Puryear, Pamela Ashworth, and Nath Winfield, Jr. *Sandbars and Sternwheelers: Steam Navigation on the Brazos.* College Station, Tex., 1976.

Ramsdell, Charles William. *Reconstruction in Texas.* New York, 1910.

Reynolds, Donald E. *Editors Make War: Southern Newspapers in the Secession Crisis.* Nashville, 1966.

Richardson, Rupert N., Ernest Wallace, and Adrian Anderson, *Texas: The Lone Star State.* 5th ed. Englewood Cliffs, N.J., 1988.

Richter, William L. *The Army in Texas During Reconstruction, 1865–1870.* College Station, Tex., 1987.

———. *Overreached on All Sides: The Freedmen's Bureau Administrators in Texas, 1865–1868.* College Station, Tex., 1991.

Simpson, Harold B. *The Marshall Guards: Harrison County's Contribution to Hood's Texas Brigade.* Marshall, Tex., 1967.

Tyler, Ron, ed. *The New Handbook of Texas.* 6 vols. Austin, 1996.

Wallace, Patricia Ward. *Waco: Texas Crossroads.* Woodland Hills, Calif., 1983.

Waller, John L. *Colossal Hamilton of Texas: A Biography of Andrew Jackson Hamilton, Militant Unionist and Reconstruction Governor.* El Paso, Tex., 1968.

Webb, Walter Prescott, H. Bailey Carroll, and Eldon Branda. *The Handbook of Texas.* 3 vols. Austin, 1952, 1976.

Winsor, Bill. *Texas in the Confederacy: Military Installations, Economy and People.* Hillsboro, Tex., 1978.

Wright, Marcus J., comp. *Texas in the War, 1861–1865.* Edited by Harold B. Simpson. Hillsboro, Tex., 1965.

Zlatkovich, Charles P. *Texas Railroads: A Record of Construction and Abandonment.* Austin, 1981.

## ARTICLES

Barr, Alwyn. "Black Legislators of Reconstruction Texas." *Civil War History,* XXXII (1986), 340–52.

———. "Texas Coastal Defense, 1861–1865." *Southwestern Historical Quarterly,* LXV (1961), 1–31.

Campbell, Randolph B. "The Burden of Local Black Leadership During Reconstruction: A Research Note." *Civil War History,* XXXIX (1993), 148–52.

———. "Carpetbagger Rule in Texas: An Enduring Myth." *Southwestern Historical Quarterly,* XCVII (1994), 587–96.

———. "The District Judges of Texas in 1866–1867: An Episode in the Failure of Presidential Reconstruction." *Southwestern Historical Quarterly,* XCIII (1990), 357–77.

———. "George W. Whitmore: East Texas Unionist." *East Texas Historical Journal,* XXVIII (1990), 17–28.

———. "Grass Roots Reconstruction: The Personnel of County Government in Texas, 1865–1876." *Journal of Southern History,* LVIII (1992), 99–116.

———. "A Moderate Response: The District Judges of Dallas County During Reconstruction, 1865–1876." *Legacies: A History Journal for Dallas and North Central Texas,* V (1993), 4–12.

———. "Scalawag District Judges: The E. J. Davis Appointees." *Houston Review,* XIV (1992), 75–88.

———. "The Whig Party of Texas in the Elections of 1848 and 1852." *Southwestern Historical Quarterly,* LXXIII (1969), 17–34

Cantrell, Gregg. "Racial Violence and Reconstruction Politics in Texas, 1867–1868." *Southwestern Historical Quarterly,* XCIII (1990), 333–55.

Crouch, Barry A. "'All the Vile Passions': The Texas Black Code of 1866." *Southwestern Historical Quarterly,* XCVII (1993), 13–34.

———. "The Freedmen's Bureau in Beaumont." *Texas Gulf Historical and Biographical Record,* XXVIII (1992), 8–27.

———. "A Spirit of Lawlessness: White Violence; Texas Blacks, 1865–1868." *Journal of Social History,* XVIII (1984), 217–32.

Duty, Tony E. "The Home Front—McLennan County in the Civil War." *Texana,* XII (1974), 197–238.

Ericson, J. E. "The Delegates to the Convention of 1875: A Reappraisal." *Southwestern Historical Quarterly,* LXVII (1963), 22–27.

Hopkins, Richard J. "Occupational and Geographic Mobility in Atlanta, 1870–1896." *Journal of Southern History,* XXXIV (1968), 200–13.

Miller, Worth Robert. "Harrison County Methods: Election Fraud in Late Nineteenth-Century Texas." *Locus: Regional and Local History of the Americas,* VII (1995), 111–28.

Moneyhon, Carl H. "Public Education and Texas Reconstruction Politics, 1871–1874." *Southwestern Historical Quarterly,* XCII (1989), 393–416.

Oates, Stephen B. "Texas Under the Secessionists." *Southwestern Historical Quarterly,* LXVII (1963), 167–212.

Russ, William A., Jr. "Radical Disfranchisement in Texas, 1867–1870." *Southwestern Historical Quarterly,* XXXVIII (1934), 40–52.

Shook, Robert. "Toward a List of Reconstruction Loyalists." *Southwestern Historical Quarterly,* LXXVI (1973), 315–20.

Smith, Thomas H. "Conflict and Corruption: The Dallas Establishment vs. the Freedmen's Bureau Agent." *Legacies: A History Journal for Dallas and North Central Texas,* I (Fall, 1989), 24–30.

Timmons, Joe T. "The Referendum in Texas on the Ordinance of Secession, February 23, 1861." *East Texas Historical Journal,* XI (Fall, 1973), 12–28.

Townes, A. Jane. "The Effect of Emancipation on Large Landholdings, Nelson and Goochland Counties, Virginia." *Journal of Southern History,* XLV (1979), 403–12.

Wiener, Jonathan M. "Planter Persistence and Social Change, Alabama, 1850–1870." *Journal of Interdisciplinary History,* VII (1976), 235–60.

Wooster, Ralph A. "The Battle of Galveston." *Texas Gulf Historical and Biographical Record,* XXVIII (1992), 28–38.

## THESES, DISSERTATIONS, AND UNPUBLISHED PAPERS

Baggett, James Alex. "The Rise and Fall of the Texas Radicals, 1867–1883." Ph.D. dissertation, North Texas State University, 1972.

Block, W. T., Jr. "Captain George W. O'Brien: A Torchbearer of Our Texas Civilization." Unpublished paper.

———. "A History of the W. T. 'Will' Block, Sr., Family of Port Neches." Unpublished paper.

Briscoe, Eugenia Reynolds. "A Narrative History of Corpus Christi, Texas, 1519–1875." Ph.D. dissertation, University of Denver, 1972.

Graf, LeRoy P. "The Economic History of the Lower Rio Grande Valley, 1820–1875." Ph.D. dissertation, Harvard University, 1942.

LaPlante, Christopher. "Reconstruction in Dallas County, 1865–1873." M.A. thesis, University of Texas at Arlington, 1974.

Smith, Melinda D. C. "Congressional Reconstruction in Dallas County, Texas: Was It Radical?" M.A. thesis, University of North Texas, 1992.

# INDEX

Miller, James F., 123
Miller, John C., 44
Miller, Richard, 209
Miller, Samuel R., 207–209
Miner, Fred W., 91–92
Missouri, Kansas, and Texas Railway
  Company, 88, 91
Moderate Republicans, 16–17, 19, 22,
  44–45, 84–86, 122, 151, 179–90, 206
Monroe, Armistead T., 85
Moon, William M., 94
Moore, George F., 137–38
Moore, Henry, 122, 125
Moore, John M., 214
Moore, Lewis, 174
Morgan, R. S., 158
Morris, William H., 180
Muckleroy, Mike, 56
Mullins, Shepherd, 172, 174–75, 179–
  80, 182, 190, 192
Munden, John, 110, 116
Murphy, J. B., 215
Murphy, P. F., 213
Mustang Island, 196
Myers, Meredith, 86

Neal, Benjamin F., 198–200, 204
*Neches Valley News*, 156, 158
Neches River, 142
Newcomb, James P., 48, 124, 155, 158,
  179, 183, 186–87
Newcomb, S. B., 218
Nichols, H. J., 121, 123–25
Noessel, Felix, 212, 214
Norton, Anthony Banning, 78, 80–83,
  88–89
Norton, D. O., 75, 78
Norton, Henry, 80
Norvell, Lipscomb, 159
Nueces County, 2, 4, 160, 220–25, 227,
  229–30. *See also under* Civil War,
  Congressional Reconstruction, Cot-
  ton production, Democratic Party,

Economic elite, Freedmen, Freedmen's Bureau, Presidential Reconstruction, Radical Republicans, Redemption, Republican Party,
Taxation, Unionists, Voter registration

Oakes, Wallace E., 168–69, 174, 189,
  222
Oakes, William E., 175
O'Brien, George A., 176, 187
O'Brien, George W., 144, 147–49, 157–
  58
O'Callahan, T., 197–98
Odom, Morgan, 149
Ogden, Edward C., 154
Ogden, Lemuel P., 153
Oliver, John W., 183–87
Osterhout, J. P., 189
Overbay, Eugene L., 52

Parsons, Albert R., 182–84, 186
Parsons, William H., 165–66
Patten, George W., 184, 187
Patten, Nathan, 171–75, 179, 184
Patton, S. C., 55
Payne, G. W., 149
Pease, Elisha M., 10–11, 15, 19, 35, 42,
  70, 75, 110, 148, 169, 200
Pedigo, Henry C., 145–46, 151, 159
Perry, Solomon R., 103–104, 110, 112,
  114, 116–17, 121, 131, 133, 135
Perry, Z. T., 122
Pickett, E. B., 153, 159
Pipkin, Allen, 150, 153, 161
Pipkin, J. F., 150
Pipkin, Woodson, 161
Plato, Nelson, 200, 206, 211, 213, 215
Poland, W. H., 123–25
Polk, Milas R., 207–208
Pope, Alexander, 119
Powell, John S., 104–105
Powers, Stephen, 212